AF517260

Constitutional Evolution in NEPAL

Constitutional Evolution in NEPAL

Edited by

Saurabh & N P Chaudhary

INDIAN COUNCIL OF WORLD AFFAIRS

PENTAGON PRESS

First Published in 2012

Copyright © Indian Council of World Affairs

All rights reserved. No part of this publication may be reproduced, stored in a retrieval system, or transmitted, in any form or by any means, electronic, mechanical, photocopying, recording, or otherwise, without first obtaining written permission of the copyright owner.

The responsibility for facts and opinions in this publication rests exclusively with the authors and their interpretations do not necessarily reflect the views or the policy of the Indian Council of World Affairs, New Delhi.

Published by

PENTAGON PRESS
206, Peacock Lane, Shahpur Jat
New Delhi-110049
Phones: 011-64706243, 26491568
Telefax: 011-26490600
email: rajan@pentagonpress.in
website: www.pentagonpress.in

Cataloging in Publication Data—DK
Courtesy: D.K. Agencies (P) Ltd. <docinfo@dkagencies.com>

Constitutional evolution in Nepal / edited by Saurabh & N.P. Chaudhary.
p. cm.
Contributed articles.
Includes bibliographical references and index.

1. Constitutional law—Nepal. 2. Constitutional history—Nepal. 3. Nepal—Politics and government. I. Saurabh. II. Chaudhary, N. P., 1951. III. Indian Council of World Affairs.

DDC 342.5496 23

Printed at Chaman Enterprises, Delhi.

Contents

Preface

Nepal is passing through a very critical phase of its nation building process. The election of the Constituent Assembly (CA) of Nepal has established the primacy of participatory politics. So, both the process of making a new constitution and its contents must open up opportunities for all the people to participate in the designing of new institutions of the state. The future of Nepal will depend fundamentally on how this matter is resolved. Nepal's legislature-parliament elected Baburam Bhattarai, Vice-Chairman of the Unified Communist Party of Nepal (Maoist), new Prime Minister of Nepal. Prime Minister Jhalanath Khanal resigned on August 28, 2011. There was increased pressure on Mr. Khanal to quit from leaders of his own party, the Communist Party of Nepal (Unified Marxist Leninist), who were upset with him for swearing in new Maoist Ministers against the party directive. Baburam Bhattrai's candidature was supported by the United Democratic Madhesi Front (UDMF), an alliance of five Madhesi parties. In the House of 594 MPs, 575 members participated in the election and around 340 voted for Dr. Bhattarai, helping him secure a simple majority. The other candidate, Nepali Congress Parliamentary Party leader Ram Chandra Poudel, got 235 votes. The NC was supported by the Communist Party of Nepal (Unified Marxist Leninist). Baburam Bhattarai government decided to bring in a proposal for constitutional amendment to enable term extension by three more months. All parties supported the proposal. This is the third extension of the Constituent Assembly, whose original two-year term ended on May 28, 2010. The CA's term, which would have ended on August 31, 2011, will now expire on November 30, 2011. Many of the parties supporting Bhattarai also warned him that the support was conditional: he would have to deliver on his party's promise that it would take the peace process forward in 45 days, especially dismantle the Maoists' People's Liberation Army.

Chairman of the UCPN-Maoist, Pushpa Kamal Dahal said he sees a slim chance of formation of the national consensus government in spite of week-long rigorous discussions for this. Similarly, a collective responsibility was needed for the peace process. Only Maoist should not be blamed. The political parties are near consensus on the number, modality and rehabilitation package regarding the army integration, he added. A PMO source revealed that the Maoists would actively participate in the meetings of the Special Committee for Supervision, Integration and Rehabilitation of the Maoist combatants to find an agreement on contentious issues. The number of combatants to be integrated, the modality of integration, rank harmonization, norms of entry, and nature of rehabilitation packages remain unresolved. The Maoists have said they are willing to 'regroup the combatants' based on those to be integrated and those opting for rehabilitation by the end of August. It is revealed that there are disputes within the Maoists. Senior vice-chairman, Mohan Vaidya 'Kiran' has emphasised that entering the peace process was essentially a 'tactical' step, not a 'strategic' shift. The party should remain committed to completing the 'revolution' and prepare the ground for this by "sharpening the political polarisation." But Baburam Bhattarai believes that the main task for now is to institutionalise the "federal democratic republic," which requires close collaboration with all other parties, especially the Nepali Congress. Mr. Kiran and Dr. Bhattarai insisted on a fresh "power-sharing" arrangement within the party, with greater responsibility to other leaders. Two factions, who had long fought an ideological battle, came together because they felt Mr. Prachanda had maintained his strength by playing them against each other. Another vice-Chairman, Narayan Kaji Shrestha 'Prakash,' and party general-secretary Ram Bahadur Thapa 'Badal' supported this campaign.

The political parties are in disagreement over several issues including the return of the seized property during the Jan Andolan II (1996-2006) to its rightful owners, abide by the past political agreements and understandings, and scrapping the structure of the Young Communist League (YCL). It is important to note that YCL is a fusion of the UCPN (Maoist) Party's military and political wing and comprises of People's Liberation Army (PLA) members who have interest in politics. Most of the YCL members are reported to be combatants whom the CPN-Maoist did not want confined in the barracks under the regulation of the United Nations Mission in Nepal (UNMIN). Some of the members who have the experience in fighting during the insurgency era (1996-2006) were trained by the CPN–Maoist. But, the most important part of the political deal is the plan to send PLA into the Nepal Army. Also, there is a proposal to send some PLA members to the Forest Security Force, where they would work with army units, presumably to combat poaching of wildlife. The remaining PLA men and women would be given a 'rehabilitation' package that includes education and job training. The Maoists have demanded that the leadership of the mixed force under the NA directorate be given to a former PLA commander; this force should have a combat role; and the entry of combatants should happen 'unit wise.' There are substantive differences between the Maoists and other parties on who would lead the new force, what would be its mandate, the standard norms, rank harmonisation, and form of rehabilitation packages and cash handouts. In the best case scenario, the parties should aim to bridge these differences and initiate the process of regrouping combatants before August 31. Concluding it by then is impossible. But even beginning it would signal that the peace process has moved to an "irreversible stage," and reassure the others that the Maoists are getting detached from their coercive apparatus.

Generally, the people of Nepal are disappointed over the political stalemate in Nepal. Most of the people feel that all political parties are motivated by usurping political power rather than drafting the constitution. Also, there is a sense of fear and apprehension that the country might again plunge into political turmoil. The donor community (including UN, US, UK etc) which has significantly funded the state agencies and non-government sectors for the initiatives on constitution writing, too, is concerned about the delay in the drafting of the constitution. Overall, the general public believes that political parties must redress the existing 'trust deficit' among themselves in order to move forward on the drafting of the constitution.

At this crucial juncture of drafting of constitution and nation-building in Nepal, India should extend its support wholeheartedly for a national consensus in Nepal and to facilitate the writing of a new constitution. As an important neighbour, India should reach out to all political parties in Nepal and express its willingness to support for the success of peace process. However, it is important that India should assure the people of Nepal that it is not interfering in their internal affairs. A stable and prosperous Nepal is critical for maintaining political, economic and social ties between the two neighbours and also for South Asia. Perhaps, the most important issue for India, is not which party, leader or coalition rules Nepal in the name of 'national government', but the issue is 'will Nepal get its much desired peace and stability'? It would be pertinent to mention there is no alternative to consensus, conciliation and cooperation among the three main political parties to draft the constitution. Chapters 1 and 6 analyses the historical perspective of the constitution making in Nepal. Party and development relations are dealt by different contributors in the Chapters 3, 5, 7-8, 11, 14, 17, 19-22 and 26-28. State and society issues are discussed in the Chapters 9-10 and 18.

Different authors have dealt with Chinese dynamics in Chapters 23-25. Implications of the outgoing impasse in Nepal is dealt in the Chapters 2, 4, 12-13 and 16.

The present venture would not have been possible without the contributions made by a large number of experts in the field. We would like to express our sincere gratitude to each of them for the valuable contributions. We sincerely own the lapses that may have occurred inadvertently in the editing of this work. However, the ideas expressed are those of the individual authors, not of ICWA or Government of India.

Saurabh
N P Chaudhary

Contributors

Prof. Sri Krishna Jha, former Professor & Head, Department of Political Science, Pandit Din Dayal Upadhyaya Gorakhpur University, Gorakhpur, Uttar Pradesh, India

Prof. Nalini Kant Jha, Professor & Director, Southern Asia Studies Programme & UNESCO Madanjit Singh Institute for South Asia Regional Cooperation, Pondicherry University, Puducherry, India

Prof. B C Upreti, Professor, Department of Political Science, South Asian Studies Centre, University of Rajasthan, Jaipur, Rajasthan, India

Prof. Navin Mishra, Professor, Department of Political Science, Tribhuwan University, Kathmandu, Nepal

Ms. Veena Sinha, Secretary, Madheshi Mahila Forum, Kathmandu, Nepal

Dr. Ram Prakash, Reader, Department of Political Science, LS College, Bhim Rao Ambedkar Bihar University, Muzaffarpur, Bihar, India

Prof. Rohitashwa Dubey, Professor, University Department of Political Science, Bhim Rao Ambedkar Bihar University, Muzaffarpur, Bihar, India

Dr. Upendra Mishra, Reader, University Department of Political Science & CCDC, Bhim Rao Ambedkar Bihar University, Muzaffarpur, Bihar, India

Prof. R N Kumar, Former Professor, University Department of Political Science, Bhim Rao Ambedkar Bihar University, Muzaffarpur, Bihar, India

Dr. Anil K Ojha, Reader, University Department of Political Science, Bhim Rao Ambedkar Bihar University, Muzaffarpur, Bihar, India

Dr. Sachidanand Singh, Lecturer, Department of Political Science, Tribhuwan University, Kathmandu, Nepal

Dr. C D Amar, Reader, University Department of Political Science, Bhim Rao Ambedkar Bihar University, Muzaffarpur, Bihar, India

Dr. Manjari Verma, Reader, Department of Political Science, LS College, Bhim Rao Ambedkar Bihar University, Muzaffarpur, Bihar, India

Dr. Kumari Kiran, Senior Lecturer, Department of Political Science, RLSY College, Bettiah, Bhim Rao Ambedkar Bihar University, Muzaffarpur, Bihar, India

Prof. Vikas Narayan Upadhyay, Reader, Department of Political Science, RDS College, Bhim Rao Ambedkar Bihar University, Muzaffarpur, Bihar, India

Dr. Sadhana Thakur, Reader, Department of Political Science, Sri Arvind Mahila College, Patna, Magadh University, Bodhgaya, Bihar, India

Dr. Madhu Singh, Senior Lecturer, Department of Political Science, RBBM College, Bhim Rao Ambedkar Bihar University, Muzaffarpur, Bihar, India

Prof. Rajkumar Singh, Professor & Head, University Department of Political Science, Bhupendra Narayan Mandal University, West Campus, Saharsa, Bihar, India

Dr. Naresh Kumar, Reader, University Department of Political Science, Bhim Rao Ambedkar Bihar University, Muzaffarpur, Bihar, India

Nam Seong Mun, Research Scholar, Banasthali Vidyapeeth, Banasthali, Rajasthan, India

Dr. B K L Das, Reader, Department of Political Science, KCTC College, Raxaul, East Champaran , Bihar, India

Dr. Dilip Kumar, Former UGC Research Fellow, University Department of Political Science, Bhim Rao Ambedkar Bihar University, Muzaffarpur, Bihar, India

Dr. Anjana Jha, Reader, University Department of Political Science, Bhim Rao Ambedkar Bihar University, Muzaffarpur, Bihar, India

Dr. Bipin Kumar Rai, Senior Lecturer, University Department of Political Science, Bhim Rao Ambedkar Bihar University, Muzaffarpur, Bihar, India

Dr. Rajesh Kumar, Assistant Professor, Department of Political Science, School of Social Sciences, Guru Nanak Dev University, Amritsar, Punjab, India

Dr. Satish Kumar, Assistant Professor, Department of Political Science, Central University of Haryana, Mahendragarh, Haryana, India.

Dr. Sanjeev Kumar, Research Fellow, Indian Council of World Affairs, Sapru House, New Delhi, India

Dr. Saurabh, Research Fellow, Indian Council of World Affairs, Sapru House, New Delhi, India

1

Nepal's Recent Constitutional Crisis in Historical Perspective

SHREE KRISHNA JHA

Recent constitutional crisis in Nepal is not a new phenomenon of politics. Constitutional crisis is somewhat perennial to the volatile and other turbulent politics of this small state, wedged between two giant neighbours, India and the People's Republic of China. The range of Nepal's constitutional history is no longer than fifty years. Till 1959, the country did not have a constitution as such in operation. This was inspite of the fact that this tiny state alone had the prestigious record of surviving as a non-colonial state in this part of the world. On the other hand, it was also the predicament of the country to remain for long under a medieval political system of monarchical absolutism isolated from the world outside.

The territory which is known as Nepal was brought into being as a single political unit during 1967-69. Prior to that it was a conglomeration of numerous principalities under small but independent rulers. Prithivi Narain Shah, the ruler of one such principality viz., Gorkha, conquered and integrated them into a centralized system under his dictatorial rule himself as the God Incarnate king as per the Hindu tradition.[1] This royal absolutism was later substituted by the automatic rule of the Ranas. In 1846, Jung Bahadur Rana usurped power from the Shah king by resorting to what is known as *Kot Massocre*. He however allowed the institution of the King to continue unhindered as a divine and fictitious sovereign authority. Thus, Nepal lived under a highly personalized, familial and autocratic rule of the Ranas for nearly a century without having any constitutional code.

However, towards the end of the first half of the twentieth century, there was a widespread movement for freedom and democracy in this part of the world, especially in Nepal's southern neighbour, India, with whom it has had pervasive cultural and social linkages. Hence when India became independent and established a democratic system, the Nepalese people rose in revolt against their autocratic rules in order to bring democracy in their country too. It was undoubtedly a danger signal for Ranacnacy. Hence, the then Rana Prime Minister, Padma Shamsher came forward in 1948 with the offer of a constitution to the Nepalese people. The 1948 constitution—the first ever in Nepal—had been officially termed as the "Government of Nepal Act, 2004 Vs." Modelled on the pattern of the Government of India Act, 1935, the constitution had been drafted by two Indian constitutional experts, Sri Prakash and Professor R.U. Singh, who had been invited by the Rana Prime Minister. It was specifically mentioned in the constitution: "I, Maharaja Padma Shamsher Jung Bahadur Rana, do hereby ordain and promulgate this Constitutional Act." The constitution did provide for some modest rights to the people (designed though as subjects, not citizens) and their superficial participation at local level.[2] However even this token of freedom to the people was not acceptable to some hardcore power-wielding members of the Rana family. Hence, the implementation of the constitution was sabotaged.

Later on, when Moham Shamsher, the next Prime Minister, who had so vehemently opposed the constitution in 1948, tried to enforce it in 1950 out of nervousness in new of the growing movement for political reforms. But it was too late by then. There was a volcanic eruption of the movement resulting from the dramatic flight of the King to New Delhi in 1950 in conspiracy with the Nepalese political leaders and the Indian Ambassador in Kathmandu which caused the sudden collapse of the Rana rule. Subsequently the King returned to Kathmandu as a result of the Delhi Settlement which promised the formation of a democratic government in Nepal.[3] Accordingly on 18 February 1951 King Tribhuban issued the historic Proclamation which was called the Interim Constitution or the Interim Government of Nepal Act, 2008 Vs. The underlying spirit and provisions of this constitution were in conformity with a true democratic set up and they categorically provided for a Constituent Assembly consisting of the people's representatives to draft the constitution of the country.

However, the promise failed to be fulfilled. The collapse of the Rana dictatorship provided the fertile ground for mushrooming of the political parties. Most of them were devoid of any ideology whatsoever and intended to capture power. The adventurous leaders of such parties as well as the top leaders of the Nepali Congress indulged in selfish and nasty rivalries and conflicts vitiating the political atmosphere. The political chaos thus created, distressed and compelled King Tribhuvan, to issue ultimately a Royal Proclamation on 10 January 1954 in which he asserted the Royal supremacy. This undoubtedly proved a death-blow to the prospect of democracy in Nepal. Soon his death in 1955 encouraged and emboldened his successor, King Mahendra, who was known for his distaste for democracy, to sabotage the agreement for having a Constituent Assembly to draft a constitution for the country. Instead, he boldly asserted his royal prerogative to grant a constitution to the people. Hence, for nearly five years, this became a contentious issue between the political leaders and the King as to whether the proposed constitution of Nepal be drafted by a Constituent Assembly consisting of people's representatives or granted by the King. The political leaders finally lost the battle and the King won it establishing his sovereign authority to grant the constitution.

Thus, the 1959 Constitution of Nepal, the first one in the history of the country was a gift from the monarch and it was clearly based on the absolute authority of the King. The constitution suffered from an inherent contradiction in the sense that it provided for a parliamentary set-up under a sovereign monarch. Democracy recognises the sovereignty of the people and the rule of law and not the rule of a person. Against this background, a General Election based on the principle of universal adult franchise was held in 1959 for the first time in the history of the country. Surely, it was a historic event for the people who had never experienced even he semblance of recognition as citizens. Under the charismatic leadership of Late B.P. Koirala, the Nepali Congress secured absolute majority in the election. He was nevertheless, reluctantly and belatedly appointed Prime Minister by the King and the worst of all, he was not allowed to continue in power for long. On 15 December 1960, the King staged a coup, abrogated all the institutions of parliamentary democracy, banned the political parties and the press and imprisoned all political leading including the Prime Minister. Nepal was thus put under the direct rule of the King. Subsequently on the 16 December 1962 the King bestowed on the country a new constitution which was "a rather odd but ingenious combination of certain features of the National Guidance System in Egypt and Indonesia, the Basic Democracy System in Pakistan, the Class Organisation System in Egypt and Yugoslavia and the Panchayat System in operation in several Indian states."[4] The constitution provided for the establishment of a panchayat democracy which was subsequently organised on a four-tier structure. This was indeed to cover-up the dictatorship of the monarch rather than to foster political participation of the people.

The constitution declared Nepal as an independent, indivisible and sovereign monarchical state and designated the people as King's subjects. The 1962 constitution was framed and enforced in an atmosphere of haste and uncertainty. The author of the constitution King Mahendra, who had usurped all pawn was indeed afraid whether he would be in a position to hold on. He faced violent opposition in the beginning for his adventurous effort to make the institution of monarchy politically omnipotent. The 1962 constitution was actually a device to formalise and legalise this process and also to delude the Nepali people that the country was heading toward a real democracy. The whole thing was quite intricate and delicate which needed considerable calculations and planning. But the situation also demanded immediate step to bolster up support for the King. Therefore, the original format of the constitution was neither final nor complete. It was only after five years of its operation when the people at large approved of, or at least acquires, the basic philosophy of the constitution, it was given the final touch through the first amendment. As such, the first amendment was not an amendment in the real sense of the term, but completion of the constitution-making process itself. On 27 January 1967 King Mahendra in accordance with the amending authority vested in the King, promulgated the first amendment on the recommendations of a special committee of the National Panchayat under Article 82 of the constitution. There was no public or legislative demand for amendment. In fact, the King himself had realized the need for this amendment.[5]

According to the amendment, the Panchayat system was described as "partyless and democratic" in the preamble to the constitution. Fundamental rights were redefined to include freedom to form associations and organisations, but no political parties or organisations with political objectives. Provisions for laying special emphasis on the decentralisation of administrative authority, maximum public participation in the economic progress of the nation and proper protection to private enterprises were included. The amendment also provided for a Council of Ministers "to aid and advise His Majesty in the discharge of his functions" and the appointment of a Prime Minister, if the King so desired. Ministers and Prime Ministers were made collectively and individually responsible to the King. King Mahendra's constitutional measures could not conceal the starke reality of his authoritarian rule. Nor could they make the new system immense from attacks of the opposition. Nevertheless, so long as he was alive, his authoritarian rule continued. His death in January 1972 looked like a challenge for his successor,

King Birendra, who was then in his twenties only and who was also known to be favourably disposed lowering to democracy. Gradually, he appointed a Seven-Member Royal Commission on 9 February 1975 for suggesting constitutional reforms. Accordingly on 12 December 1975, the King introduced certain changes in the constitution, known as the Second Amendment, by promulgating an ordinance. This further fortified the system and enhanced the powers of the King.[6]

The second amendment failed to smoothen and strengthen the functioning of the system. The system's failure on various front and the increasing corruption and high-handedness in administration pushed it to the point of collapse during the nation-wide violent upsurge in June 1979. In utter confusion, the King announced on 24 June 1979 a referendum on the question whether the people wanted the system to continue with suitable reforms or would prefer a multi-party system instead. Further, in order to allow the people and the same political parties to participate in the referendum freely and fearlessly, the King, albeit without any formal amendment to the constitution de facto libralised the system substantially. The banned political parties, the press and the people were permitted to function without any let or hindrance. Despite this, the protagonists of the multi-party system lost and the royalists won the battle in the referendum. Soon after the announcement of the result, King Birendra declared in his proclamation over Radio Nepal on 14 May 1980:

> He consider the sacred will of the entire people to retain the partyless Panchayat system with timely reforms ...... We shall introduce amendment in the constitution within sometime according to these proposal, in consultation with all side.[7]

Barely a weak after this proclamation, the King announced the formation of an Eleven-Member Constitution Reforms Commission which soon started functioning by collecting public response to the questionnaires prepared by it. After examining the wide ranging responses to the questionnaires, the commission submitted its recommendation to the King. The King referred them to the Special Committee comprising the member of the Standing Committee of the National Panchayat to prepare the draft of the amendment. Accordingly on 15 December 1980, the King promulgated the third amendment to the constitution. The wide-ranging changes introduced by the third amendment, provided the complexion of a parliamentary form of government to the continuing system.[8] But they in no way affected the paramount position of the King in the system. Hence, although it was widely appreciated it could not satisfy the hardcore democrats.

However, it cannot be denied, that as a result of the referendum and the third amendment, the political system and political atmosphere in Nepal underwent some worthwhile changes conducive to the prospect of democracy. Nepal no longer remained a regimented society. As such, the gradual increase of critical opinion took the robust form leading to the great political uprising under the vanguard of the communists in 1990. The ultimate result was the collapse of the authoritarian system. The King was now compelled to help the establishment of a democratic system. The result was the new constitution of 1990 which made a bold declaration:

> To enact and enforce this constitution made with the widest possible of the Nepali people, to guarantee basic human rights to every citizen of Nepal; and also to consolidated Adult Franchise, Parliamentary system of Government, Constitutional Monarchy and Multi-Party democracy… and also to establish an independent and competent system of Justice…; keeping in view the desire of the people that the state authority and sovereign powers shall ... be exercised in accordance with the provisions of this constitution.

The adoption of this constitution was indeed a landmark in the constitutional development of the country. However, the fact remains that some loophole had still been left for the King to assert his powers. Notwithstanding their disturbing features, a free and fair election was held according to the provisions of the Constitution in 1991 and the government of the majority party i.e., the Nepali Congress was formed under the leadership of G.P. Koirala without any hitch or hindrance on the part of the King.

To sum up, Nepal's exercise in constitution making from 1948 to 1990 was charaterised by the conflict between the country's tradition of authoritarianism and the people's aspiration for democratic government. The King remained the stumbling block to democracy till 1990. Therefore inspite of the fact that the 1990 constitution bestowed effective powers on the popularly elected Prime Minister as the head of the government, the apprehension that the King would sabotage the functioning of democracy did continue. Not unnaturally, the left parties, which had by then become quite strong, had forcefully demanded the abolition of the institution of monarchy at the time of framing of the 1990 constitution. The King belied this apprehension. Nevertheless, the democratic government under the 1990 constitution could not function smoothly. It was because tolerance, restrainting and adherence to norms on the part of political leaders required for the successful function of democracy found lacking. The result was the utter instability of government. No government survived for more than two years since 1991 as no party secured the absolute majority or the parties become accustomed to coalition culture. From 1990 to this day. 17 Prime Ministers were installed in office besides the King's direct rule for sometimes during the early years of Gyanendra's Kingship.[9]

The recurring instability in fact encouraged the militant section of the communists in Nepal known as the Maoists to resort to a largescale violence to capture power. For quite some time arson, loot and murder made the life hell for people in some party of the country. It war a kind of civil war causing distress not only to the people and government of Nepal, but to other countries friendly to Nepal which wanted democracy to flourish there. Amidst all their country the most tragic and ghastly incident, worse than even the Kot massacre, when King Birendra along with the members of his family was brutally murdered in his palace. His younger brother, Gyanendra took over us the King who made a Kain effort to restore peace through his direct rule. Instead, there was widespread opposition and protests against his rule which further worsened the situation. In April 2006, the movement brought about a change in the nation's governance. An Interim constitution was promulgated with the King giving up power, and an Interim House of Representative was formed with the Maoist members after the new government held peace talks with the Maoist rebels. The number of parliamentary seats were also increased to 330. The UCPN-M entered into a peace deal with the seven parliamentary parties and in April 2007 they joined the government. Maoist guerrillas gave up their arms and were housed in UN supervised cantonments, with the promise that they would be integrated into the army in future.

On 10 December 2007, the Interim Parliament passed a bill that would make Nepal a federal republic with the Prime Minister becoming the Head of the State. Accordingly on 10 April 2008 the first election in Nepal for the Constituent Assembly took place. The Maoist emerged as the single largest party in the election though failing to secure a simple majority in parliament. The Constituent Assembly had been elected to facilitate the transition of the country to a democratic republic. Its members were entrusted with the task of drafting a constitution that would guarantee fundamental rights and governance based on the rule of law to the citizens. On 28 May 2008, the parliament legally abolished the 239 years old monarchy and declared the country a republic by an overwhelming majority. Following this, Prime Minister G.P. Koirala tendered his resignation to the Constituent Assembly i.e., the parliament.

On 19 July 2008 voting for the election of the President and the Vice-President took place in the Constitution Assembly. Parmanand Jha was elected as the first Vice-President of Nepal, but Dr. Ram Baran Yadav and Ram Raja Prasad Singh the two leading Presidential candidate failed to secure the required minimum votes in the first round. In the second round, however, Dr. Ram Baran Yadav of the Nepali Congress won and the Maoist candidate Ram Raja Prasad Singh was defeated. Subsequently, on 15 August 2008, the Maoist leader Pushpa Kumar Dahal, popularly known as Prachanda, was elected as Prime Minister. However, he could not remain in office for long. The President did not approve his decision of sacking the Army Chief, who was opposed to the large-scale integration of the Maoist combatants into the Army. In reaction to it, Prachand resigned on 4 May 2007. Madhav Kumar Nepal of CPN-UML became the next Prime Minister. Eversince Prachand's resignation, Nepal has plunged into a constitutional crisis. The Assembly's mandate of framing a new Constitution was to be realized by 28 May 2010 after the extension by one year. Hence just on the verge of the expiry of the date, a three-point agreement was reached and signed by the representatives of the three major parties viz., Prachand, Sushil Koirala and Jhalanath Khanal. It was agreed:

1. We are committed to moving ahead with consensus and cooperation to take the peace process to a meaningful conclusion to carry out all the remaining works related to the peace process and to accomplished the historic responsibility of completing the task for writing of the new constitution.
2. Though a significant progress has been made in the constitution writing process it has not been completed yet. Therefore, we have agreed to extend the tenure of the Constituent Assembly by one year.
3. Based on the agreement to fulfil these responsibilities and works as soon as possible, we are ready to form a national consensus government and for that the Prime Minister of the incumbent coalition government is ready to resign without delay.

Hence, just two minutes before the deadlock of 28 May 2010, a resolution was passed to extend the term of the Constituent Assembly for another year. Nepal's present constitutional crisis is more political than constitutional. It is a kind of power-struggle based on ideological differences. Maoists are putting to much emphasis on large-scale integration of their guerrillas into the army. The other parties especially the Nepali Congress, are apprehensive of the Maoist motives. While they agree to the integration of Maoist combatants in the army, they are opposed to their number being 19000. Moreover, they want the return of the seized property by the Maoist guerrillas and disbanding of the paramilitary structure of the YCL. Further, they differ in their concept of democracy. The Nepali Congress suspect that the Maoist would like to erect the structure of dictatorship in the name of democracy. Not surprisingly, the constitution writing apart, the parties have failed to arrive at a consensus for having a Prime Minister to translate the proposal of the national government.

END NOTES

1 Shah rulers are believed to be high-born Rajputs who fled to the Himalayan region as a consequence of the Muslim conquest of Rajasthan in the Fourteenth Century.

2 For details, See, Shree Krishma Jha, *Nepal's Experiments in Constitutionalism: 1948-1981*, Occasional Papers Series 5, Centre for the Study of Nepal, BHU, Varanasi

3 *Ibid*, pg.16

4 Bhuwan Lal Joshi & Leo E Rose, *Democratic Innovations in Nepal: A Case Study of Political Acculturation*, California University Press, Clifornia, 1966; Mandala Book Point, Kathmandu, 2004, Reprint, pg.396

5 *Gorkhapatra*, Kathmandu, 23 January 1967

6 Jhapaha Pond, Kathmandu, *no. 2*, pg.23

7 *Gorkhapatra*, Kathmandu, 15 May 1980

8 For detailed provisions of the Third Amendment, See, Jhapaha Pond, Kathmandu, *no. 2*, pg.39

9 K P Bhattarai (Thrice), G P Koirala (Four times), Man Mohan Adhikari (Once), Sher Bahadur Deuba (Thrice), Lokindra Bahadur Chand (Twice), S B Thapa (Twice), Pushpa Kumar Dahal "Prachand", Madhav Kumar Nepal, Jhalanath Khanal and Baburam Bhattarai (Once)

2

Political Impasse in Nepal: Implications for India

NALINI KANT JHA

Since the election of the Constitution Assembly in Nepal in April 2008, very little has been achieved towards deliberating over the framing of the Constitution of the country. While Prime Minister Madhav Nepal resigned on June 30, 2010, almost two months after Maoist led crippling strike during May 2-3, Nepal still does not have a new Government. With two candidates on the fray, Ram Chandra Poudel of Nepali Congress and Pushpa Kamal Dahal of Unified CPN-Maoist, they tried 16 times to elect a new PM, without success. Because of the lack of support from other parties, chiefly Communist Party of Nepal (United Marxist-Leninist) and a few Terai-based parties, who abstained from voting or remained neutral, none of the candidates garnered the required majority votes in the CA of 6001. Dahal withdrew his candidacy on September 26, after contesting for the 8th time. Part of the reason was the party's vote buying scandal involving China, made public via the leaking of the infamous Mahara wiretap. Poudel was the sole candidate for the top post and ran the race until the end, i.e. 15th time, until the Supreme Court on December 18, 2010 ruled that lawmakers in Parliament could no longer choose to remain neutral or abstain from voting in the election for the prime minister. The deadlock has only helped lengthen the life of the caretaker government of Mr. Nepal, till now.

The Roots of the Impasse

The roots of the present political impasse can be traced to the deep trust deficit between the Maoists and non-Maoists; issue-based and personality-driven differences within parties, a complex arithmetic in Parliament where no party has a majority, and a troubled India-Maoist relationship. Large sections of the Nepali Congress, the Communist Party of Nepal (Unified-Marxist-Leninist), and Madhesi parties do not trust the Maoist commitment to democracy. They cite the Maoist reluctance to 'give up the PLA'; the presence of a militant youth wing; the Maoist track record of 'attacking' institutions while in government; and 'undemocratic' constitutional proposals as proof of their totalitarian mindset. The fact that the Maoists are stronger than many of the older mainstream parties put together adds to their fear.

Maoists, on the other hand, feel cheated out of power despite being the largest party in the house. They allege that older parties have allied with the Nepal Army and external powers. Maoists point to their participation in elections and the constitutional process, and willingness to keep their army in cantonments as visible proof of commitment to peace and democracy. Even as other parties have made Maoist leadership of Government conditional on immediate resolution of the Maoist armed forces, namely, Peoples Liberation Army (PLA) issue, the Maoists argue that movement on PLA and Constitution writing should happen simultaneously, for they fear other parties may back out of writing a 'progressive constitution' if they give up the army. Besides the timeline, there is also a difference in the way both sides envisage the nature and modalities of the integration and rehabilitation process, with the Maoists linking it with the 'democratisation of the Nepal Army.'

This trust deficit is complicated by divisions within parties. The Maoists suffer from an ideological crisis, when a pragmatic faction believes that they should seek to 'preserve existing achievements' while another hardliner group continues to harbour goals of a 'people's republic'. Party Chairman Pushpa Kamal Dahal 'Prachanda' and his old comrade, Dr. Baburam Bhattarai now share a competitive relationship with both vying for leadership of the Government. The NC and the UML are as mired in ideological and personal feuds too. Both have strong right wing factions, though officially the parties remain committed to the 2006 political framework. In the UML, Chairman Jhalanath Khanal is closer to the Maoists while influential leaders like K.P. Oli and Madhav Nepal are closer to the NC and India. Khanal was a candidate in the first round of elections for prime minister, but had to withdraw since his party's central committee, controlled by Oli and Nepal, had made his candidature contingent on obtaining a two-thirds majority. There are factional feuds between Sher Bahadur Deuba and acting president Sushil Koirala in the NC, though it has put up a coherent front for now by nominating Ram Chandra Poudel as the official candidate.

It is in this polarized context that the numbers game in Parliament is being played out. Prachanda can form a majority government if the Madhesi parties with 82 seats in the house back him. The NC's Ram Chandra Poudel needs the support of both the UML and the Madhesi front to get to the majority figure of 301 seats, which will essentially be a continuation of the previous anti-Maoist coalition under a new leadership. Torn between Khanal's 'pro left' and Oli's 'pro democracy' factions, the UML is neutral for now and so are the Madhesis—the reason why there has been no result in the past two rounds. Now add to this maze the unsaid, but major factor, for the political impasse —the troubled India-Maoist relationship. For the past year, India's energy in Nepal has been directed at isolating the Maoists politically. The relationship had dipped when Prachanda was PM—rising Chinese engagement, the perception that the Maoists were going back on their commitment to democracy, and efforts to reshape the Nepal Army were seen as potentially harmful to Indian security interests. India played an active role in blocking the Maoist move to dismiss the then army chief and putting together the Madhav Nepal Government. The Constitution-writing and the larger peace process India helped initiate in 2005-06 became secondary to the task of 'democratising' the Maoists. Indian strategists felt the former rebels had to undergo a 'course correction' by moving on PLA largely on terms set by the Nepal Army and other parties, disbanding the Young Communist League, renouncing violence, and ending 'anti-Indian' activities and rhetoric. Officials also let it be known informally that they would prefer Dr. Baburam Bhattarai, seen as a more pragmatic leader. A split in the Maoist party was, in the Indian scheme, a desirable objective.

To deal with the Indian stance, Prachanda adopted a dual strategy. Privately, he tried to reassure India he was committed to democracy, would respect India's core interests, and gradually deliver on the conditions laid out. Besides using normal diplomatic channels, the Maoist chairman met senior RAW officials in London, Singapore and Kathmandu to convey the same message. But they did not buy it. At the same time, Prachanda publicly blamed India for the fall of his government; said the Maoists would never follow Indian diktats; hinted darkly that India was involved in the death of UML leader Madan Bhandari in the early 90s in a car accident and the royal massacre in 2001; and said India had propped up the Madhav Nepal government. Prachanda's public position obviously did not win him any friends in the Indian establishment. Bureaucrats circulated his speeches as proof of why

Nepali Maoists had to be kept out. Hence, Delhi has used its leverage with its supporters in the UML, and Madhesi parties to block either a Prachanda-led or Khanal-led left Government, and trying to keep Maoists in general, and Prachanda in particular, out of state power.

Departure of the United Nations Mission in Nepal (UNMIN)

The political impasse has got further fillip with the departure of the United Nations Mission in Nepal (UNMIN) on January 15, 2011. UNMIN's exit has come at a time when there is a growing recognition that Nepal may fail to meet its extended deadline of writing the Constitution by May 28, 2011. Though a new process to elect a Prime Minister will begin soon, its outcome remains uncertain. All formal structures of the 2006 political framework though which republican Government in Nepal has been framed after the ouster of the Monarchy, suddenly appear fragile, as UNMIN has been an integral component of Nepal's peace agreements. For the past four years, it has monitored 19,000-plus combatants and 3,000-plus weapons of the Maoist People's Liberation Army (PLA) and a limited number of personnel and arms of the Nepal Army (NA); chaired the Joint Monitoring Coordination Committee (JMCC) that acts as a mechanism to resolve disputes between the NA and the PLA; and has been a symbolic deterrent against the resumption of violence.

While the caretaker Government led by Madhav Kumar Nepal has been able to ink a last-minute accord with the Maoists before the pullout, agreeing that a Special Committee headed by the Prime Minister will take over UNMIN's task, the issue of who will be monitored is yet to be settled. The Government insists that there is no need to monitor the NA anymore as the context has changed, but the Maoists argue that the same arrangement applies to both armies in accordance with the Agreement on the Monitoring of the Management of Arms and Armies. Another issue that needs to be settled is who will resolve the disputes on the code of conduct and its violations? UNMIN did so in JMCC quietly and efficiently out of media glare but no alternative neutral mechanism is in place yet. The impact goes well beyond the technical aspects, about which the parties may well find an agreement at the last minute. UNMIN's absence will increase the possibility of even a small incident going out of control. The Maoists have already said this takes the country back to a 'ceasefire' situation. UNMIN leaves at a time when the most complex task of this process—integration and rehabilitation of the former combatants—has not even started. Its expertise and good offices could have played an important role in guiding the process. Peace has held in Nepal because Nepali actors, including the Nepal Army and the Maoists, have behaved with restraint and responsibility, but UNMIN's exit will make this task more difficult. Surprising though it may appear, mainstream political parties in Nepal has worked in close cooperation with India to outs the UNMIN from Nepal. For, after the abolition of Monarchy in Nepal, these political parties, especially the Nepali Congress and the Communist Party of Nepal (Unified Marxist Leninist), now see the NA as an ally and are deeply suspicious of the Maoists' intentions and their commitment to democracy. UNMIN began to be viewed as providing a "safety blanket" to the former rebels for, it treated them as a 50 per cent stakeholder in the peace process and recognised their army. The NA has always been furious with UNMIN for "equating the NA and the PLA," and was lobbying hard to be removed from UNMIN's monitoring.

As regards India, it has traditionally disliked international actors in its 'backyard.' In the beginning, New Delhi worked hard to ensure that UNMIN had a limited and weak mandate but more recently it has been lobbying with other international capitals, and now with fellow members in the Security Council, to wrap up the mission. Washington and London were happy to follow the Indian lead on Nepal, even though the Secretary-General in his report stated conditions for UNMIN's departure were not optimal. This formidable coalition—of India, the US and the UK internationally and the non-Maoist parties and the Nepal Army domestically—argues that UNMIN's presence allows the Maoists to drag on the peace process; its exit will remove a safety valve and bring pressure on them, in turn, forcing them to "reform" and "disarm."

Pushing UNMIN out is in line with India's broader Nepal policy, the key tenet of which is to isolate the Maoists and exclude them from the formal power structure as the only way of democratising them. Indian officials believe that the Maoists have used the peace process only "tactically;" harbour authoritarian ambitions and cannot be allowed back to power until they undergo a "course correction," which would include giving up the PLA. Otherwise, it is argued, they would consolidate power and subvert all democratic institutions, and it would be impossible to dislodge them. To this end, India has invested enormous political capital in galvanising the anti-Maoist forces together, and ensuring that Prachanda did not get to the majority mark in the prime ministerial elections. There is a section in New Delhi and Kathmandu which believes that like UNMIN, the Constituent Assembly, where the Maoists command 40 per cent of the seats, is another "safety blanket" for the former rebels. This school tried hard to ensure that the CA did not get an extension last May. They are now hoping for its dissolution by the May 28 constitutional deadline, in order to "isolate" the Maoists from the only formal state structure in which they have space—the legislature. The those who have adopted this approach, are forgetting that it only strengthens the dogmatic branch within the Maoist party, and underestimates the intensity of the conflict Nepal will be engulfed in if the constitutional process fails. It is true that the Maoists have dragged their feet on the integration and rehabilitation of the former combatants, which makes the other parties insecure about their democratic commitment. At the same time, the Maoists are insecure too far, they are being asked to surrender a major source of power, largely on the Nepal Army's terms, while in the Opposition. The hardliners within the party are quick to point out how "bourgeoisie democracy" is a sham as the largest party cannot form a government, how "Indian expansionists and Nepali reactionaries" have ganged up on them and are conspiring to dissolve the CA, and how the party should not give up the PLA at such a time reminding the cadres of the Mao dictum, "without the army, people have nothing."

The reluctance of the non-Maoist parties to share power, the Maoist dogma, and India's hardliner approach—all feed on one another and have contributed to mutual insecurities and belligerence on all sides, limiting the space for compromise. The Nepali Congress' withdrawal from the prime ministerial race, and the imminent initiation of a new process to elect a prime minister, have opened up one final opportunity to reengineer the consensus needed to push the peace and constitutional process forward.

Conclusion

Bridging the trust deficit between Maoists and Nepali Congress, and Maoists and India requires enormous political management but is critical to completing the peace process and writing the constitution. Forming a majority Government, with either the Maoists or the NC remaining in opposition, will not solve any of the fundamental problems. The main onus, of course, is on the Maoists to resolve their ideological battles once and for all, fulfill peace process commitments, reassure the other side, and be flexible on issues of leadership in the government. At the same time, non-Maoist parties too have to realize this is a process, not an event. Isolating the largest party in the country just creates a situation of dual power on the ground, and adds to the instability. If they are worried about the undemocratic tendencies of the Maoists, the only way to counter it is by building their steadily diminishing political strength on the ground. For its part, India should analyse whether there are other ways to exert leverage on the Maoists to be mindful of their core concerns, without destabilising the broader process, for the present stalemate is not helping India achieve any of its tangible interests in Nepal.

Hence instead of aiding the polarisation, India needs to play a constructive role in enabling a deal on power-sharing and the peace process, in which the Maoists will be accommodated while locking them into handing over their coercive apparatus. This is essential for Constitution-writing. Otherwise, this May could well mark the collapse of Nepal's ambitious experiment in political transformation.

REFERENCES

1. *apdnepal.org.np/index.php/constitution-making-support-program*, accessed on October 11, 2011
2. *asd.org.np/en/transition/constitution*, accessed on February 10, 2011
3. *biz.nepaltrekkinginformation.sajha.com/sajha/html/openthread.cfm?...*, accessed on November 16, 2011
4. *blog.com.np/.../drafting-of-statute-for-the-republic-of-nepal-formall...*, accessed on November 11, 2011
5. *community.indigenousportal.com/_Nepal...Constitution/.../109225.ht...*, accessed on November 12, 2011
6. *en.wikipedia.org/.../Women's_representation_in_the_Parliament_of_...*, accessed on February 1, 2011
7. *gorkhapatra.org.np/rising.detail.php?article_id=58508&cat_id...*, accessed on January 23, 2011
8. *hamropalo.com/nepal.../maoists-intensify-works-on-constitutionmaki...*, accessed on October 7, 2011
9. *issat.dcaf.ch/.../Post-Conflict-Peace-Building-and-Constitution-Makin...*, accessed on November 6, 2011
10. *kathmandumetro/.../delay-in-constitution-craftin.*, accessed on February 8, 2011
11. *lesliechand.blogspot.com/2011/04/constitution-making-in-nepal.html*, accessed on February 8, 2011
12. *manjeet.com.np/.../global-climate-talks-and-constitution-making-in-n...*, accessed on February 19, 2011
13. *mumbai.academia.edu/.../Nepali_Constitution_making_adop to_ada...*, accessed on November 3, 2011
14. *nccnepal.org/Document_Uploads/.../1061471298858416l606.pdf...*, accessed on July 11, 2011
15. *newsclick.in/international/one-more-lifeline-ca-nepal*, accessed on March 29, 2011
16. *nhrcnepal.org/project1.php?ProjNo=4*, accessed on February 25, 2011
17. *np.china-embassy.org*, accessed on August 19, 2011
18. *story.nepalnational.com/index.php/ct/9/cid/.../id/16378389/*, accessed on November 4, 2011
19. *swiss-nepal.ch/downloads/newsletters/nl_FinalN97-p04.pdf*, accessed on February 16, 2011
20. *trulynepalivideos.meronepalma.com/people-blame-parties-for-delay-...*, accessed on March 21, 2011

3

Restructuring the State in Nepal: Issues in Framing the New Constitution

B C UPRETI

The framing of a new constitution in Nepal is an issue of high significance for several reasons. It has indeed generated new hopes and challenges for the transitional politics in Nepal. While it is being visualized that the new constitution would realize the goals of envisaging a new political set up for the country based on the principles of democracy, the political process that has taken place in the post 2006 phase has aroused a large number of expectations and demands thereby raising new challenges for the Constituent Assembly. The very fact that the Constituent Assembly has not succeeded in framing the constitution even in the extended time frame clearly indicate at a complex political situation, rise of conflicting interests and struggle for power. How to reach to a political consensus that would help in timely completion of the constitution has become a serious issue in Nepal. It is interesting to note that even after Nepal's transition to democracy, modernization and development in 1950, the traditional state continued.[1] The Nepalese ruling elite always tried to create a balance between the tradition and modernity. However, the continuation of the traditional political elite as a 'modernizing elite' made the democratic institutions and processes merely a cover to the political supremacy of the traditional elite under the leadership of monarchy. The 1950 democratic transition though installed a democratic system under a new constitution; it failed in restructuring the state.

It was for the first time in the 2006 democratic movement that the Nepalese state faced a serious challenge. In fact the moist movement raised the issue of restructuring the Nepalese state and it acquired a broader political acceptance.[2] In the subsequent years the issue of restructuring of the state became a major component of the areas of political transformation in Nepal. The abolition of the age old institution of monarchy and declaring Nepal a republican state was a significant development which indeed set a tone for the structural changes in the Nepalese political order. The Constituent Assembly is entrusted with the task to frame a new constitution for the country in tune with the issues raised in the post 2006 Nepalese political discourse. To what extent the Nepalese state is undergoing a change in the new constitution? What are the major issues that have to be addressed? What are the positive and negative directions of the changes that are likely to come up in the politico-constitutional structure of Nepal?

Historical Foundation of State in Nepal

The modern state of Nepal came into existence in 1769. Before this, Nepal was divided into several small principalities. There were forty six small states in the east and the west of Kathmandu valley known as Baise and Chaubisi states, representing different ethno-religious groups and communities. These apart, there were tribal states of kosi and Gandaki basins, the Newar rulers of Kathmandu valley and the Sen of Palpa. Prithvinarain Shah a ruler of the Gurkha principality took up a military adventure and invaded and defeated various principalities and the rulers of Kathmandu. He then founded the Kingdom of Nepal in 1769. King Prithvinarain Shah was conscious of the fact that the new Kingdom was founded by a forced unification of diverse ethno-cultural groups that were inimical to and fighting with each other for their existence. It was indeed a matter of great consideration that these principalities had been brought together through a military expedition. It was not possible to sustain a Kingdom on the basis of military power alone on a long-term basis. There was a need to evolve a socio-cultural milieu that would give shape to a monolithic social order in Nepal. There was also a need to evolve a strong socio-religious base for the rule of the King.

Before the unification of the Kingdom of Nepal tribal societies divided into different clans and tribes existed in various parts of the country.[3] These tribal societies were not monolith and they had diverse forms and systems. King Prithvinarain Shah tried to define the state in religious-cultural terms.[4] It was declared that all the land resources of Nepal automatically rest under the possession and control of the king. The land was identified as Desha (the country) and the people as Realm. The King was projected as the sovereign lord and he had proprietary authority over both. He was accorded a religious basis and was declared as the representative of Lord Vishnu and that way, he got the right to rule the Desha and Realm both. Thus, the King was projected as sovereign over the land; the protector of his subjects and the territory and the source of all aspirations, rules and traditions. A multi-dimensional approach was followed by Prithvinarain Shah in order to build a strong and unified Nepali society and state. He followed a stratified hierarchical model for the society based on the Chaturvarna Hindu caste system in which the Brahmins and the Kshatriya (Rajputs) were accorded top places. All the ethnic groups were classified as other categories. On the whole there were four varnas and chattis jats (Thirty six castes) Jung Bahadur Rana further classified them in his Mulki Ain of 1854.[5] King Prithvinarain and his successors though accepted this diversity they never recognized cultural rights of these communities. They were not given any opportunity to articulate their rights and demands.[6]

It was Brahmins and Thakuris of the hills who were accorded positions of power and privilege. This bowed seeds of regional disparities as well. The Brahmins and Thakuris of the hill region became repository of the hill culture. Henceforth, identification with the hill culture and caste hierarchy became important in determining power and prestige of various social groups. The people of Tarai were encouraged to follow the hill culture traits, which they resented and consequently they got dissatisfied and felt being discriminated. Thus, there was no identification of the people of Tarai with the state. The differentiations between the hill and the Tarai people provided negative definition for Nepali national identity. It laid foundation of the conflict of hills visa-a-vie Tarai.

The Shah rulers used the Hindu religion as a source of legitimization.[7] Therefore; they started a process of Hinduaization in order to form a monolithic society. The non-Hindu tribal communities were motivated as well as forced, to accept the Hindu religion. They were categorized under the Hindu hierarchical caste order. All tribal people were placed in the lowest web of the social order. A policy of compensation and accommodation was also followed in order to bring non-Hindu communities within the fold of Hinduism. The Magars were allowed to wear scared thread as recognition to the services that they had rendered to the Palace. King Prithvinarain Shah said. "I am the King of Magrant". It was indeed an emotional attempt to assimilate Magars. The Gurungs were also rewarded for the services rendered by them to the Gurkha rulers. Autonomy was also given to Limbus for sometime. These policies and perceptions formed historical foundations for resentment among the ethnic groups. The monarchy accorded protection to Hindu temples and shrines. Crime was graded on the basis of caste and punishment was fixed accordingly. The Brahmins were excluded from capital punishment. Thus, Brahminic supremacy became hallmark of Nepali state and society. A unified religious and cultural policy was persuaded. Nepal was given the status of a Hindu state which continued even after 1950. King Prithvinarain Shah said 'Yo Asli Hindustan Hao' (This is the real Hindustan) The Gorkhli or the Kura was designated as the language of Nepali in the form of Nepali.

The Mulki Ain of 1854 promulgated by Jung Bahadur Rana as said earlier, was the first attempt to provide a legal framework to the state and the social order. The four main ingredients of state were defined as Rajan, Rajya, Praja and (social order). It also accepted the hierarchical social order. The state was to this hierarchy and it was the main arbitrator in caste to matters. The Shah and the Rana rulers adopted policy of consolidation of the tribal areas. Once the rulers were defeated Brahmins and Kshatriyas were sent in these areas the local administration in their hands. Land was confiscated from the tribal land under the Kipat land system and it was redistributed to Brahmins and the under Raikar, Birta, Guthi and Jagir systems. New settlement of the high people in the tribal areas was encouraged. A large number of high caste Brahmins and Thakuris became absentee landlords in these areas. The high caste people also encouraged to migrate to these areas. Thus, the indigenous people exploited under the new system. The policy of patrimonialism, rewards punishment continued. Thus a patrimonial state and society emerged in Nepal.[8] Actually, the ruling elite tried to lay down a foundation of a unified model under the framework of Hindu monarchy. Obviously, no efforts could be made towards the socio-economic uplifting of the backward communities, assuming that it would generate consciousness among them ultimately being detrimental to the authoritarian rule of the monarchy itself. The state thus emerged in Nepal has been viewed by scholars as a predatory Hindu state.[9]

State in the Post-1950 Era

The withdrawal of the Rana rule in 1950 paved a way for the emergence of a new political order in the country. It was expected that the democracy would take roots in the country there by changing the nature and dynamics of the state. But the foundation that was laid with this objective in the form of 1951 New Delhi Agreement made goals of democracy and development in Nepal rather complex. The systematic changes that followed ensured a political role for the traditional power elite. The monarchy and the nobility took advantage of the situation and consolidated their powers. The democratic forces that were still emerging, weak and non-experienced got marginalized. As a result the traditional elite remained the centre of politics. The political parties could not consolidate themselves and the democratic institutions failed in taking roots. The traditional political forces remained in power in the name of democracy.

It also gave protection to the traditional hierarchical and feudalistic social order. The upper caste and groups continued to remain at the helm of affairs except that their positions and roles were changed. For instance, the leadership of the political parties, higher positions of bureaucracy and army went to high caste hill people. Similarly, the member of the landed aristocracy began to take new economic roles unleashed by the process of modernization and development. Thus, it was the same traditional political elite, which acquired a central position in the new system and it was the same social and economic elite that acquired new roles and positions. The consolidation of these trends actually took place after 1955, when King Mahendra took over the reigns of power. King Mahendra wanted to see the monarchy at the helm of affairs. It required the persistence of the traditional norms of Nepali state and society. He saw democracy and political parties as main obstacles in his way to the establishment of an authoritarian political system. King Mahendra promoted the traditional bases of Nepali state and society. He also gave a new direction to Nepali nationalism that would promote and preserve Nepal's cultural identity. The anti-Indianism also became a strong force behind the new nationalism of Nepal.[10] This was considered to be essential to down the democratic forces, for whom the Indian democracy was a source of inspiration.

The panchayat system established in 1962 recognized the political supremacy of the monarch, Hindus identity of the state and the upper caste supremacy. The panchayat institutions were meant only to provide a democratic cover to the authoritarian rule of the King. The King had a vested interest in the preservation and promotion of the traditional norms of the state based on the Hindu philosophy and hierarchical social order. The Hindu identity, upper caste status, identification with the Parbatiya culture and allegiance to the King remained the bases for acquiring positions in politics, administration and army. King Mahendra thus tried to consolidate the traditional identity of the Nepali state. His new Mulki Ain of 1963 although did away with the legal recognition of caste and Nepal was accepted as a multi-structured society, in practice caste hierarchy remained the basis of social and political relations. His attempts towards land reforms also promoted interests of the Parbatiyas and the upper caste people. His slogan of one bhasa (language) and one bhesh (dress) was also based on the narrow identity of the Nepali state.

It was, however, not possible for the authoritarian rulers to contain socio-economic changes in the country. It had become imperative to respond to the process of modernization and development. Foreign aid had begun to flow into the country after 1950. Infra-structural developments began to take place. The country was opened to external economic forces. Trade and commercial activities began and new economic practices came up. The development of educational and the other such facilities took place. It is true that most of the basic facilities were urban centered and limited to the upper echelons of the society. Nevertheless, these developments gave way to social change and social mobilization. The various minority non-Hindu groups became conscious of the discrimination and deprivation that they were faced with because of authoritarian rule and the upper caste domination in politics and administration. Many of these groups and communities began to assert upon their ethno-cultural identity. These trends became more expressive after 1990, when democratic rule became operative once again. Two trends were quite visible in the post 1990 period: consolidation of the ethno-regional identities and the demands for the restructuring of the state and transforming the society. These contradictions ultimately gave rise to discontent and formation of various identities, particularly after the 1990 political change. It is clear form the above discussion that the Nepali monarchy tried to preserve the traditional norms of the state and the society so as to secure their own political interest. But they could not restrain the forces of modernization and development. It naturally produced contradictions within the Nepali society.

Discontent against the State

Widespread discontent began in Nepal against the authoritarian nature of the state. New identities had come up, which were conscious of deprivation and discrimination against them. They considered political order in the country responsible for their marginalization. The 1990 movement was an expression of the discontent against the state. However, the Nepalese rulers always tried to follow a policy of appeasement. After the 1990 movement though the basic contours of the Nepalese state and politics remained unchanged, the establishment of a democratic political system was a major breakthrough. However, the political process in the post 1990 era proved to be frustrating.[11]

Maoist Movement and the Question of Restructuring of State

The question of restructuring of the traditional Nepalese state was raised for the first time in the demand charter of the Maoists in 1996. The Maoist launched a nation wide violent movement based on the guerrilla tactics with a view to ensure a new political system for the country based on the principles of the people's democracy. They believed that the establishment of the people's democracy which they called 'Noulo Janbad' would not be possible without transforming the traditional state. They tried to win support of those groups of the Nepali society that were frustrated with the existing Nepali state, which they believed was highly authoritarians, centralized and exclusive.

The Maoist conceptualized the notion of restructuring of the Nepali state along the following lines:

1. Declaring Nepal a republican state, which would obviously meant abolition of age the old institution of monarchy.
2. Declaring Nepal as a secular state.
3. Framing a new constitution by the representatives of the people ensuring secularization, republicanism and inclusive democracy.

The issues of restructuring the state came up for the first time in Nepal. In fact, the democratic forces had also believed in the continuation of the traditional state. It was because of this reason that the institution of monarchy remained a centre of power and the project of democracy remained scarcely attended. Actually due to the powerful position of the monarchy and the weak and fragile nature of the political parties and leaders, they always looked towards monarchy for support and sustenance.

The Maoist demands were not accepted by the government and a tough militaristic attitude was taken towards them. However, the Maoist Succeeded in gaining support from different quarters and intensified the movement. The governmental actions proved to be helpless in containing the Maoist insurgency. On the other hand monarchy tried to take advantage of the situation and concentrate powers in his hand on the plea that the government was not in a position to maintain peace, and law and order. The monarchy began to assert politically since 2002 and reached to its climax with the King assuming all the political powers in early 2005. The monarchy though tried to rise as the supreme political authority in the country, his actions went against his own aspirations. The Maoists were already opposed to monarchy and now the democratic forces also realized that the institution of monarchy was the greatest obstacle to the promotion of democracy in the country. The political parties of all colours had followed a reconciliatory approach vis-à-vis monarchy in the past. But now on the one hand, the Maoist insurgency had created a complex political situation and now the steps taken by the monarchy had though exposed him but created a difficult political situation as well. This led to the polarization of political forces against the steps taken by king Gyanendra and to restore democracy in the country. Not only that the democratic political parties come to a common platform to give up insurgency and join the struggle for democracy through democratic means. In a dramatic way the Maoist declared withdrawal of their guerrilla war and declared their support to the Seven Party Alliance. Actually the Maoists had realized that the monarchy was isolated and loosing its socio-political support base fast. It was also realized that there were possibilities of realizing their political goals, through democratic means. The restoration of democracy in the county in 2006 also marked an era of peace stability and democracy. Although the post 2006 phase of Nepali politics continued to remain with uncertainty, confusion and conflicts yet the Maoists persuaded there political goals in a process of political compromises and alignments. Interestingly the mainstreams political parties also began to support the Maoist proposals of secularism, republicanism and federalism. It was in this sprit that the 2007 interim constitution was framed and (CPNM) the Maoists joined the interim government. The Constituent Assembly which came into existence in April 2008 formally declared Nepal a republican state in its first meeting on 26 May, 2008.

The Task of Framing a New Constitution

The task of framing a new constitution was assigned to the Constituent Assembly (CA) which was constituted in April 2008 on the basis of direct elections following the principle of universal adult suffrage.[12] The CA was to frame 6th constitution after 1948 when Nepal for the first time tried to frame a constitution. It is interesting to note that

1. All the constitutions had resulted due to a political change in the country.
2. All the constitutions were framed by a constitution committee constituted by monarchy. It was for the first time in 2008 that a Constituent Assembly was constituted on the basis of adult franchise although demands had been raised to frame a constitution by CA as early as 1950.
3. All the constitutions in the past tried to maintain a balance between the traditional and the modern political forces with the result that the constitution could never become an instrument of democratization process.

The Constituent Assembly which was to act as a constitution making body as well as a parliament for the interim period was to frame a new constitution within a time period of 2 years. It was given an extension of one year in mid 2010 and now again it has got some more time to finalize the constitution. The fact remains that the CA has not been able to complete its task in within the stipulated time frame. Actually these have been certain inherent difficulties. None of the political parties could gain a majority in the CA. The CPN (M) emerged as the largest party. It was frustrating to the larger political parties such as Nepali Congress and UML. It affected the working of the CA adversely. The Maoist movement and the post 2006 political process mobilized a number of groups, parties and individuals and many of them got place in the CA. They seem to have been more concerned about the interest of their communities or regions. It has indeed made formulation of national consensus rather complex.

It may also be stated here that the struggle for political power, governmental instability, the challenges of post-conflict socio-economic order, the question of rehabilitation of the Maoist combatants, etc made the political situation in Nepal non-supportive to the smooth working of the Constituent Assembly. What has been much more important is that the new constitution of Nepal has to be framed in the context of restructuring of the state. It is true that the declaration of a republican state and the consequent abolition of the age old institution of monarchy set a tone for the new constitution. But the question of restructuring of state is a complex issue. The transition from a monarchical to republican state involves several complex issues. The political transition in Nepal has aroused several ethno-religious and regional aspirations. The Maoists raised a number of issues in order to gain support from different quarters of the society. Now these have to be accommodated within the new constitution. The fact that the CA has not been able to give a constitution even within the extended time period clearly indicates that the things are not that simple. It seems that there is lack of consensus over several issues. Some of the issues have come up for the first time in the political dynamics of the country and how to address to them in the constitutional framework is a big challenge. Some of the issues relating to the restructuring of the state that needs to be incorporated in the constitution may be briefly touched up on here.

Issues in the Making of the New Constitution

The restructuring of the Nepali state and policy within a new constitutional framework was basically a demand of the Maoists that was later on endorsed by the mainstream political parties. Nepal has already been declared a republican state. As pointed out earlier the monarchy has already been abrogated and despite the uncertain political situation in the country it is certain that Nepal is adhered to a republican state structure with a parliamentary system of governance. Nepal has adhered to parliamentary system since the begriming. Secularism has been one important issue that has to be addressed properly in the new constitution. Nepal has already been declared a secular state. It will be a major departure from the past as all the constitutions of Nepal till 1990 had declared it a Hindu state. Understandably, Nepal was declared a Hindu state in order to strengthen the philosophical foundation of the institution of monarchy. The fact remains that the Nepalese society has exhibited religious tolerance and an understanding between different religions. However, with the mobilization of new groups and communities which had remained isolated so far the status of Hindu state was being questioned. In the changed context a secular state has become a necessity. However, there are several conceptual and practical aspects associated with the notion of secularism, which need to be properly defined in the new constitution.

One very important aspect that has come in the recent Nepali politics is that of federalism. It has been already committed that the notion of federalism will be incorporated in the new constitution. Nepal came into existence through a process of annexation and assimilation of various states that existed before 1769. The Shah rulers tried to establish a strong unified Kingdom. However, in the context of contemporary political transformation identity and autonomy has become a major issue. The Mongol National Organization had raised the issue of autonomy to various Mongolian ethnic groups. The people of Tarai had also been raising this issue at different time periods. However, the Maoists gave a formula of creating autonomous regions which also included some of earlier suggested autonomous regions.

It has already been accepted that Nepal will have a federal state structure. The idea of federalism has mobilized the communities and the regions to demand for an autonomous entity of their own within the proposed Nepalese federation. What should be the basis of federalism is a serious issue in the case of Nepal. Two criteria have been offered the ethnic and the regional. Both the principles have its positive and negative connotations. It is true that they provide answer to many of the problems of a plural society. But it also generated new problems. Nepal is a small country in terms of its size. So the question that too what extent federalism is viable for smaller states seems to be relevant. However, Nepal's geography is typical. It has two distinct geographical regions: Hills and Tarai (plains). Historically the Tarai region and the people of Tarai were discriminated and deprived. They now strongly believe that their identity and interest can be preserved within a federal principle only. However, Tarai people have strongly adhered to the unity of Tarai and have given the slogan of one Desh one Madhes. They would not accept division of Tarai. The people of Tarai have faced violent movements for the last two years and the question of Tarai has become a sensitive issue. On the whole federation is a delicate issue. There are other issues which need to be dealt with extensively as sharing powers between centre and state, allocation of resources, centre state relations and so on. In the recent years many more issues have come up which new to be addressed in the new constitution. The question of Dalits has become significant. The Dalit communities have organized and have been demanding special treatment to them including policy of reservation. The gender issue is important. The minority groups such as Muslims, Christians, are also asserting for their identity and rights. What is important here that the various ethnic, religious, minority, gender, ethno-regional and aspiring for the realization of their interests in the new constitution. Therefore, the constitution has to be accommodative and forward looking.

Lastly, in order to accommodate many of their interests and aspirations there is a need to accord prime importance to the principle of inclusive democracy. In the last few years the notion of inclusive democracy (Samawaise Loktantra) has become quite popular in Nepal. The aspects of inclusive democracy will have to be properly incorporated in the new constitution. To conclude it is clear that the new constitution of Nepal would be a complete departure from the past with republican, federal and inclusive politico-administrative and democratic structures. How best these issues are addressed in the new constitution is a vital matter for peace, stability and solidarity in the country because these are going to be the critical features of the Nepali politics.

As pointed out earlier, there has been a lot of horizontal and vertical mobilization of groups, communities and regions in the part. They are looking for a space in the up coming political constitutional structures. There is need to follow an accommodative approach. There are unsettled questions take the rehabilitation of the Maoist combatants. The question of socio-economic transformation is equally important. The goals of equity and justice can not be realized unless the challenges of poverty elevation, upliftment of the weaken sectors and the issues of land reforms, all properly taken up the project of restructuring of the state will not be complete. However, what is most disturbing at the moment is that the political process in the country has not supportive to constitution making process.

End Notes

1. For a discussion of some of the issues, See Bhuwan Lal Joshi & Leo E Rose, *Democratic Innovations in Nepal: A Case Study of Political Acculturation*, California University Press, California, 1966, Mandala Book Point, Kathmandu, Reprint, 2004
2. See, B C Upreti, *Maoists in Nepal: From Insurgency to Political Mainstream*, Kalpaz, New Delhi, 2008
3. R S Chauhan, *State and Society Building in Nepal*, Sterling Publishers, New Delhi, 1989, pp.1-23
4. Richard Burghart, ed., *The Conditions of Listening: Essays on Religion, History and Political in South Asia*, Oxford University Press, Delhi, 1976, pp.226-59

5. See, A Hotter, *The Caste Hierarchy and the State in Nepal, A Study of the Mulki Ain of 1854*, Wegner, California, 1979
6. Prayag Raj Sharma, *The State and Society in Nepal, Historical Foundations and Contemporary Trends*, Himal Books, Lalitpur, Nepal, 2004, pg.212
7. John Whelpton, "Political Identity in Nepal: State, Nation and Community", in David N Gellner E et al., eds., *Nationalism and Ethnicity in a Himalayan Kingdom, the Politics of Culture in Contemporary Nepal*, Harvard Academic Publishers, Amsterdam, 1997, pp.43-44
8. Rishikesh Shaha, *Nepali Politics, Retrospect and Prospect*, Oxford University Press, New Delhi, 1978
9. Harka B Gulung, *State and Society in Nepal* in David N Gellner, ed., no.7, pp.465-72
10. See, B C Upreti, *Uneasy Friends*, Kalinga Publications, Delhi, 2001, pp.55-66
11. See, B C Upreti, *Nepal: Democracy at Cross Roads*, Kanishka Publishers, New Delhi, 2007
12. See, B C Upreti, *Nepal, Transition to Democratic Republican State*, Kalpaz, New Delhi, 2010

4

Possibility of Constitutional Vacuum and its Implications in Nepal

NAVIN MISHRA

Introduction

'Political development' is the increased differentiation and specialization of political structures, and the increased secularization of political culture and its significance lay in the increased effectiveness and efficiency of the performance of the political system and its increased capabilities. The term was defined as "an institutional framework capable of continuous absorption of changes". But the words "ability", "will", "skill" and "capacity" continued to be used in a rather imprecise manner. Halpern, Huntington, Diamant, Holt, Turner, and others have developed a new approach variously known as "Will" and capacity approach, problem solving capacity, "institutionalization", and "ability to sustain new goals. Amidst universal thinking, it may be necessary to do some fresh thinking on the meaning and purpose of political development, The development that cannot fulfill these needs of the masses cannot be regarded as development in the true sense. The fulfillment of basic needs also includes other needs, other goals and other values, which are equally important, like freedom of expression, right to information, right to life and right to participation in the decision-making process.

In fact, what is regarded as development in the context of the Western societies suffered a setback in the third world. Development has not been equitable—we see under-development on one side and development on the other. It is the indiscriminate development of the Western world that is responsible for the large-scale underdevelopment of the so-called developing world; though the countries in this category can't follow or pursue wrong policies and blindly copy or imitate the West. So, the goals and meaning of development have to be redefined and we have to try to envisage such plans and theories which would better suit our environment and our needs.

Need of the Hour

What would be Nepal's political future is everyone's concern today. The comprehensive peace agreement on 22 Mangsir, 2063 B.S. between seven political parties and the Maoists has made people optimistic of political stability and a promising future. Nepal has indeed achieved maturity in its journey from absolute monarchy to a federal system. Rural people have become conscious of their rights and are discussing "State Restructuring". The 1990 Revolution in Nepal has made people aware of their role, responsibility, recognition, identity and goes against the old discriminatory system. Now people of every caste, religion, gender, and ethnicity are agitating for their demands to be addressed by the state. The Madhesi agitation in Terai, The Tharuwan agitation, the Churebhawar, Limbuwan, Khumbhuwan, OBC agitations are aimed at establishing their identity and ensuring the preservation of their rights. But their demands have not been addressed yet; on the one hand, the aspirations and expectations of people are sky-rocketing and on the other, Nepal is facing instability. The political parties have gone back on their responsibility of nation-building and the drafting of the Constitution and have reduced themselves to mud-slinging, and power politics. The relations between political parties has soured and is embittered. Madhesh-based parties are engaged in infighting. The serious challenge before the nation is to maintain national integrity and bind the people in one thread and lead the nation towards progress. This is the political need of the hour.

In the context of third world society especially Nepal, democracy and development has not been adequately understood or analysed as a value or an ideal that is a part of the overall goal of social development. Whether democracy has been given a proper chance by society to prove itself against the wishes of those who may be inclined to condemn it without proper trial, needs to be seen. The hard earned democracy is due to the success of the people and because of the sacrifices made by our martyrs time and again. The activities, trends, practices, and developments after the restoration of democracy have been a matter of concern for every citizen. Any system can be sustainable only if it is brought to practice honestly and when the people derive benefits from it. The system can have a bright future if people enjoy their rights freely and have access to the decision-making process. If we study political development the following questions arise:[1]

(i) Why did people's movement 2062/063 B.S.?
(ii) What were the ultimate achievements of the people's movement of 2007, 2046 and 2062/063 B.S.?
(iii) What were the false and fallacies of Nepali politics after 2046 B.S.?
(iv) What is federal system and what types of stake restricting will?

The struggle for democracy and political change in Nepal was due to the long-cherished desire of the people. The overthrow of 29 year-long partyless 'Panchayat' regime was something to boast about but it was very important that the appropriate model of democracy be adopted and the high expectations of the people be resolved one after another on priority basis. No system can reach its zenith without a constructive and conscious contribution on part of the citizens, parties and other internal or external factors. It is the duty and responsibility of the citizens to study, analyse and to work to uproot the unwanted trends, practices, support the positive pro-people activities so that a peaceful, prosperous and stable system can be put in place that will be tolerant and progressive. All these have been distant dreams for the people of Nepal.

Causes of Political Crisis and Conflict Prior to 2062-063 B.S. Movement

The politics of Nepal and the political system, which is in transitional phase, has been suffering from many weaknesses. It takes a long time to achieve political stability, development, cultivate and establish political culture cultivated and establish democratic principles and institutions but even a little honest effort can far reaching influence, which can get established in future. But nothing can be said with surety about Nepali politics what happens the and the people should not shirk from their responsibility. So the following are the causes/reasons for the failure of the system next moment. ... There is no doubt that the past 12 years of democracy is responsible for different kinds of crises in the system but undoubtedly the political actors and the people's movements 2062/063 B.S.[2]

(1) Lack of experienced, mature and selfless political leadership.
(2) Lack of institutionalization of political institutions and process.
(3) Inefficiency of the government to lead the country towards peace, progress and prosperity.
(4) Large-scale corruption, bribery and misuse of country's resources.
(5) Nepotism, favoritism and political criminalization.
(6) Avoidance and neglect of sovereign Parliament.
(7) Political parties were unable to deal and the Maoist demands and tactics.
(8) Inter-party and intra-party conflict and fractional politics.

Declaration of Emergency on 19 Magh 2061 B.S. forced the Maoists and seven mainstream political parties to come together in a single front and have a common agenda for the establishment of federal democratic republican state.[3] This alliance has surprised the entire world. The twelve-point agreement between the Maoists and the parties of 7th Mangsir, 2062 B.S. proved to be a landmark event.[4] This inspired the people from all sectors of national life to take to the streets to expose the outdated feudalistic autocratic sysem.[5] The seven-party alliance and the Maoists called for a nationwide general strike from 24th Chaitra to 27th Chaitra. This was aimed at forcing the king to transfer sovereignty to the people by withdrawing the Royal proclamation of 19 Magh 2062 B.S. The seven parties led the revolution peacefully from the urban areas whereas the Maoists revolutionalized the people from all over the country. The King Gyanendra Shah and his well-wishers used brutal force and different pressure tactics for 19 days but to no avail. Imposition of curfew and breaching orders was common every day. King Gyanendra Shah had no other option but to announce the reconvene the dissolved Parliament on 11 Baisakh 2063 B.S.[6] The political parties accepted his address and the reinstated Parliament held its first meeting on 15 Baisakh 2062 B.S. The second meeting of the Parliament through Royal decree passed the proposal of holding Constituent Assembly on 17th Baisakh 2063 B.S.[7]

Meeting of Restored Parliament

The first meeting of reinstated Parliament was held on 15 Baisakh 2062 B.S. The meeting began 5 hours after the scheduled time due to Prime Minister Girija Prasad Koirala's illness. Mrs. Chitra Lekha Yadav presided over the function. Mr. Koirala in his letter message invited the Maoists for Constituent Assembly elections, ceasefire and peace talks. The second meeting was held on 17th Baisakh, which passed the proposal for having a Constituent Assembly with majority. On 20th Baisakh 2063 B.S. the Cabinet withdrew the red corner notice against the Maoist leaders and the terrorist tag on them. The government also declared unilateral cease-fire complementing the existing ceasefire.

The restored Parliament passed with unanimity on 4th Jestha 2063 B.S. the restoration of sovereignty in the hands of the people and the king became a helpless spectator without any kind of authority. The historic declaration also made it clear that the Constitution of Nepal 2047 B.S. would be regarded as null and void to the extent that it opposes the declaration. This declaration of the House of Representatives is taken as the landmark event. It was no less than the Magna Carta of United Kingdom and Bill of Rights of the USA.[8] The Government of Nepal and the Communist Party (Maoist) sat for summit talks on 12 Jestha 2063 B.S. for the first time and on 1st Asar 2063 B.S. and decided to formulate an Interim Constitution, to hold Constituent Assembly elections by constituting an interim government and six other points.[9]

Peace Agreement, 2006

The long-cherished desire of the people to have self-rule and a people's Constitution through people's movement to establish democracy, peace and changes in the socio-economic, culture and political sectors is very near to being a possibility. To endorse the 12-point agreement among the parties, an 8-point deal, a 22-points deal and the ceasefire agreement between the government and the Maoists, and a comprehensive peace accord was signed on 5th Mangsir 2063 B.S. by Prime Minister Girija Prasad Koirala and Pushpa Kamal Dahal alias Prachanda. It contains 10 Articles. It paved the way for a triangular agreement to manage the arms and the combatants in PLA organized by CPN (Maoist).[11]

Terai Movement

There was happiness and confidence for peace, progress and prosperity after the success of the second Jan Andolan. Newly formed groups and parties of the Terai movement blamed the government for its betrayal towards democracy; the continuing discontent cost loss of life and about 60 per cent of the total GDP. National and international trade collapsed and the industrial sector suffered the most. India reasserted its stance that the solution for the Madhesi movement should be sought through the Constituent Assembly, the political parties and the Madhesi groups. The Madhesi Forum reached an 8-point agreement to end the deadlock in the southern part of the country. The government and the other political parties expressed their deep commitment towards an amicable solution. The compromise created the environment for elections to the Constituent Assembly.

Constituent Assembly Election—Emergence of New Political Power

The election was contested by all together 54 new and old political parties including the CPN (Maoist) and some royalists as well. Large-scale violence, clashes between the cadres created an environment of fear and insecurity but couldn't keep the voters away. Apart from few incidences of irregularities, the election process was free and fair, according to the international observers. The political parties also accepted the results and declared the elections to be a milestone for the country. The first to win the election was Prakash Man Singh of the Nepali Congress from Kathmandu constituency No. 1. The results were not up to the expectations of the Nepali Congress and the

Communists (UML). 50 per cent of the Maoist candidates, 15.5 per cent of Nepali Congress 13.75 per cent of CPN (UML) and 12.5 per cent of MPRF won the direct election from their respective constituencies.[12] The results of proportional representation, indirect elections were even more surprising—CPN (Maoist) could win 100 seats, Nepali Congress 73, CPN (UML) had 70 seats, MPRF 22, TMDP 11 seats, and others had marginal success.[13] Altogether, CPN (Maoist) emerged as the largest political party with 220 seats, Nepali Congress had 110, CPN (UML) 103, whereas MPRF had 52 and TMDP could get 20 representatives into the Constituent Assembly.[14] There are about 170 Constituent Assembly members from different ethnic tribes and more than 50 members from the dalit, about 150 Madhesi members and 200 were women: this has been what Nepal was looking for, its new dimension of inclusiveness and participatory democracy coming into practice in the real sense. New hopes and aspirations have arisen for a peaceful conversion of old Nepal into a new peaceful, progressive and prosperous Nepal.[15]

Constituent Assembly—New Dimension

The dream, desire and the demand of the people of Nepal to have a Constituent Assembly came true on 28th Chairta, 2064 B.S. The people's voice to have their own Constitution during their struggle for democracy was even endorsed by the Ranas as well as the Delhi accord: in fact, the convening of a Constituent Assembly had been part of the agreement worked out in Delhi in 1950/5/A.D. and had also been promised to the people in King Tribhuwan's proclamation of 18 February 1951 and in the 1954 representation of the People's Act. The successful conduct of the Constituent Assembly election has set an example for the rest of the world and the whole world is eyeing Nepal with great curiosity. The landmark event achieved after the misery, suffering and sacrifices is expected to change the political façade of the country. It will not only help to rebuild the nation but also will redefine the meaning of revolution for the country.

Achievements of the Constituent Assembly Election

- *Right to Draft full fledged democratic Constitution:* The people's dream came true with the opportunity to participate in drafting of the Constitution. The people of all castes, races, religions, ideologies, professions, regions and genders caste their valuable votes to choose their representatives for drafting the Constitution. For the first time in Nepal's history, people exercised their sovereignty.
- *As a tool of meaningful conclusion of peace process:* The Constituent Assembly has always and everywhere been viewed as the forum which

drafts the Constitution according to which the country is ruled, but Nepal's experience has been somewhat different. It is the integral organ of thed comprehensive peace accord as well as of the peace process. Without drafting and the enactment of a meaningful people's Constitution, the peace process of Nepal would never be possible; so, it should be viewed not only as the principle process of the drafting of new Constitution but also as the means to transform war into peace. So it is the roadmap of peace, progress and future prosperity of Nepal and the Nepalese people.

- *Emergence of New Political Forces:* The Constituent Assembly election rewarded the revolutionary forces, advocating far-reaching changes in society, economy, culture and politics of the country. The power of the state has shifted towards a new tribal revolutionary class, a marginalized community, the Madhesis, and women. Those who were neglected till now are in Constituent Assembly, to end dynastic rule. The Constituent Assembly has ensured at least 33 per cent representation for women and this would end the patriarchal male domination and empower them. The qualitative and quantitative emergence of new political forces can be regarded as a historic event.
- *Abolition of feudalistic monarchial system:* The abolition of 240 year-long deep rooted monarchy and the establishment of a Republican state is a unique event in the world. Never ever has the institution of monarchy been outdone by the Constituent Assembly but the then king rejected the people's movement and remained in the palace until Jestha 2064 B.S., and was finally driven out of the palace. Though desperate efforts were made by the monarchy, nothing could stop the people from getting what they desired, i.e., the complete abolition of the monarchy.
- *Democratization of the Maoists:* The coalition of armed Maoists and the mainstream political parties with their faith in the democratic parliamentary system for political change is also a novel experiment. The Maoists inspired the people in the remote rural areas, the Seven-Party Allaince, and the urban settlers, and led the movement. These coalition partners had signed the 8-point, 12-point and 22-point agreements for the restoration and strengthening of the democratic system. The Communists who believed in the seizure of power, expressed their faith in the ballot and showed inclination towards peaceful transformation. The guns of the People's Liberation Army had found their way to the Cantonment under U.N.M.I.N.S. supervision.

- *Expression of People's Desire for Peace, Progress and Prosperity:* The large-scale participation of the people in the Constituent Assembly election reflects their deep concern for peace, stability and 'loktantra'. The people expressed their sovereignty for the first time in a fearless manner, free from the insecurity, confusion and uncertainty that had hitherto prevailed in the national and international arena. The unexpected participation of the women, Dalits, Madhesis and the marginalized communities sent a clear message that there was no alternative to peace.

Conclusion and Recommendations

Development is a concept, which will perhaps never be defined fully to everybody's satisfaction or effectiveness. The idea of development as we understand and pretend to practice it, did come from the outside world. For most of the thinkers except the economists, development is a complex process that can take different meanings and characteristics and therefore, require different approaches in different cultural spaces and times. It is often confusing and a cause for disagreement. However, Nepal's own cultural and intellectual heritage has much to recommend for the meaning, character, complexity, contradictions and importance of what we call development.

It needs to be reaffirmed that development as understood in Nepal is an idea and practice that has grown by virtue of the country's interaction and participation as a member of the modern international community. Our acceptance of the paramount importance of the principles of market economy has attained its current recognition as the new method. It is the convergence of interests between the national and international power centres that has played an influential role. It is now taken as a process of integration with the global economy or pursuit of "liberalization" in the interest of economic efficiency. Nepal today, in this view, has strayed from the path. Nepal's development has failed; it was because of its basic strategy. The nation has been plagued by near stagnation. The political events and trends we have lived through in the period when Nepal has been striving for development, if we recall, will help us to understand better the influence of "politics" on the mission, motives and outcomes of development. In the process we can also ponder whether democracy has been given a proper chance by the society to prove itself against the wishes of those who may be inclined to condemn it without proper trial. There are well known facts and tendencies in the country's political history that should underline how comparable the political events and actions are to the country that experienced them in its experiment with democratic politics and development.

If we draw the inter-period parallels in attitude and events, we will be able to recognize the common factors contributing to the malaise of the first and second experiment with democracy during the first and second Jan Andolans. We also see how little has changed in the "balance a power" between the three major political forces until 2062/063 in spite of the momentous changes in the regime structure. The three forces may be broadly identified as the palace, the people along with the political parties and the external forces.

However, there were circumstances when people seemed to enjoy certain civic and political rights including freedom of expression and the right to dissent. Significant reforms were also introduced in the administrative and judicial system, which were archaic and not conducive to a society gearing itself for development. The political parties actively engaged in the competition for political power, some of them would demand early election for Constituent Assembly till 2017 as well as after 2052 B.S., the start of Maoist insurgency. At times they competed for favour of not only of people and the palace but also of India and U.S. whenever required. A unique system of government was emerging where a virtually absolute monarch ruled over a society that could never enjoy the benefits of democracy. The king enjoyed such exclusive status because of the relatively weak condition of the political parties, which he exploited under the policy of divide and rule. Accordingly, despite the fundamental rights, the lower classes, which were in overwhelming majority, did not have a voice and in the absence of a meaningful middle class, the upper classes would support any regime that was not a threat to their interests.

Of, the three forces the palace, the people and the external powers, the people have generally become a subject of manipulation by the other two. A political culture befitting the time and the objective of the state could not evolve. Nor could a realistic system of mutually beneficial role between the 'leaders and the people, the citizens and the state' and 'the palace and the political leaders' get progressively institutionalized. In the years after the restoration of democratic process in 2064 there was plenty to cheer about despite all the frustrations, calculations and alliance for petty internal gains; the division on party lines of even the most trusted civil society, professional groups, advocacy groups and the human rights organizations with few exceptions, are some of the problems of Nepali society which can be said to be destabilizing the political development of Nepal. The ultimate paradox in political development was, how far the political change in Nepal was driven by the masses rather than merely by involvement of the elites? We should also think whether it was the product of internally generated demands or external forces? Lastly, what did political change mean to those who struggled for it? The obvious answer would be the revolution of 2007 B.S. which was entirely the work of external forces and some conscious elite while the revolution of 2046 was principally a Nepalese movement and marked the beginning of mass politics in the country. The third concern is the concept of democracy entertained by politically conscious Nepalese and the extent of which these were realistic in the context of Nepalese society. Nepal has been facing a crisis of legitimacy in government. Not even a single government after restoration of democracy could provide good governance, efficient, effective and corruption-free administration and complete its term. They lacked the legitimacy. Nepal's continuing existence as a poverty-stricken democracy is a sorry scenario and it is still true that economic and social change is urgently required.

The people have seen that it is one thing to establish democratic aspirations emanating from injustices and inequalities are another matter. These have given rise to a query among those interested in politics: Whether and how a new political culture is likely to grow as an integral part of democratic convergence in Nepal and how an political socialization can be imparted? We should also understand Nepal's political development, the character and degree of support it may provide to the development of the society depends on the success to promote transparency and accountability in public affairs as a prerequisite for good governance and development. The voters have always been seen resisting this kind of shift in political bureaucratic culture.

Corruption had been a very old legacy in Nepal as it is everywhere else. But its current scale and dimension seems to be threatening the newly established democratic norms and values. The future Nepal or New Nepal can never be secured until the country's leadership makes up its mind and has strong determination that it is a disease that can be cured or at least reversed. Corruption is not only about misuse of public resources and unethical or illegal acts that enrich some at the cost of others. It is about how we order our values, about democracy, the rule of law, social discipline, professional self-respect, collective security and national honour. It is eating into the vitals of the state, so measures have to be taken by the government to end it. Nepalese political development has been suffering over the years due to the primacy of the personal gains over ideology, which still, also remains strong at the grass-root level. The people still vote for the candidate because he/she is 'aphno manche' (one's friend, or relative) but not for a good candidate. Factionalism has been a feature of Nepalese polity. Ever since the early days till today, the leaders are grouped into one or the other faction that is ready to takeover the other, which has been the reason for most of the political deadlock in the country. The continued political infighting and the failures of the party leaders to bring improvement in people's everyday life has brought about widespread disillusionment.

Another obstacle to the institutionalization of democracy has been the 'andolan mentality'. The temptation to take everything to the streets can be hazardous for the country's transition towards a new system of governance. A potentially more serious problem in the making of a peaceful progressive and prosperous New Nepal is the Terai and 'madhesi' religionalism. The open border, cultural similarities and the free flow of people across the border remained a cause of concern. The fear of a regional uprising in the pretext of avoidance, neglect, disrespect and domination can really be a concern for Nepal's integration and unity. The discontent among the people in the Terai actually started at the time of Referendum of 1980 with the question of citizenship rights. The parties are still fighting to get citizenship for 13 per cent of the Terai population who are living and looked upon as Indians though they have always been in Nepal. Violence erupted in the Terai region after the revolution of 2062/063 in the name of Madhesi movement, causing great damage to life and property. But the leaders of the Madhesi movement along with the major political parties are trying to address their justified demands and they are justified in doing so. It is their responsibility to give an equal share to everyone; only then can Nepal remain intact, strong, united and peaceful.

There has been a chequered history of political development. Prithvi Narayan Saha of Gorkha unified the small and petty states of Baise, Chubise, which was continued by Rajendra Laxmi, Bahadur Shah and also by Bhimsen Thapa. Nepal had to bear insult and great humiliation in anglo-Nepal war, which ended with singing of incorrect and unjust Sugauli treaty. But this couldn't lessen the nationalist feeling among the Nepalese. After the downfall of Bhimsen Thapa, the history is full of plots, conspiracies and intrigues with the policians lacking patience and competency. After the untimely demise of people's leader B.P. Koirala, the democratic movement suffered great loss. Satyagraha movement of 2042 B.S. got withdrawn due to violent bomb incidence of Janawadi Morcha. But the oppressive regime couldn't sustain long. The united people's movement of 2046 B.S. under the supreme commandership of Ganesh Man Singh paved the way for democratic changes but here too people didn't get their wish met. Monarchy continued and became even more unpopular especially after the royal massacre of Jeshta 19, 2058 B.S. The people's war led by Communist Maoist was becoming more and more successful and aggressive. There arose grave situations for the people, parties and the palace.

The government couldn't maintain law and order, peace and security and couldn't conduct elections. So, king Gyandendra Singh, the ambitions king, dismissed the parliament and recommend by Primer Sher Bahadur Deuba. Different rounds of peace talks were proving futile. So there was yet another "Cool and calm take over" by king dismissing Deuba in the charge of being inefficient on Asoj 18, 2058 B.S. He seized all the executive power in his own hand. The gulf between the political parties and the palace widened. The people didn't like King's action though they didn't express it, as the disconnect that lay latent in them. The palace tried in its extreme desperation to remain clung to the authority but destined was different. The twelve-point agreement between the political parties and the Maoist rebels might have shocked the king and his dear ones. This paved the way for the people's movement 2062/063 because of which the 237 years of old feudalistic monarchical system got abandoned. The people continued their movement led by the maintained seven political parties and the communist (Maoist) for 19 days. The use of brutal force, imposition of curfew didn't have impact upon, so king had to give up through his proclamation of 8th Baisakh 2063 B.S. People didn't tale rest, understanding there might be yet another "befooling game" with them. So, another declaration for the reinstallation of the dissolved parliament came on 11th Baisakh, 20634 B.S.

The first meeting of reinstated parliament held on 15th Baisakh, 2063 B.S. and the second meeting of 17th Baisakh, passed the proposal for constituent assembly and Nepal proceeded with the process of making people's constitution with maximum possible participation of the people. Our transition towards a full flagged democracy has some historic documents like historic declaration of the parliament, historic peace agreement 2063 and tripartite arms management treaty between the government of Nepal, Maoist revels and UNMIN. Interim constitution promulgated on Magh 1, 2063 suspended all the right but the very day violence erupted in the Terai region in pretext of Terai/Madesh movement. The five constitutional amendments till now have been carried out which, though temporarily able to manage the voice raised in different parts of the country but if not dealt seriously can prove to be very fatal for the nation. The question of proper model of federalism and the sensitive issue of inclusiveness has to be thought of very carefully so that not even a single ethnic tribe or caste feels left out or humiliated. Empowerment of one at the cost of the other can never be acceptable. Nepal has been declared as the "Independent, indivisible, sovereign, secular, inclusive, federal, democratic, republican state by the Interim Constitution which provides the vision of a New Nepal. But the present political leadership of the country should learn from the past in the larger interest of the people and the nation, to keep Nepal as it has been envisaged by its innumerable martyrs.

END NOTES

1. *The Himalayan Times*, Kathmandu, 15 Chaitra, 2064 BS
2. Mishra, Navin, *Nepal: Democracy in Transition*, Authors Press, New Delhi, 2006
3. *Republic,* Kathmandu, 20 Magh, 2061 BS
4. *Nagrik,* Kathmandu, 8 Mangsir, 2062 BS
5. *Himal,* Kathmandu, 16-30 Mangsir, 2062 BS
6. *Gorkhapatra,* Kathmandu, 12 Baiszkh, 2063 BS
7. *Kantipur,* Kathmandu, 18 Baisakh, 2063 BS
8. *Kantipur,* Kathmandu, 5 Jestha, 2063 BS
9. *The Rising Nepal,* Kathmandu, 25 Baisakh, 2064 BS
10. *Nepal Samachar Patra,* Kathmandu, 13 Jestha, 2063 BS
11. *Gorkhapatra,* Kathmandu, 22 Kartic, 2063 BS
12. *Election Result Buletin of Nepal,* Kathmandu, 29 Chaitra-6 Baisakh, 2064 BS
13. *Gorkhapatra,* Kathmandu, 4 Baisakh, 2064 BS
14. *Rastriya Samachar Patra,* Kathmandu, 11 Baisakh, 2064 BS
15. *Himal,* Kathmandu, Jestha 16-30, 2064 BS

REFERENCES

1. *asiafoundation.org/.../nepal-averts-constitutional-crisis-hope-for-dem...*, accessed on August 18, 2011
2. *azad-kashmir.com/.../constitution-making-to-complete-in-3-months-...*, accessed on September 16, 2011
3. *community.indigenousportal.com/_Nepal... Constitution/.../109225.ht...*, accessed on November 12, 2011
4. *en.wikipedia.org/.../Women's_representation_in_the_Parliament_of_...*, accessed on February 1, 2011
5. *hdr.undp.org/en/reports/nationalreports/.../nepal/name,3287,en.html,* accessed on January18, 2011
6. *himalaya.socanth.cam.ac.uk/.../IDEA_Creating_Constitution.pdf,* accessed on February 21, 2011
7. *lancau.org.np/home/download_pdf/16*, accessed on February 1, 2011
8. *lawandotherthings.blogspot.com/.../constitution-making-in-nepal.htm...*, accessed on February 10, 2011
9. *monthlyreview.org/.../womens-role-in-the-nepalese-movement,* accessed on February 11, 2011
10. *mrzine.monthlyreview.org/2010/yami080310.html,* accessed on September 16, 2011
11. *news.oneindia.in/.../constitution-making-difficult-koirala-121014900...*, accessed on June 19, 2011
12. *newsclick.in/international/one-more-lifeline-ca-nepal,* accessed on March 29, 2011
13. *unsr.jamesanaya.org/.../22-nepal-alleged-exclusion-of-indigenous-pe...*, accessed on June 17, 2011

14. *video.ezinemark.com/voices-from-below-constitution-m... - United States,* accessed on June 19, 2011
15. *wn.com/Voices_from_Below_Constitution_Making_in_Nepal,* accessed on June 18, 2011
16. *www.bippi.org/bippi/menu_left/conflicts/Nepal/Nepal.htm,* accessed on October 31, 2011
17. *www.brahmand.com/news/China-announces-Rs...Nepal.../14.html,* accessed on October 17, 2011
18. *www.butterfliesandwheels.org/2010/secular-nepal—-challenges-ahead,* accessed on August 21, 2011
19. *www.cin.org.np/inner.php?pagename=about,* accessed on April 29, 2011
20. *www.citizenside.com/.../nepal-a-demonstration-for-constitution-by-a- ...,* accessed on September 30, 2011

5

Constitutional Development in Nepal : The Legal Status of Women

VEENA SINHA

After the end of monarchy and the establishment of the republic, the country is engaged in the process of the constitution-building so that an outline of a new Nepal can be decided. The women of the country are working hand in hand with the men for the constitutional development of the country. Today, every woman in Nepal dreams of a well-organized, united country without any differences. They are hopeful that the prominent presence of women members in the assembly (197) will provide them the opportunity of getting recognition for women and fulfilling their needs and rights, so that Nepali women too will be make an identity and a place for themselves at the international level. According to human rights, women are men and equal in every society. Both have an equal right to an environment which enables them to use their economic, sociological, cultural, political, human rights and the rights of a citizen. However, since Nepalese society is a patriarchal and predominantly Hindu society, men have been using women according to their needs—from personal to political and public realms, from the home to the fields, schools, streets, marketplace and the workplace.

The Status of Women According to the Law in the Past

The convention of worshipping women as living goddesses is being followed in our country since ancient times. Similarly, there was a convention of Sati—to burn a widow alive with her dead husband on his funeral pyre was also followed but through the Muluki Ain of 1853-54, this practice was banned and only then did the widows of this country get a right to live. In 2004, following the struggle by women to get the right to vote, they not only got the right to choose their representatives but also to fight elections.

In VS 2007, in the interim constitution governance law, the limited rights of women were put down in writing. This was the first document to put down women's rights in writing. A legal ban was placed on child marriage, polygamy, and mismatched marriages but these bans could not be put to practice. The legislative of the interim constitution made after the people's movement of VS 2046 also signed on the international treaty based on the elimination of all types of discrimination over women and about a dozen others related to human rights. But all these signatures remained only theoretical; could not be implemented into practice. According to the interim constitution 2063 of Nepal, the following arrangements have been put down in writing for women:

- The provision of getting citizenship in the name of the mother under section 8.
- Under Section 13, there will be no discrimination in the state on the basis of gender.
- Under Section 18, the provision of right to social security and employment.
- Under Section 20, the provision of the rights of a woman related to procreation/reproduction and crime against women was declared as illegal.
- Under Section 21, equal rights to a son and daughter over ancestral property, according to right to social justice and based on the right of women for inclusion in an equal proportion, the right to be participants in the creation of a state. Similarly, according to Section 29, right against exploitation, according to Section 33(d) it is the responsibility of the state to abolish all discriminatory practices which have been a part of tradition and continue to exist as social laws.
- The provision of special arrangements to me made for the education of women, their health and employment, and social security. Arrangements for the payment of allowances to old and weak women and the unemployed.
- Under Section 65, the arrangement to have minimum one-third of the candidates for election to the constituent assembly as women and under Section 154, arrangements for the establishment of a commission to look after the rights and welfare of women were made.

The Condition of Women in the Present Constitution

The interim constitution of VS 2063 made extensive legal arrangements to safeguard the rights of women, but it did not help much in improving the condition of women. According to the National Census Report VS 2058, whereas the population of men in Nepal was 49.965, that of women was 50.45. Despite that, the presence of women in any field is minimal. Even today, the life of women revolves around the kitchen, household chores and the fields. Every year 12,000 women become victims of sex trade whereas 43 per cent of the women face sexual harassment in the workplace. According to the 2066/67 report released by the women's commission, 137 cases of crime against women were registered and according to the PrahariPradhanKaryalaya, 983 cases of violence of various kinds were reported within one year. Even today, almost 70 per cent of the female population is forced to live below the poverty line. 85.2 per cent of the women are actively engaged in agricultural labour, but only 10.84 per cent of them own agricultural land and 5.5 per cent are masters of their own houses. Similarly, due to the lack of education in the services; only 11.29 per cent are teachers, 2.04 per cent work in the field of Communication and Justice and 2.01 per cent are active in business related activities.

According to the census of VS 2058 (2001), out of a population of 1,92,50,000 Nepalis in the age group 6-45; 76,65,000 Nepalis are illiterate, out of which 42,20,997 are women, i.e. 34.45 per cent. From amongst Nepali women, the condition of those who live in the valleys/marshy areas and are known as 'madheshi' women is worse. They have been subjected to social discrimination for centuries now. They are completely dependent socio-politically and economically. In the same way, tribal women form 37.50 per cent of the female population. They are subjected to three kinds of discrimination—firstly because they are women, secondly because they are tribal women and thirdly because they are economically backward and dependent on others. The condition of Dalit and Muslim women is also pitiable. They are subjected to discriminatory oppression in the name of tradition.

Participation of Women in the Political Field

The participation of women in the political field has been extremely low. The four constitutions till now, i.e. VS 2004, 2007, 2015 and 2047 have been prepared without the participation of women; whereas for the structuring of the constitution in VS 2019 only one woman participated. After the formation of the interim constitution assembly, eight parties made fifty-seven women its members, which was less than even ten per cent of the total number.

Rulings in the Interim Constitution with Respect to Women Rights

In the interim constitution of VS 2063/ 64, the following provisions have been made with respect to women rights:

1. Section (20)—no discrimination on account of gender,
2. Rights related to health and childbirth for every woman,
3. Punishment by law for violent actions, physical or emotional/mental, against women and equal rights in paternal property to both sons and daughters.

Similarly, in section 21, women who lag behind due to social and educational approach, have been provided for being a participant in the structuring of the state on the basis of proportional and inclusive theory. Also, arrangements have been made therein to give allowance to single and old women; under subsection 5 of section 63, there is a compulsion for direct and proportional appointment for candidature to thirty-three per cent women. Consequently, 197 women were elected for the current constituent assembly from various parties. Legal and Constitutional arrangement related to women rights in present times:

1. Recognition on independent identity for women,
2. Priorities to widows in case of hearing,
3. First right of guardianship to mother,
4. Godson/daughter to have equal rights,
5. Complete right over part-property,
6. Recognition as owner of the house,
7. Ban on gender-based abortion,
8. Punishment on coercion by HIV infected person or on women living captive,
9. Punishment against allegation of witchcraft,
10. Provision of giving citizenship to sons and daughters on mother's name,
11. Citizenship of Nepal based on birth,
12. Provision for citizenship to a child born to a Nepali woman with a foreign citizen,
13. Allowance to women in Nepal Army,
14. Twenty per cent reservation in sentinel services,
15. Reservation in Nijamati service.
16. Foreign woman married to a Nepali man to be given citizenship within fifteen days of the marriage,
17. No discrimination, reservation and special facilities to women in foreign trade.

Women Rights and Legal Arrangements in the Forthcoming Constitution

In the upcoming constitution, there is a need to include women rights with even more strength and open mindedness, based on priority. It is necessary to also include the following rights for women in the constitution that is being made:

1. Ensuring indiscrimination—on political, social, financial and cultural basis. Also, 'indiscrimination' will have to be clearly defined in the constitution and will have to be implemented not only in theory but in practice as well.
2. Under the similarity of opportunities, the similarity in access and results will have to be established. It will have to be clearly mentioned in the constitution how rights to equality for women will be established in all fields.
3. The upcoming constitution will have to stipulate for girls also equality on the basis of education, and provision for free education by the state.
4. There will have to be a provision for declaring violence against women a crime under fundamental rights; to punish the culprit and to give compensation to the sufferer as needed, will have to be assigned as responsibilities of the state.
5. Under fundamental rights, there should be a provision for constraint and boycott for those indulging in sexual harassment, dowry, witch, purchase-sale, making servants, and child labour.
6. With respect to wealth/ property, to bring into practice the right to equality for daughters (girls), it will have to be added to the constitution as a fundamental right.
7. Provision for adding the right to familial-rights and selection of dwelling place as equal for women, like men, and to be added under human rights.
8. Legal provision for ending discrimination in distribution of paternal property as well as familial property.
9. A woman is biologically/physically different from a man. Thus, there will have to be a constitutional provision for creating an appropriate environment for her health and child-bearing.
10. Fifty per cent rebate in revenue on land ownership and transference of rights for women.
11. Constitutional provision for equal rights in control and reach for establishing identity with respect to water, forest, land, along with natural resources.

12. Violence in private establishments, society or family will have to be declared crimes and the concerned person or establishment will have to be held completely responsible and punished.
13. To make the reach of women simpler in Nijamati services, provision for increase in number of reserved seats.
14. Constitution will have to make provisions to ensure economic rights for women.
15. Provisions to put into practice all regulations related to women.

Conclusion

Today, nation's politicians, experts and members are converged in the historical task of writing the constitution for grooming the nation's future; but any work or change or structuring of the constitution would remain incomplete if half of the nation's population is kept at bay, it won't be obtained fully. Today, women in Nepal are fully capable to work for building and leading the family, the society and the nation. Thus, they should be given appropriate rights and authority to enable them to be a part of the nation's renewal. Although appropriate arrangements have been made by the interim constitution to give women complete patronage and rights, keeping in mind their rights and interests; but when all of the nation's processes are nearly blocked, in such a situation no statutory arrangement can be effectively put into practice/ use. This is the reason that despite women-related constitutional orders having been passed, the women in the country are still neglected.

REFERENCES

1. *asiafoundation.org/.../nepal-averts-constitutional-crisis-hope-for-dem...*, accessed on August 18, 2011
2. *biz.nepaltrekkinginformation.sajha.com/sajha/html/openthread.cfm?...*, accessed on November 16, 2011
3. *blog.com.np/.../drafting-of-statute-for-the-republic-of-nepal-formall...*, accessed on November 11, 2011
4. *hamropalo.com/nepal.../maoists-intensify-works-on-constitutionmaki...*, accessed on October 7, 2011
5. *himalaya.socanth.cam.ac.uk/.../IDEA_Creating_Constitution.pdf*, accessed on February 21, 2011
6. *manjeet.com.np/.../global-climate-talks-and-constitution-making-in-n...*, accessed on February 19, 2011
7. *martinchautari.org.np/research-dis-2009.html?tmpl=component*, accessed on May 15, 2011
8. *mumbai.academia.edu/.../Nepali_Constitution_making_adopt to_ada...*, accessed on November 3, 2011
9. *nccnepal.org/Document_Uploads/.../1061471298858416l606.pdf...*, accessed on July 11, 2011

10. *nepal.usembassy.gov/ep-12-17-2008.html,* accessed on November 1, 2011
11. *research-db.ritsumei.ac.jp/Profiles/91/0009023/books_e1.html,* accessed on March 21, 2011
12. *southasiamonitor.org/detail.php?type=n&nid=418,* accessed on November 5, 2011
13. *unsr.jamesanaya.org/.../22-nepal-alleged-exclusion-of-indigenous-pe...,* accessed on June 17, 2011
14. *www.acdi-cida.gc.ca/cidaweb%5Ccpo.nsf/projEn/A034688001,* accessed on May 10, 2011
15. *www.adb.org/documents/CPSs/NEP/2010.../CPS-NEP-2010-2012.pd...,* accessed on January 31, 2011
16. *www.campaign.org.np/activity_summary.php,* accessed on June 10, 2011
17. *www.constitutionnet.org/.../international-conference-dynamics-consti...,* accessed on February 15, 2011
18. *www.ekantipur.com/the-kathmandu-post/2010/05/03/.../207904,* accessed on November 1, 2011

6

Constitutional History and the Present Crisis in Nepalese Constitution Making: An Analytical Survey

RAM PRAKASH

Nepal was first settled by Buddhist people migrating from the Tibetan Plateau and later by Hindus moving up from Northern India. The Hindu migrants mostly settled in the fertile downland valleys of the south and west while the Tibetans occupied the uplands regions of the Himalayan foothills to the north and east but the culture of Nepal has increasingly been a blend of Hindu and Buddhist influence. The region was dominated from the 13th to 17th centuries by the rulers of the Malla dynasty. The Mallas were overthrown by the Shah dynasty in the 18th century and the country was unified in 1768 by Prithvi Narayan Shah. The country was protected at the time by the tough Gurkha warrior people of central Nepal though this did not prevent Nepal being annexed by the British in 1817. The aid of the Gurkhas in helping the British to crush the Indian mutiny in 1857 led to Nepal being given back much of its old territory and sovereignty and for 100 years the country developed in isolation from western influences. The Rana family dominated the Nepalese up to 1951, reducing the king to a puppet during that time. From 1846 to 1951 Nepal was in effect ruled by a family of hereditary Rana prime ministers who pursued a policy of close cooperation with the British Power in India. Agitation by the Nepali congress party in the 1940s for a more democratic government led to a revolution, through which the royal line represented by king Tribhuvan returned to power. A general election on the style of western democracies, held in June, 1959 delivered an overwhelming victory to the Nepali congress party headed by B.P. Koirala. However, towards the end of 1960, King Mahendra who had succeeded his father king Tribhuvan, dismissed the country's first parliamentary government and inaugrated personal rule through the medium of the partyless panchayat system. King Mahendra died in 1972 and was succeeded by his western educated son, Birendra who was officially crowned in 1975. Some four years later, Birendra announced that Nepal's political system would be put to the vote. A national referendum was held in May 1980, resulting in a narrow mandate for the continuation of the panchayat system with democratic reforms. Three important reforms were introduced at that time:

(a) The election of the Rashtriya (national) Panchayat and of the lowest tiers of government (village or town) on the basis of universal adult frachise;
(b) The government's accountability to the public through the national legislature; and
(c) The king announced his decision to bring about decentralization and administrative power and development responsibilities down to the village or town panchayat level. The crown, however, retained tremendous political and executive powers.

In March 1990, violence erupted in Nepal, when the people protested against the autocratic role of King Birendra. He then appointed Mr. K.P. Bhattarai to lead the cabinet representing both the congress and the communists. By November 1999, the King finally announced a new constitution, lodging sovereignty in the people and instituting democracy through elections. The senseless slaughter of King Birendra and Queen Aishwarya of Nepal on June 1, 2001 along with the rest of their family members was another sad and unwelcome development for the political system in Nepal. In Feb, 2005 King Gyanendra suspended parliament and assumed direct rule over the country. But this constitutional crisis finally resulted in his ouster from the Nepalese politics. Though many people still viewed the King as a reincarnation of the god Vishnu, the monarchy's reputation declined after unfortunate episode of 2001. Ultimately king Gyanendra had to abdicate the throne due to violent agitation of the Maoists and Federal Democratic Republic of Nepal was formed. The Communist Party of Nepal (Maoist) was founded by Pushpa Kamal Dahal 'Prachandra' in 1994. In November 2006, the then Prime Minister of Nepal Girija Prasad Koirala and Prachandra signed a peace deal, ending a civil war that killed over 13,000 people. In august, 2008 Prachandra formed coalition government. He was elected the first prime minister of the Federal Democratic Republic of Nepal but he had to resign on May 4, 2009 after a highly politicized battle with the chief of army staff. Senior leader of the Communist Party of Nepal (Unified Marxist Leninist) Madhav Kumar Nepal on May 23, 2009 became the second Prime Minister of the Federal Democratic Republic.

Nepal's Constituent Assembly is working for framing a new Constitution since May 28, 2008. It was initially contemplated that the work would be finished by May, 2010—a term of two years. But Article 64 of the Interim Constitution was amended on May 28, 2010 so as to extend the Constituent Assembly's tenure by one year. Nepal's Constituent Assembly has a strength of 601 members and the three major political parties control over 450 seat in the house—the Unified Communist Party of Nepal (CPN-Maoist)—229, the Nepali Congress—115 and the Communist Party of Nepal-United Marxist Leninist (CPN-UML)—108. Unlike other Constituent assemblies that led countries such as South Africa or India through successful transitions to progressive constitutional democracies, no one political party in Nepal holds even a simple majority of seats in the House. Hence Nepal's Constituent Assembly lacks a cohesive political and historical vision that such a process requires.

The people of Nepal have had neither the benefit of politicians who display a sense of history, nor a political party that could push through its brand of constitutionalism, by virtue of a sheer majority. Sadly for Nepal, a leader who projects a moral force and enjoys national credibilitylike a compassionate, dignified and always civil Nelson Mandela or a sober legal mind—like India's Ambedkar is nowhere to be found. Nepal has stepped uncertainty into what now be its sixth constitution-making exercise, but with some differences from before-the absence of an authoritarian monarch and the involvement of what is now the largest political force, the erstwhile Maoist rebels. Unfortunately, there is nothing to indicate that the performance of the Assembly during the 12-month extension will be any different than that of the preceding 24 months. There are many fundamental issues relating to the constitution that will have to be resolved. Agreement is yet to be reached on major issues like the devolution of power, Form of Government (Presidential, Parliamentary or Hybrid), the role of the Head of State (Ceremonial or executive), powers of President and Prime Minister and their relationship, elections system, structure of legislation, the federal structure (the number of states to be formed and the basis of state formation), the appointment and removal of judges (one proposal is to reflect the political parties' strength in the House), inter-relationship of the judiciary,existence and role of the opposition, delineation of boundaries of the provinces and the parliament etc. There are also other constitutional issues like integration of Maoist combatants,dissolution of the YCL of the Maoists and the return of seized properties of the Maoists. Hence, Nepal is positioned no differently than many other countries have been during similar constitutional exercises. The following suggestion may prove fruitful in this exercise:

(a) The relationship between the Constituent Assembly members and the body politic needs to be enriched and made more transparent to enable a consistent and cordial dialogue.
(b) The process needs to be clearly explained to ensure public knowledge and requisite participation in crafting the legal framework that will define the country's future.
(c) Progress made and areas where there is still conflict between the drafters needs to be shared publicly.
(d) A civility of dialogue and disagreement needs to characterize the discourse that exists among the various political parties within and outside the assembly.

Nepal is a poor country with GNI per capita $400, adult literacy rate at 57.9 percent and an infant mortality rate of 85.5 deaths for every 1,000 children under the age of five, given the looming spectra of famine in many districts, massive unemployment, and a domestic economy brought to its knees by power shortages and labour stoppages, a shared sense of history and compassion toward the public is required rather than platitudes to party ideology.

REFERENCES

1. *blog.com.np/2009/03/25/nepali-constitution-in-search-of-excellence/*, accessed on April 10, 2011
2. *gorkhapatra.org.np/rising.detail.php?article_id=58508&cat_id...*, accessed on January 23, 2011
3. *hamropalo.com/nepal.../maoists-intensify-works-on-constitutionmaki...*, accessed on October 7, 2011
4. *icj.org/dwn/database/NEPAL_ESC_rights_FINAL_30July2009.pdf*, accessed on September 22, 2011
5. *idsn.org/.../user.../Nepal/Nepal_UPR_session_-IDSN_analysis.pdf*, accessed on September 25, 2011
6. *lawandotherthings.blogspot.com/.../constitution-making-in-nepal.htm...*, accessed on February 10, 2011
7. *martinchautari.org.np/research-dis-2009.html?tmpl=component*, accessed on May 15, 2011
8. *nccnepal.org/Document_Uploads/.../1061471298858416l606.pdf...*, accessed on July 11, 2011

9. *nepalicount.com/.../25-america-nepal-society-interaction-program-* ..., accessed on April 10, 2011
10. *nepalicount.com/.../25-america-nepal-society-interaction-program-* ..., accessed on April 17, 2011
11. *trulynepalivideos.meronepalma.com/people-blame-parties-for-delay-*..., accessed on March 21, 2011
12. *www.campaign.org.np/activity_summary.php,* accessed on June 10, 2011
13. *www.constitutionnet.org/.../The-CA-of-Nepal-An-Agenda-for-Women*..., accessed on November 2, 2011
14. *www.cwish.org.np/.../1307433589newsletter1_2011draftversion.pdf,* accessed on June 19, 2011
15. *www.freedomforum.org.np/.../WorkingPaper_Constitution_RTI_* ..., accessed on July 1, 2011
16. *www.igd.org.np/pages.php?section=pages&page_id=96,* accessed on September 20, 2011

7

Present Constitutional Crisis in Nepal

ROHITASHWA DUBEY

This paper attempts at an analysis of present constitutional crisis in Nepal. The paper views this crisis as a long-drawn process of the transfer of power from absolute monarchy to the people. In this context it treats the promulgation of the constitution of the kingdom of Nepal in 1990 as starting point of this continuum. The paper will present a statement of the various events and developments since 2006 leading to the overthrow of monarchy and election of a constituent assembly and problems confronting it. An in-depth analysis of the reasons and factors behind the ongoing imbroglio have been made, India factor being one of them. It concludes with a message loud and clear that establishment of people's authority is irresistible and irreversible howsoever painful and prolong the process may be.

In the hitherto history of the world there has been a consistent and natural process of the transfer of power from the absolute monarchy to the people. In some cases it has been through devolution and in others through forceable overthrow. With the advent of modern knowledge and reason, Nepal, though belatedly, experimented it in 1962 when riding on a popular wave B.P. Koirala of the Nepali Congress headed the first elected government. But it was short-lived. Gauging the people's mood the king dismissed it and ruled the country uninterruptedly till the singeling masses compelled the king in 1990 to concede to the transfer of sovereignty to the people with multi-party democracy and be content with mere constitutional authority.[1] This latter came to be known as Jan Andolan-I. But taking recourse to various lacunae as also the constant bickering and disagreement among the political classes the king continued to enjoy the clout.

This, however, could not stop the march of the people towards establishment of its complete authority. The second phase of people's movement (Jan Andolan-II) by the Nepali political classes spearheaded of course the Maoists was launched in 2006. This created an extraordinary situation by ending the direct rule of the monarch. Rising against the power of the state and going beyond what the political parties were willing to settle for, the people this time had sought to create a new paradigm. A new parliament was formed through a process of negotiations which promulgated an interim constitution. The preamble reads, "We, the people of Nepal, in exercise of sovereign powers and state authority inherent in us ... now, therefore, do hereby promulgate this interim constitution of Nepal, 2063 (2007), prepared through a political consensus enforceable until a new constitution is framed by the Constituent Assembly in order to institutionalise the achievements of the revolution and movements till this date."[2]

Elections to the 601 members Constituent Assembly (CA) was held in April 2008. The C.A. which also functions as the country's interim parliament had a mandate to provide a constitution in two years. Ironically, the mainstream political parties hoped that the Unified Communist Party of Nepal (Maoist) headed by Pushpa Kamal Dahal 'Prachand' would not fair so good in the elections. But against the forecasts, the Maoists won 30 per cent of the votes and 40 per cent of the seats. The Nepali Congress (NC) and the Communist Party of Nepal (Unified Marxist Leninist) or UML, the hitherto mainstream parties, trailed behind, with each bagging about 20 per cent of the seats. The rest of the seats were won largely by a combination of Madhesi parties. Thus the results gave the Maoists twice as many seats as either the UML or the N.C. Instead of being gradually weaned into politics, the Maoists were now thrust into governance. They were thus allowed to form a new government in August 2008, and Prachanda was elected Prime Minister. The people may or may not have voted for the Maoist manifesto, but they certainly, and most demonstrably, voted for change. They wanted delivery on the pent-up expectations. That the Maoists could gauge the mood of the people was also seen in the representation they gave to the middle and lower castes of society, to women and to younger people-in each category for outstripping the other major parties.

And it is here that the trouble started. As Prime Minister Prachanda recommended for the dismissal of the Army Chief. Sensing a discreet game plan in Prachanda's move, President Ram Baran Yadav simply did not oblige. Prachanda resigned in May 2009. Taking stock of the nine months of Maoist governance it can be safely deduced that it did not stand up to the expectations of the people. It was not marked by any significant achievement, even taking into consideration obstructive approach of other parties. With the support of 22 parties, Madhav Kumar Nepal of UML was then elected the Prime Minister. The ensuring period saw little progress in the primary task of drafting a constitution. The Maoists staged nationwide protests and caused disruptions in parliament demanding the resignation of Madhav Nepal. With the Constituent Assembly's two-year term coming to a close at the end of May 2010, hectic negotiations were started. These resulted in a three-point all party agreement. Firstly, providing for the extension of the Assembly's term by a year to enable it to complete its task of drafting the constitution; secondly, the resignation of Madhav Nepal; and thirdly, the continuation of the peace process, notably integration of the Maoist cadre into the security forces, return of seized properties and disbanding of the Youth Communist League. Ofcourse, there were differences on the sequence of implementation of the terms of the agreement.

However, Madhav Kumar Nepal resigned after a month in the larger national interest. The Maoist are accused of non-implementation of the third element of the agreement where action is required from them. Even after six months of the resignation of Madhav Nepal as Prime Minister, Nepal's parliament is yet to find a successor. The seventeen rounds of voling yielded no majority for the two contestants for the post-Prachanda (Maoist) and Ram Chandra Poudel (N.C.). Various rounds of voting demonstrate an obstinate behaviour of the representatives and their lack of the sense of accountability towards long-term national interest. Going through the motion of periodic voting results in *petitio principii*. Principle involved in this stand off are not always clear. The Maoist claim that as the largest political party they have a right to form the government while the N.C. claims that as the two parties have already got the chance it is now its turn to nominate a Prime Minister. As a matter of fact, only a grand coalition can steer clear of this impasse. If Maoists, who accounts for 40 per cent of the seats, want to have their nominee as Prime Minister, they will have to win support of either N.C. or UML. Likewise, the latter two should come together if either candidate is to be elected.

Betrayal of the People's Will

But while so doing they will be chasing out a chimera. In ultimate analysis the people's will should be kept in sight while treading on any course of action. The minutiae of the arithmetical calculations detract from the purpose that informed the Nepali political classes in 2006 in launching the Jan Andolan-II (People's movement II). The operative approach of this movement was one of political consensus. It is this consensus that has ceased to exist, leading to the current connundrum.

Sad aspect of the whole issue is that all the energy of the political classes in Nepal has been centered round the election of the Prime Minister. But election of a Prime Minister, even if it happens in the days to come, does not resolve the political problems for, heading a government for just 4-5 months should not become the be all and end all of political strategy. All constitutions are living documents. If the Maoists win a majority in the next election, they can always try and improve the constitution. Seven months of the extended Constituent Assembly for one year period has already passed. Even if a draft constitution is formulated, it cannot be adopted without a two-thirds majority which, given the present numbers, will be possible only through a consensus.

UNMIN

Meanwhile, United Nations Mission in Nepal (UNMIN), which monitors more than 9000 former Maoist combatants of the People's Liberation Army (PLA) and 3000 weapons in seven cantonments and 21 camps as well as a restricted number of Nepal Army (NA) personnel and arms, has decided to pack up as its term ends on January 15, 2011. Differences have sharpened among Nepali political forces on Unmin's future and alternative arrangements. The caretaker government led by Madhav Kumar Nepal has expressed its will not to request the United Nations Security Council (UNSC) for another extension. The government has argued that peace agreements require the Maoists to transfer the PLA to the All Party special Committee for supervision and Rehabilitation of Maoist armed personnel. The committee recently constituted a 12 member secretariat, which has proposed a mechanism consisting of retired and serving state security personnel to be stationed in the 28 Maoist camps to monitor arms and personnel—the task performed by U.N. arms monitors.[3] While Maoist members are a part of the secretariat, they have opposed the proposal that is silent on the monitoring of the Nepal Army personnel and arms. Instead, Maoist have demanded another extension for Unmin, and have warned they may send a unilateral request to the UNSC if the government does not agree. "Unmin's exit before the conclusion of the peace process will create complications as it is an important part of past agreements", according to Maoist Vice Chairman Narayan Kaji Shreshtha.[4]

Dissentions Within

Problems also stem from the differences within the Maoists themselves. These are often conflicting and paradoxical. In fact, they are going through a deep existential crisis. This was most starkly reflected in the separate political documents presented by different high functionaries of the party at an extended party meeting. At the end, the Maoist expressed their commitment to peace and the constitutional process but paradoxically also decided to prepare for a revolt if their aims were not met.[5] But the real difficulty lay in the party's failure to resolve the fundamental ideological and political differences within it. Be it democratic-republic path, or People's Federal Democratic Republic or nationalism or democracy, differences are sharp and real. The three leaders of the party-Prachanda, Mohan Vaidya 'Kiran' and Baburam Bhattarai also differ as regards principal contradiction, the correct revolutionary line, the immediate tactics and the problems facing the organisation.

India Factor

The other political parties and India accuse Maoists of turning their back on democracy, and say they cannot be trusted with power till they detach the party from the PLA. For their part, the Maoists accuse India and other parliamentary parties of collaborating to "isolate" them despite their proven electoral strength and subvert progressive political change including the democratisation of Nepal Army.[6] Prachanda also claimed that India had choreographed political opposition to the Maoist move to dismiss the army chief, blocked political agreement between Nepali actors, stopped Madheshi parties from supporting him in the recent Prime Ministerial elections, begun intimidating the Nepal media, and was hatching conspiracies to dissolve the C.A.[7]

The Maoist deliberations, thus, could further complicate the prospects of a fresh political settlement in Nepal. In seeking to maintain his supremacy and revolutionary image Prachanda has incorporated several elements from the Maoist strand, limiting negotiating space with other parties on issues such as the PLA. The radical rhetoric of the Maoist leadership in front of the cadre has only strengthened the right wing hawks who have been itching for a confrontation.[8] This will have unforeseable consequences both for Nepal and its neighbours. Ironically, in recent days, there has been talk of Maoist support for restoration of a cultural monarchy, with suggestions that the monarchy was removed at the behest of a foreign country. But these may be wishful thinking or pressure tactics. Even though their views on the current political crisis varied sharply, virtually all the politicians agreed that Indian interference in Nepal politics had reached a new high. Many blamed this interference for the failure of these parties to establish some sort of *modus vivendi* among themselves. So far the stand of the UML is concerned a rightist faction led by K.P. Oli shares the official Indian antipathy toward the former insurgents but party leader Jhalanath Khanal believes that only a consensual approach towards the Maoists will allow the C.A. to finish its work.[9]

As elsewhere in the world, march of democracy in Nepal, though belatedly, cannot be stopped. The genie of people's expectations cannot be put back and must receive some measures of satisfaction. No less important, the culture of subservience ingrained in a feudal society has dissolved, never to be recreated. It can only be hoped that all the political parties will rise beyond political arithmetic and look to the future of Nepal. For this it would be necessary for the Maoists to display, by both words and action, their commitment to non-violence and democracy, and for the others to eschew the manipulative and personalised politics of the past and seek greater connectivity with the people's aspirations. The Maoists should bear this in mind that all constitutions are living documents. If they win a majority in the next election, they can always try and improve the constitution. On their part, the N.C. and the UML, and the Indian establishment should stop looking at the Maoists as an 'insurgent' outfit. Integrating them into a democratised national army would be a win-win all round. In exchange for the loss of dedicated party cadres, 5000-8000 PLA men would never be able to stage a coup or subvert a lakh strong force. The Maoists want the national army to be ethnically inclusive and brought firmly under civilian control. Surely, that is something everyone out to back whole-heartedly. India might have been a reluctant midwife these past few years but it always managed to come out on the right side of the changes Nepal was undergoing. It should again live up to its past credential. For their part, Nepali political classes should not always look for convenient escapade in India for all their failings.

END NOTES

1. See the analysis of the Constitution in *Nepal News*, November 15, 1990
2. Deb Mukharji, "Elusive Horizon", *Frontline*, September 2010, pg.51
3. Prashant Jha, "Vacuum as UNMIN Prepares for Exit", *The Hindu*, December 31, 2010
4. *asiafoundation.org/.../nepal-averts-constitutional-crisis-hope-for-dem...*, accessed on August 18, 2011
5. Prashant Jha, "Maoists in Nepal: Differences Within", *The Hindu*, December 6, 2010
6. Prachanda named India as its main enemy; See Prachanda's views in *Kantipur Times*, 28 November 2010
7. Siddharth Varadarajan,"The Danger in India's Nepal policy", *The Hindu*, 16 August 2010. Also see Prashant Jha, *no.5*
8. *Ibid*, See also Deb Mukharji, *no.2*, pg.53
9. *gorkhapatra.org.np/rising.detail.php?article_id=58508&cat_id...*, accessed on January 23, 2011

8

Dimensions of Constitutional Crisis in Nepal

UPENDRA MISHRA

Nepal, a landlocked country at the southern slope of the Himalayas, has been a great laboratory for different kinds of ideals and systems such as kingship (Dynastic), Ranashahi, Parliamentary system, Partyless Panchayat System, multi-party system and unstable political culture of coalition governments. Its strategic importance has made it a centre of attention not only for India and China but also for the superpowers of the world. India has a close historical, geographical, social and political relation with Nepal. With the establishment of the Rana Constitution in 1948, the process of constitutionalism began in Nepal. Its second Constitution came into existence in 1951 which was of course an interim one. Nepal's third Constitution was inaugurated in 1959. It was a parliamentary Constitution and it lasted for only two years. In 1962, Nepal saw the establishment of its long-serving partyless Panchayati Constitution which remained in force for about 30 years. During this period Nepal could not keep itself immune for a long time from the impact of changes that were taking place around the world under the influence of globalisation and from the impact of Indian democracy in particular. Taking a cue from the survival of the British monarchy, King Birendra declared a democratic Republican Constitution which was the fifth Constitution of Nepal. Under this parliamentary Constitution, a multi-party general election was held on May 12, 1991 and a new democratic government under the Prime Ministership of Girija Prasad Koirala was formed on the basis of the majority obtained by his party, the Nepali Congress.

It is important to mention here that this Constitution was the product of the first popular people's movement (Jan Andolan-I) which was launched in

1989-90 for the restoration of multi-party democracy on the lines of Indian democracy. After this, Nepal went through a period of political turmoil and instability. During this period (1991-2005) Nepal witnessed the formation and fall of 10 governments apart from three general elections and a palace massacre. All this led to a mass revolt which is popularly known as Jan Andolan-II and which was launched to re-establish democracy and abolish monarchy completely from the Himalayan kingdom. Jan Andolan-II saw the emergence of the Maoists on the political horizon of Nepal under the leadership of Pushpa Kamal Dahal alias Prachanda, giving up their underground insurgency and joining the political mainstream. A 12-point Comprehensive Peace Agreement (CPA) was concluded between the Maoists and the Seven-Party Alliance (SPA) in November 2005. An important milestone of Jan Andolan-II was the promulgation of an Interim Constitution by the Maoists and the Seven-Party Alliance on January 15, 2007. In accordance with the provision of this Interim Constitution an interim government headed by Girija Prasad Koirala assumed office in Nepal in April 2007.

Genesis of the Present Constitutional Impasse

Following the promulgation of the Interim Constitution, elections to the Constituent Assembly were held in April 2008. The Assembly was mandated to provide a Constitution within two years. There was general relief in Nepal that the insurgency was over and the country could look forward to a stable future after years of violent conflict. There was satisfaction that the Maoists had been persuaded to give up arms and join parliamentary politics. The mainstream political parties hoped that the Maoists would not do too badly in the elections and thus be disheartened. But the results were unexpected. It gave the Maoists twice as many seats as either the UML or the NC. The Maoists won 30 percent of the votes and 40 percent of the seats. The NC and UML trailed behind with each getting about 20 percent of the seats. The rest of seats were won largely by a combination of Madhesi parties.

The Maoists being the largest party were allowed to form a government in August 2008 with 'Prachanda' as Prime Minister. But in less than a year, in May 2009, Prachanda resigned after President Ram Baran Yadav refused to dismiss the Army Chief as recommended by the Prime Minister. Madhav Kumar Nepal was then elected Prime Minister with the support of 22 parties. The ensuing period saw little or no progress in the principal task of drafting a Constitution. The Maoists called country-wide protests and demanded the resignation of Madhav Kumar Nepal.

With the Constituent Assembly's two-year term coming to a close at the end of May 2010, hectic negotiations resulted in a three-point all-party agreement literally at the stroke of midnight, providing for the extension of Assembly's term by a year to enable it to complete its task of drafting the Constitution, the resignation of Madhav Kumar Nepal as Prime Minister and the continuation of peace process, notably the integration of PLA into the national army and disbanding of Youth Communist League. But differences remained regarding implementation of terms of agreement. However, Madhav Kumar Nepal resigned after a month in larger national interest. Six months after the resignation of Prime Minister Madhav Kumar Nepal, Nepal's Parliament is yet to find his successor. The sixteen rounds of voting yielded no majority for the two contestants for the post-Pushpa Kamal Dahal 'Prachanda' (UCP-Maoist) and Ram Chandra Poudel of the Nepali Congress. The present constitutional crisis is the result of the lack of trust and differences in vision among the forces that are at work in Nepal. The following factors merit attention in this context:

Two Armies

Five years have passed since the Nepali political forces signed the Comprehensive Peace Agreement (CPA). But the country continues to have two armies—the official Nepali Army (NA) and the Maoists People's Liberation Army (PLA). The future of these two armies is at the heart of the peace process and is directly linked to both government formation and Constitution drafting. An agreement between the government and the Maoists was reached on September 13, 2010 for integration and rehabilitation of Maoist combatants within the next four months. But it seems very difficult to achieve given the deep differences between two sides on the issue.

In pursuance of a provision of the CPA, a Special Committee for the management, integration and rehabilitation of Maoist combatants was set up towards the end of 2008 by the Maoist-led government which is now chaired by the caretaker Prime Minister Madhav Kumar Nepal. But no tangible result has been achieved towards integration and rehabilitation of Maoist combatants. Though all political parties agree that PLA must be brought under the control, direction and supervision of the Special Committee, there are major differences among them at least in three areas, namely, numbers, modalities and timing. These differences could be resolved if all parties display the necessary political will because the reform of the National Army and bringing it under strong civilian control are part of the peace accord. The Nepali Congress and the Unified Marxist Leninists should refrain from playing the army's card because they see it as an ally in their fight against the Maoists.

They should also stop isolating the Maoists because it will aggravate their fear that reactionaries are out to eliminate them and will make them reluctant to give up their coercive apparatus. The Maoists should also stop using PLA as a bargaining chip. If they want a new Constitution, they will have to make compromises on their political-military structure because other parties are justifiably feeling insecure. If the question of two armies remains unresolved, there will be little chance of Nepal drafting a Constitution or institutionalising democracy.

Hostile Relationship Between India and Kantipur Media House

The Indian Embassy in Kathmandu is also accused of creating controversies. It is accused of gross interference and attacking freedom of press in another country, and faces censure from a Parliamentary Committee, politicians across the spectrum and civil society groups. The hostile relationship between the Indian Government and the Kantipur group—the biggest media house in Nepal—has contributed in creating a perception that India is interfering in the affairs of Nepal. While Kantipur media house has its own vested interest in 'anti-India' reporting which was linked to the ban on advertisements by the Indian Embassy, it succeeded in getting support of political parties, media organisations and civil society in its opportunistic and chauvinistic reporting. However, the Indian Government should seriously rethink its attitude towards the constitutional crisis in Nepal. It must stop strong-arm tactics against the media in a country where it claims to be supporting democratic forces. It should also stop using Indian big business operating in Nepal for questionable purposes. India finds itself ranged against not only the country's biggest political party, the Maoists, but also its biggest media house, Kantipur. It has opened up so many fronts all in the name of national security that its traditional allies find it difficult to defend India. Therefore, India should not underestimate the depth of resentment against it and should strive hard to create a consensus on the complicated issue so that process of Constitution-drafting may move forward in Nepal and it should do whatever it can to remove the constitutional crisis in Nepal.

Differences Among the Big Three

The ideological differences among the big three—the Unified Communist Party of Nepal (Maoist) Chairman Pushpa Kamal Dahal 'Prachanda', senior Vice-Chairman Mohan Vaidya 'Kiran' and another Vice-Chairman and ideologue Baburam Bhattarai—are also contributing in the present constitutional impasse. These differences came to the surface at a party meeting in Palungar of Gorkha district. In 2005 in the Chunbang meeting the Maoists adopted the 'democratic republic path', which led to an alliance with other political parties against monarchy, the 2006 People's Movement, entry into the peace process, the Constituent Assembly elections and the abolition of monarchy. After taking over the reins of government in 2008, the Maoists met at Kharipati, on the outskirts of Kathmandu, and announced that their aim was to establish a 'People's Federal Democratic Republic'. If Chunbang was the result of an alliance between Prachanda and Bhattarai, Kharipati saw Prachanda come closer to the dogmatic ideologue Mohan Vaidya Kiran. Since then the political peace and constitutional process have been stalled. India and other political parties of Nepal accuse the Maoists of turning their back on democracy. The Maoists, on the other hand, accuse India and other parties of collaborating to isolate them despite their proven electoral strength and subverting progressive political change including democratisation of Nepali army.

It was in this background the differences between the big three regarding the 'Principal Contradiction', the correct 'revolutionary line' the immediate tactics and the problems facing the organisation, assume significance. According to Prachanda the principal contradiction of the Nepali people is the alliance between India and domestic reactionaries. Kiran also agreed with Prachanda's assessment that India was the main enemy. On the other hand, Bhattarai emphasised that the principal contradiction was with the remnants of feudalism, domestic reactionaries, Comprador bourgeoisie and brokers who received Indian protection. He argued that it would be incorrect, besides being tactically naive to label India the enemy until it had militarily invaded Nepal. Thus, the Marxists' differences have further complicated the prospect of a fresh political settlement in Nepal. In his desire to maintain supremacy and his revolutionary image, Prachanda has incorporated several elements from the Marxist strand and thereby limited the negotiating space with other parties on issues such as PLA. He should show true statesmanship and reiterate the Maoist commitment to past agreements, stick to federal democratic republic as the goal, move to fulfil the Maoist promise towards the peace process and Constitution drafting. India and other democratic parties in Nepal, on their part, should introspect whether their actions have contributed to Maoist insecurity and belligerence.

The excitement of the emergence of a Nepal out of People's Movement is getting blurred. The excitement of the possibility of a new Nepal emerging out of the people's movement and the harsh lessons learnt from the insurgency has been overtaken by the politics of old in Kathmandu to which all parties today seem subject. Any attempt to turn the clock back would be a betrayal of what Jan Andolan II stood for. In recent days there has been talk of Maoist support for the restoration of a cultural monarchy with suggestions that the monarchy was abolished at the behest of a foreign power. This may be a wishful thinking or pressure tactics. The genie of people's expectations—be it from the Madhesis, the Janajatis or other ethnic groups—cannot be put back. It is high time that all political parties rise above petty political considerations and put their heads together for the future of Nepal. It is necessary for the Maoists to display by both words and actions their commitment to non-violence and democracy and for others to abjure the manipulative and personalised politics of the past and seek greater connectivity with people's aspirations. Only then can they fulfil the democratic aspiration of the people of Nepal as espoused by Jan Andolan II.

An important step to resolve the present constitutional impasse was taken when on February 3, 2011, Jhalanath Khanal, Chairman of the CPN (Unified Marxist-Leninist) was elected Prime Minister by securing support of 368 MPs in the House of 601. Khanal was supported by the Maoists whose chairman Pushpa Kumal Dahal 'Prachanda' decided to withdraw from the contest just before the voting. The victory of Khanal has brought into existence a new 'left-alliance' between the UML and the Maoists replacing the previous 'left democratic' alliance between the UML and the Nepali Congress. This alliance is the result of a seven-point behind-the-scenes agreement between the two communist parties of Nepal. Both parties agreed to draft a Constitution that would "institutionalise [the] republic, restructure the state and adopt federation, strengthen people's inclusive democracy, end all forms of feudalism and strengthen national independence." Both parties also agreed to "create a separate force of Maoist combatants or [a] separate force that includes Maoists combatants and personnel of other security organs. They further pledged to build a long lasting partnership and "lead the government rotationally in future."

The agreement between the two communist parties drew sharp critical reactions from the Nepali Congress and sections of the UML. NC leader and Prime Ministerial candidate Ram Chandra Poudel said that "the creation of a separate force is not mentioned in the CPA. We will never accept this. This is a great betrayal." Similarly, UML leaders from the Madhav Kumar Nepal and K.P. Oli factions alleged that they had not been consulted at all. Unified Communist Party of Nepal (Maoist) Vice-Chairman Baburam Bhattarai also registered a note of dissent on sharing power with Khanal. Perhaps due to these differences Prime Minister Khanal was unable to form a small cabinet as per his original plan. There is also a difference between the two parties on who would get the Home Ministry. The rotation in Prime Ministership has put Khanal in a hot spot within his own party. In spite of differences and criticisms it may be assumed that the election of Jhalanath Khanal as Prime Minister of a majority Left coalition government offers the young Republic the best chance it has had in 20 months to finish the task of drafting a new Constitution and completing its peace process. Top priority must now be given to crafting a new Constitution which means resolving key issues, notably reforming the new state's federal structure and political system. Of equal importance is the peace process. With the departure of the United Nations from Nepal, the fate of the Maoist combatants is now entirely in the hands of a special all-party committee headed by the Prime Minister. It is in the interest of democracy that Maoist combatants be either integrated into a democratised Nepali army and into the security forces or demobilised and suitably rehabilitated.[35] Political parties in Nepal must come forward to reach a political consensus so that the process of a stable democratic system may be firmed up.

REFERENCES

1. *hdr.undp.org/en/reports/nationalreports/.../nepal/name,3287,en.html,* accessed on January18, 2011
2. Deb Mukharji, "Elusive Horizon", *Frontline,* Chennai, September 24, 2010, pp.51-53
3. *icj.org/dwn/database/NEPAL_ESC_rights_FINAL_30July2009.pdf,* accessed on September 22, 2011
4. Archana Kumari, *Nepal-Rajniti, Samvidhan Evam Prajatantra Ka Vikas,* MPS Publishers and Distributors, Delhi, 2008, pp.9-11
5. Prashant Jha, "Maoists in Nepal: The Differences Within", *The Hindu,* November 11, 2009, Delhi, pg.7
6. *blog.com.np/2009/03/25/nepali-constitution-in-search-of-excellence/,* accessed on April 10, 2011
7. *en.wikipedia.org/.../Women's_representation_in_the_Parliament_of_...,* accessed on February 1, 2011
8. *nccnepal.org/Document_Uploads/.../1061471298858416l606.pdf...,* accessed on July 11, 2011
9. *www.acdi-cida.gc.ca/cidaweb%5Ccpo.nsf/projEn/A034688001,* accessed on May 10, 2011
10. *www.can.gov.np/en/committees/view/14,* accessed on May 10, 2011
11. *www.constitutionnet.org/.../The-CA-of-Nepal-An-Agenda-for-Women...,* accessed on November 2, 2011
12. Prashant Jha, "India and the Kantipur Saga", *The Hindu,* Delhi, September 3, 2010
13. *www.idea.int/.../Nepal%20-%20workshop%20paper%20-%20Yash%...,* accessed on April 9, 2011
14. *www.indianexpress.com/news/will-guarantee-security...nepal.../0,* accessed on August 22, 2011
15. *www.ilo.org/kathmandu/whatwedo/projects/WCMS.../index.htm,* accessed on February 1, 2011
16. *www.ipcs.org/.../nepal/constitutional-rumblings-in-nepal-three-scenar...,* accessed on September 18, 2011
17. *www.nepalitimes.com/blogs/thebrief/2011/10/.../visit-successful-pm/,* accessed on February 25, 2011

9

Ethnic, Cultural and Social Diversity and Framing of New Constitution of Nepal

R N Kumar

Like most of the nation-states Nepal is also a multi-ethnic, multi cultural and a country having social diversity. Jan Andolan-I brought the Interim Constitution of Nepal in 1990 and it accepted the sovereignty of the people. After Jan Andolan-II the monarchical system of government was replaced by a Republican form of government. A Constituent Assembly has also been elected by the people to frame the new Constitution, which will replace the Interim Constitution framed after Jan Andolan-II. But the framers of the Constitution are facing many challenges. Out of these challenges, accommodating the demands of different ethnic, linguistic and cultural groups besides social diversity are the major ones. The model of nation-state has been under considerable scrutiny in the post-war period because no nation-state in present times has ethnic, cultural, religious or linguistic homogeneity. The language and culture of the majority is in a dominant position in almost all the nation-states resulting in resentment among the ethnic, cultural or religious minorities. Thus identity crisis of such minority communities has been a major cause of concern for almost all the nation-states today. The framers of the Nepali Constitution are also faced with such a crisis.

During the long period of Sah dynastic rule or Ranas' autocratic rule different ethnic communities of Nepal had their own leadership. There was no written rule. Only customs dominated their social structure. After Jan Andolan-II Nepal is facing new problems as the marginalized communities are demanding not only the recognition of their languages and culture in the

Constitution but also greater representations in state institutions. With this background it is also essential to briefly discuss Nepal's racial and ethnic diversity.

Social Diversity

Ethnic, linguistic and cultural diversity is a characteristic feature of Nepal as a state. Primarily they may be divided into three major groups—(i) The Aryan Nepalis, (ii) Tibeto-Mongol Nepalis, and (iii) Indigeneous Tribal Nepalis. The first group consists of the people of hill and Tarai Brahmins, Chhetris, Thakurs and Dalits. They are inhabitants of fertile hills, river-valleys and Tarai plains. The second major group comprising communities of Tibeto-Mongol origin are the occupants of higher hills from west to east. The third comprises of several indigenous communities as Tharus, Chepangs, Botes, Rauts and Santhals. The hill castes are about 40 per cent of the population followed by non-tribal Tarai groups (30 per cent) and tribal groups 25 per cent. Academicians have divided them into five major cultural groups—(i) Hindus, (ii) Newars, (iii) Janjaris, (iv) Muslims and (v) others.

Social and political Brahmins are high ranking Thakurs, Rajputs and Chhetris among the Aryan Nepali group and they dominated the nation socially, politically and economically. The Dalit community although Aryan, is socially ostracized, politically excluded and economically deprived. The indigenous communities, consisting of about sixty-one nationalities are excluded politically. The second and third groups, known as indigenous nationalities are politically excluded although there are about hundred castes and ethnic groups in this category. As per the 2001 Census of Nepal there are 92 languages and cultures inseparably connected with each other and these influence each other. A system of governance and development should reflect each language and culture. But recognition of Nepali as the lone official language has resulted in the exclusion of all other languages from the official list. As a result of this, a large segment of population has been deprived of the advantage of services and other opportunities provided by the state. As per the 2001 Census 86.5 per cent of the total population consists of Hindus, 7.78 per cent Buddhists and 9.35 per cent Muslims. A small section of population is tribal. But this figure of the followers of different religion has been challenged by several nationalities as they have not been classified properly as followers of Buddhists, Muslims or Christians and have randomly been named Janatis (indigeeous population) consisting of Magars (7.14 per cent), Tharus (6.75 per cent), Line bus (1.58 per cent) and Rais (3.94 per cent) of the total population, and have their own religious rituals. But they have been classified as Hindus. These indigenous communities together with

Buddhists and tribal groups constitute a significant part of the population not governed by the Hindu faith. The Hill Brahmins, Chhetris and Thakurs, the major Hindu groups, approximately constitute 30 per cent of the total population of Nepal. The Tarai population is also by and large Hindu, although there are some Muslims groups also.

Exclusion of Indigenous Population: Its Nature and Extent

The exclusion of the indigenous population (of Dalits and tribal groups) has been a deep-rooted problem in Nepal as their exclusion has been institutionalised by the Constitution and the law. Their exclusion has been of different kinds. The Kamali zone is one such excluded range where arable land is extremely limited. Its upper reaches are covered by snow round the year. The entire zone suffers from illiteracy, poverty and serious health problems. There has been no government aid for this area so far. There are 13 to 20 per cent of Dalits in Nepal. They have been ill-treated for generations. Their exclusion is primarily socio-economic and political as well as psychological in nature. There are nearly 40 per cent of indigenous people in Nepal who have been displaced from their native habitats and their linguistic and cultural identities are under threat. Besides, there are over thirty small tribal groups who are socially and economically extremely backward. Most of them, if not all, are landless, jobless and disenfranchised having no say in politics. Only the dominant groups consisting of Brahmins/Chhetris and Newans have dominated the politics at different levels. On the other hand, the marginalized groups are at the bottom of the ladder where such activities are concerned. This is evident from the Table 1.

These patterns of exclusion had the following broader implications:

- The dominant groups had monopolised the state activities. Other linguistic or cultural groups had neither any say in the political system nor in the system of governance.
- For the masses civil or political rights were meaningless. The exercise of these rights by women, Dalits, tribal groups etc. was effectively barred by the presence of upper class political elites, the bureaucracy and the army.
- Social and economic rights were not to be considered basic or fundamental rights. The state had failed in providing life of dignity to its citizens.
- With the change in regime and establishment of democracy, there was new hope and aspiration amongst the marginalized groups in Nepal. They now demanded their rightful place not only in the society but

TABLE 1

	Dominant Groups		*Marginalized Groups*				
	Brahmin/ Chhetri	*Newar*	*Madhesi*	*Janjati*	*Dalit*	*Others*	*Total*
1. Court	77	136	76	17	0	0	236
2. Constitutional Bodies	56	24	12	28	0	0	25
3. Cabinet	625	94	196	125	0	0	32
4. Parliament	60	76	174	136	15	0	265
5. Public Administration	77.6	37	12	0	0	0	245
6. Party leadership	58.8	109	198	152	0	0	165
7. Leadership Local Elected Bodies	56.5	15.7	16.2	12	0	0	191
8. Leadership Commerce Industry	16.7	47.6	36.7	0	0	0	42
9. Leadership Education Area	77.3	11.3	72	21	1	1	9710
Leadership Culture Area	69.1	17.9	0.49	0	0	0	1231
Science & Technology	58.1	29	9.7	3219	0	0	621254
Civil Society Leadership	75.9	14.8	7.4	19	0	0	54
Total	665	15.2	112	7.1	0.3	1	
Population (%)	31.6	56	3.9	222	87	1	
Difference from Population (%)		+34.9	+9.6	-197	15.1	-84	-1

Source: Neupane, Govinda, 2000, Nepalese Jetiya Prasad (Question of Caste/Ethnicity in Nepal), Kathmandu, Centre for Development Studies.

also in the governance of the country. The provisions of the Interim Constitution were inadequate and they were of the view that through amendments their demands could not be fully met, Janajatis and Madhesis have entered into an agreement with the government and they were not clear how their demands would be met.

Now the basic question is what do the marginalized communities hope to achieve in the Constituent Assembly? What are the main issues that should be addressed in the new Constitution? In this context, is also pertinent to note that the issues that the different marginalised groups want to be incorporated in the Constitution are not one and the same. Their issues and demands vary from each other. For example, Dalits want reservation in both the public as well as the private sector. They want to minimise the number of seats reserved in the legislature and the educational institutions. Thy also want elimination of untouchability and caste-based discrimination. They favour adoption of economic and social rights.

On the other hand the main demands of Janajatis is creation of a federal state based on 'ethnicity, language, geographic region, economic indicators and cultural distinctiveness'. They are in favour of right of self-determination for each federating unit. They also want constitutional recognition of local languages with Nepali. Likewise, they want formation of Indigenous People's Parties which was prohibited in the 1990s and by the Interim Constitution. They want representation in the Assembly and other bodies on the basis of gender, class, region and community based on their population. They also want a secular state. (This has already been achieved). The Kamaiyas want a permanent solution to bonded labour. They want the restoration of their land which was improperly taken away by the upper-caste settlers. The major demand of the Madhesis is federalism with substantial powers (power of autonomy), preferably with the whole of Tarai region as one of the states in the federation. They also want better distribution of revenue—a significant part of which is generated in the Tarai—to the Tarai and other underdevelopment areas. At the same time, they have proclaimed their commitment towards the sovereignty and integrity of Nepal. At the same time, they have been deprived so far, although they have inhabited the Terai region for centuries. They also want proportional representation in the legislature, executive and judiciary and in the public service, at the national level. They want adoption of the three language policy comprising: (i) native language, (ii) Nepali language, and (iii) English language in government, business, and education. Hindi has recognition, which is an important language in Madhesh. They also want national recognition of their language, culture and customs.

These demands of the marginalised groups are not merely demands for the recognition of linguistic or cultural diversity. They desire that their claims should have support of the political parties. They want re-structuring of the state and re-allocation of political power and economic resources. They also want recognition of their group rights. These demands were also made before the commission that drafted the 1990 Constitution. But all such demands were rejected at the time. But now, these longstanding demands have once more been voiced by different marginalised groups. How to accommodate them in the basic framework of the democratic Constitution of Nepal is a complex problem, as accommodation of such vast but different claims would not be an easy task. It may even weaken the unity and integrity of the country.

The root cause of discontent in Nepal lies in the hitherto economic, social and political exclusion of different communities. There is a close correlation between a person being poor and being a member of the minority ethnic group. But a powerful case for a more inclusive state system is based on the perceived threat to the cultural autonomy. In such a situation, the framing of the new Constitution for Nepal has become a very difficult task; since Constitution is about a nation-building, an undertaking in which the process is as important as the substance. The second stage of state restructuring follows the framework in which the first stage is resolved.

In recent times, in a number of states, new norms have been set by emphasising the virtue of diversity, re-conceptualization of political communities and equitable division and sharing of sovereignty. The framers of the Nepali Constitution should take note of ongoing changes in different nations across the world. They can adopt different approaches to resolve ethnic claims and conflicts. They must recognise the political rights of the ethnic groups, if they want to build a strong and united Nepal. For their purpose, they may think in terms of a strong federation in which different groups have a definite say without a right to secede from the federation. Their cultural identities together with linguistic identification must also be accommodated to the extent possible. In this respect, some of the suggestions made by Mahendra Lawoti in his article "Democracy, Domination and Engineering" should also be taken into consideration to the extent possible. He has narrated in his work that through a federation, electoral reforms, democratization of political parties, economic and social rights, the executive system, gender rights, empowerment of communities through civil and political rights and through fair citizenship rules, these problems can be thought over as per the Nigerian model, to accommodate claims of different communities in the Constitution.

REFERENCES

1. For detail see, Nepal's constitutional history by Bipin Adhikari in Yash Ghai, ed., *Creating the New Constitution: A Guide for Nepali Constitution*, Kathmandu, 2008
2. Census Report of Nepal, Kathmandu, 2001
3. Yash Ghai, *op.cit*, pg.94
4. Govinda Newpane, Nepalles Jatiya Prasar, Centre for Development Studies, Kathmandu, 2000
5. *www.gorkhapatra.org.np/gopa.detail.php?article_id=51673&cat...*, accessed on September 19, 2011
6. *www.citizenside.com/.../nepal-a-demonstration-for-constitution-by-a- ...*, accessed on September 30, 2011
7. *www.interpeace.org/index.../constitution-making.../about-the-authors*, accessed on April 18, 2011

8. *www.international-alert.org/sites/.../Consolidating_Peace_Nepal.pdf*, accessed on February 10, 2011
9. *www.mediahubsouthasia.com/.../nepal-constitution-making-at-stake-i...*, accessed on May 20, 2011
10. *www.minorityrights.org/.../minorities-and-the-constitution-building-...*, accessed on February 1, 2011
11. *www.myrepublica.com/portal/index.php?action=news_details*, accessed on February 8, 2011
12. *www.norway.org.np/.../Norway-supports-public-debate-on-the-const...*, accessed on September 19, 2011

10

Party System and Democracy in Nepal

ANIL K OJHA[1]

Twenty first century Nepal witnessed unprecedented People's War launched by the Communist Party of Nepal (Maoist) [CPN(M)] that led to the dethronement of King Gyanendra and reaching of an agreement between CPN(M) and other political parties for restoration of peace and democracy in the country. An interim constitution was framed in 2007 and an election for the constituent assembly was held in 2008. The process of transition towards a democratic republic through a consensually arrived written constitution is proving immensely difficult in Nepal. The tenure of the constituent assembly has to be extended twice and a third extension appears inevitable. An attempt has been made in this chapter to diagnose the events and trends that make political consensus elusive. It is sought to be accomplished through the role played by political parties in the process.

Context

Having unique geo-strategic location of being placed between India and China, Nepal has an area of 147181 square kilometres. It is a landlocked country having 1690 kilometres of land boundary with India and 1236 kilometres with China. India and China driven by their national interest remain concerned with the socio-political developments in Nepal. The population of Nepal stood at 2,89,51,852 at the last counting. Its demographic distribution is as following: Hindus 80 percent, Buddhists 10.7 percent, Muslims 4.2 percent and rest are from Kireet and others. As regards linguistic preferences, government recognises a large number of languages, among them are Nepali, Maithili, Bhojpuri, Tharu, Tamang, Newari, Hindi, Gurung, and

Limbu-Nepali. Nepali is the official language, which is the primary language of about 50 percent of the population. However, 12.1 percent of the population speak Maithili, 7.4 percent Bhojpuri, and 2.4 percent Awadhi also. Nepal celebrates its Republic Day on 29 May, Democracy Day on 24 April. Its legal system runs on Hindu legal concepts and English Common Law. Every Nepali citizen of 18 years of age has voting right.

Historical Background

Following the June 1, 2001 murder of King Birendra and the royal family, the US intervened militarily in Nepal. At first India closely coordinated with the US strategy of military defeat of the Maoist-led People's War in Nepal, and China acquiesced. But starting in the spring of 2004 both India and China came to reject the US anathema of the Nepali Maoists as "terrorists" and accept them as legitimate actors. With the 12-point agreement in November 2005, the success of the April 2006 urban insurrection, comprehensive peace agreement in 2006, the Maoist entering the government in early April 2007, the circumstances changed completely.[2] The overall consequences of government's reliance on army to deal with Maoists had exacerbated problem. Declaration of emergency in November 2001 was a counter-productive step. Glaring inequality and centralisation of power was the root cause of the problem. Maoists demanded constituent assembly[3] Comprehensive Peace Agreement (CPA) signed on November 8, 2006 between seven-party alliance and the CPN (Maoist) was a milestone in the evolution of constitutional democracy in Nepal. Besides Nepali Congress (NC) and Communist Party of Nepal (United Marxist Leninist) [CPN (UML)], other parties in the seven-party alliance for democracy were NC (Democratic), Janamorcha Nepal, Nepal Sadbhawana Party (Anandidevi), Nepal Mazdoor Kisan Party and Samyukta Bam Morcha Nepal.

Interim Constitution 2007

The interim constitution produced after the CPA has 25 parts, two schedules and 167 articles. it terminated the 1990 constitution of the kingdom.[4] Its preamble stated the goal of competitive multiparty democratic rule. Certain basics of the Nepali State are summed up as: independence, indivisible, secular, inclusive, sovereignty vested in Nepalese people and fully democratic state. It declares Nepal as a multiethnic, multilingual, multi-religious and multicultural state. Article 12(3)(c) of the interim constitution granted freedom to form political parties or organisation subject to reasonable restriction on acts that undermine sovereignty and integrity of Nepal or might jeopardise the harmonious relationship subsisting among people of various castes, tribes, religion or communities. Political parties are mentioned in Part 18. Article 141 prohibits imposition of restriction on political parties and article 142 prescribes requirement of 10000 supporters for registration and securing recognition for the purpose of contesting election. As regards the election of the prime minister, the interim constitution prescribed consensus and if no consensus could be achieved then two-thirds member could elect PM. This condition was revised to absolute majority, when after 16 unsuccessful rounds of election process; a successor to caretaker PM Madhav Nepal of Communist Party of Nepal (United Marxist Leninist) [CPN (UML)] running a coalition with Nepali Congress (NC) could not be elected for several months in 2010-2011.

Constituent Assembly Elections 2008 and the Evolving Party System

Constituent Assembly has 240 directly elected members, 335 elected on the basis of proportion representation and 26 are nominated. Seventy four parties are registered with the election commission. A mixed electoral system was adopted to guarantee a better chance of representation to diverse ethnicities in the CA elections. It offered opportunity to several minor parties to win seats in the CA. Only nine parties won seats in First-Past-the-Post System, while twenty five could secure seats through Proportional Representation. Multiplicity of parties offers enormous opportunity for expression of diverse political preference. In the CA elections, the Communist Party of Nepal (Maoist) emerged as the single largest party with 239n seats, while the NC and CPN (UML) came second and third with 115 and 108 seats respectively. Madhesi Janadhikar Forun could get 54 and Terai Madheshi Loktantrik Party could secure 21 seats. All other parties could get seats ranging from one to nine. The table 1 shows the parties represented in the Constituent Assembly.

Nepal has seen emergence of new parties and decline of old parties. Among the new parties CPN (Maoist), Madheshi Janadhikar Forum, Tarai Madheshi Loktantrik Party and Sadhabhawana Party are noteworthy. Nepali Congress, Communist Party of Nepal (Unified Marxist Leninist), Nepal Sadhabhawana Party (Anandidevi), Rashtriya Prajatantra Party, RPP Nepal and Rashtriya Janashakti Party faced decline. Three parties having support base in areas close to India—Madheshi Janadhikar Forum, Tarai-Madheshi Loktantrik Party and The Sadabhavana Party—have reached to an electoral understanding and launched a front called United Democratic Madheshi Front (UDMF) before the CA elections.

Table 1: Parties Represented in the Constituent Assembly

Party	*FPTP Vote % & seats*	*PR vote % & seats*	*Nom. Seats*	*Total Seats in CA*
Unified Communist Party of Nepal (Maoist)	30.52/120	29.28/100	9	239
Nepali Congress	22.79/37	21.14/73	5	115
Communist Party of Nepal (Unified Marxist Leninist)	21.63/33	20.33/70	5	108
Madheshi Jana Adhikar Forum	6.16/30	6.32/22	2	54
Tarai Madheshi Loktantrik Party	3.25/9	3.16/11	1	21
Sadbhavana Party	1.69/4	1..56/5	—	9
Communist Party of Nepal (Marxist-Leninist)	1.63/0	2.27/8	1	9
Rashtriya Prajatantra Party	3.01/0	2.45/8	—	8
Janamorcha Nepal	1.33/2	1.53/5	1	8
Communist Party of Nepal (United)	0.38/0	1.44/5	—	5
Nepal Workers Peasants Party	0.64/2	0.69/2	1	5
Rashtriya Janamorcha	0.91/1	0.99/3	—	4
Rashtriya Janashakti Party (Surya Bahadur Thapa)	0.77.0	0.95/3	—	3
Communist Party of Nepal (Unified)	0.50/0	0.45/2	—	2
Nepal Sadbhavana Party (Anandi Devi)	0.44/0	0.52/2	3	5
Nepali Janata Dal	0.17/0	0.46/2	—	2
Rashrtiya Janamukti Party	0.37/0	0.50/2	—	2
Sanghiya Loktantrik Rashtriya Manch	0.35/0	0.67/2	—	2
Chure Bawar Rashtriya Ekta Party Nepal	0.13/0	0.27/1	—	1
Dalit Janajati Party	0.30/0	0.37/1	—	1
Nepal Loktantrik Samajwadi Dal	0.10/0	0.23/1	—	1
Nepal Parivar Dal	—	0.22/1	—	1
Samajwadi Prajatantrik Janata Party Nepal	0.13/0	0.33/1	—	1
Independents	1.20/2	—	—	—
Other Registered Parties	1.50/0	—		
Total	98.50/248			

Post-election Power Sharing

Government formation required a strong coalition culture, a culture of compromise and coexistence. In order to isolate the CPN (Maoist), other parties reached an understanding. Nepali Congress candidate for the post of president, Dr Ram Baran Yadav, romped home being supported by the CPN (UML) and the MJF. Parmanand Jha from the MJF was elected the vice-president of the republic, while the chairman of the Constituent Assembly was elected from CPN (UML). Its nominee, Subas Chandra Nemwang was elected. The president and the vice-president were elected on July 23, 2008. Fractured mandate with no party garnering even simple majority led to a series of unstable government. It is imperative to have a brief discussion about major parties.

Nepali Congress

Nepali Congress was established in 1947. Having led the democratic movement in 1950 and successfully ending the discredited Rana Regime, it acquired an unparallel aura. However, faced with the royal coup of 1960 it saw its leader, the then prime minister B.P. Koirala, getting imprisoned. During the period from 1960 to 1989, political parties were prohibited in the country, which was being run through a titular Panchayat Democracy under the guardianship of the King. A draconian act, Association and Organisation (Control) Act, 1963, was in vogue. In the national referendum called by the King in 1980, the NC had supported multiparty system in opposition to panchayat democracy. Its leader B.P. Koirala passed away in 1982; thereafter a troika of Ganesh Man Singh, Krishna Prasad Bhattarai and BP's younger brother Girija Prasad Koirala dominated the party. Though faced with defection, factionalism and external pressure, Nepali Congress remained undeterred and again vigorously participated in the democratic movement of 1990 to end monarchy and reinstate parliamentary democracy, though in partnership with the Leftists. It could install its leader G.P. Koirala as the prime minister after the 1991 parliamentary election. Krishna Prasad Bhattarai was defeated in that election. G.P. Koirala remained its president from 1996 till his death.

On November 22, 2005 it has reached a twelve-point agreement with CPN (UML) and CPN (Maoist) that had led to successful reinstatement of parliament and shift towards the goal of Federal Democratic Republic. As regards intra-party affairs, it has faced split on 22 September 2002 when Sher Bahadur Deuba formed Nepali Congress (Democratic). But, the splinter group merged with the parent party on 25 September 2007. Girija Prasad Koirala, K.P. Bhattarai and Sher Bahadur Deuba were its leading players. After the death of GP, Sushil Koirala was elected working president on 20 March 2010. Veteran leader KP Bhattarai was opposed to fake republicanism. Party's 12th convention was held between 17 and 21 September 2010 at Kathmandu, where Sushil Koirala was elected President; while Ganesh Man Singh's son, Prakash Man Singh, was elected general secretary. After the declaration of resignation of CPN (UML) leader Madav Nepal-led coalition, the party projected Ram Chandra Poudel as its candidate. Presently Deuba is aspiring for leadership role. Ram Chandra Poudel of the Nepali Congress termed the February 2011 seven-point power-sharing agreement between UML and Maoists as unacceptable and great betrayal by the UML. He particularly mentioned that the creation of a separate force of Maoist combatants was not mentioned in the comprehensive peace agreement. The NC leadership is often accused by Maoists as acting at India's behest.

Unified Communist Party of Nepal (Maoist)

Emerging as the largest party in the Constituent Assembly elections of 2008, its leader Pushpa Kamal Dahal 'Prachanda' became the Prime Minister of Nepal. He remained in power till May 4, 2009. For reaching consensus, it is reconciled to the aim of federal democratic republic. It was once in the terrorist list in the West. It entered into pro-democracy alliance with other mainstream parties of Nepal. Prachanda has outlined a new path of peace and constitution to attain its path of people's democracy. Prachanda propounded this line after having realized that none of the proletarian revolutions of the past could be carried out in Nepal.[5] One of its splinter group Communist Party of Nepal (Unity Centre-Mashal) had merged with it in January 2009. At party's conclave in late 2010 at Bhaktapur, Prachanda said that the party should move ahead creating a new statute in favour of the people and a tactical slogan for People's Republic. When isolated and out of power in 2009-10, it used to accuse other parties of defying the interim constitution and also of disregarding the mandate expressed in the constituent assembly elections. Though, it now seeks the integration and rehabilitation of its People's Liberation Army (PLA) into Nepal Army (NA), but not before the completion of the constitution making process. Its reluctance tot to disarm the PLA creates scepticism among other parties. The Maoist party emphasises sovereignty, territorial integrity and independence of Nepal and self-respect of Nepali people. It affirms understanding of the sensitive geo-political location of Nepal and particular state of population distribution. Maoists entered into a seven-point power-sharing pact with CPN (UML) and a coalition led by Jhalanath Khanal was installed in early February 2011. Maoists delayed nominations of its members in the government. It insisted on its MP and former deputy chief of PLA Barsha Man Pun Ananta inclusion as defence minister.

The year 2011 witnessed intense factional feud within the CPN (Maoist). Chairman Prachanda faced challenge from all the top leaders of the party. Senior Vice-chairman and a hard-line ideologue Mohan Vaidya Kiran held the view that a suitable time has come for popular uprising and setting up a people's republic. Party should remain committed to completing the 'revolution' and prepare a ground for this by sharpening the political polarisation. According to him, entering the peace process was essentially a 'tactical' step, not a 'strategic' shift. While another vice-chairman Baburam Bhattarai, who is now being projected as the party's potential candidate for the office of the prime minister of the national unity government, perceives institutionalising the federal democratic republic as the main task. He views close cooperation with other parties, especially the Nepali Congress, as the prerequisite of such progress. Mohan Vaidya Kiran had earlier accused him and Prachanda of being trapped into bourgeoisie politics, when they enabled the Maoist entry into open politics and pushed for a republic instead of people's democracy. On Kiran's prodding Prachanda as prime minister had attempted to dismiss army chief Katawal. Their failure to accomplish it had led them to threaten people's revolt. They stated that revolution's principal contradiction was now with India and its "brokers".

In the meantime Bhattarai had teamed up with Kiran as he was marginalised by Prachanda. Though, Bhattarai and Kiran had fought long ideological battle in the past; they came together because they felt that Prachanda had maintained strength by playing them against each other. Bhattarai felt that Prachanda had blocked his chances of becoming prime minister in 2010. He also harboured resentment at being branded as Indian agent. He criticised Prachanda in mid-2011 for encouraging a culture of personality cult around him. Focussing on internal party management, they insisted on fresh power-sharing arrangement within the party. Another vice-chairman Narayan Kaji Shrestha Prakash and general secretary Ram Mahadur Thapa Badal also supported their move. Prachanda faction termed their deal as unnatural alliance. Prachanda, nevertheless, command the loyalty and support of all top PLA commanders who argued that this was not the time to weaken the chairman since only he could complete the peace process.

A tentative compromise was worked out among warring factions of the Maoist party. It was decided that Baburam Bhattarai would be the head of the party's parliamentary board and his name would be proposed as party's official prime ministerial candidate to lead the national unity government, while Prachanda would continue to be the party's chairman and parliamentary party leader. Further, Kiran would be the head of party's organisational and disciplinary departments while Badal would look after party's military affairs. Meanwhile, it was also decided that a new team of CPN (Maoist) ministers representing all factions and giving an equitable share to women and marginalised would be sent to Khanal's government including Prakash as the Deputy Prime Minister and Home Minister. These political proposals were ratified by the party's central committee as well. However reshuffle helped the fragile internal compromise to survive, it has caused complications in negotiations with other parties.

Communist Party of Nepal (Unified Marxist Leninist)

It had faced several splits. Over Mahakali Treaty with India done by the Prime Minister Manmohan Adhikary, Bam Deo Gautam faction had formed CPN Marxist-Leninist) in 1998. However, it reunited with the parent party on February, 2002. After the Constituent Assembly elections, in a power sharing arrangement its nominee got the post of chairperson of the Constituent Assembly. Its nominee Madhav Kumar Nepal was the Prime Minister till February 2011. Its President Jhalanath Khanal entered into a seven-point agreement with CPN (Maoist) President Prachand in early February and secured majority in the CA. Main points of the agreement were: (i) to write a Constitution that would institutionalise Republic, restructure the State and adopt federalism, (ii) strengthen people's inclusive democracy; (iii) end all forms of feudalism; (iv) strengthen national independence; (v) to create a separate force of Maoist combatants, or a separate force that includes Maoist combatants and personnel of other security groups; (vi) to build a long lasting friendship; and to lead the government in the future. It also included a commitment for rotational leadership of government between two parties.

On 6th February 2011 Jhalanath Khanal took oath as prime minister. He formed a cabinet of only four, assigning finance portfolio to his party colleague Bharat Mohan Adhikary, home to Bishnu Poudel, and education to Gangadhar Tuladhar. Cabinet expansion was delayed for a fortnight due to Maoists insistence on Home and defence portfolios. Narayan Kaji Shrestha stated that they were in favour of a comprehensive deal on power-sharing and sending a small cabinet along with the PM, but UML needed more time to resolve intra-party differences. It could be resolved when a commitment note was signed by Khanal and Prachand to rectify some of the contentious points of the seven-point agreement including formation of separate force for PLA and rotational leadership of the government. The signing of seven-point agreement caused dissension within the CPN (UML). Factions led by Madhav Kumar Nepal, K.P. Oli etc. criticised it vehemently alleging non-consultation by Khanal. K.P. Oli could not meet PM Khanal when he went to his official residence. He was turned away by the security forces deployed there. In late May 2011, during consultations among parties for the extension of the term of the CA, Prime Minister Jhalanath Khanal had agreed to resign to make way for national unity government. Though initially reluctant to include new ministers from their party; PM Khanal asked Maoist leadership to focus on the peace process. But on Maoists insistence, PM Khanal reshuffled his cabinet in August 2011. Cabinet reshuffle was opposed by the NC in the parliament terming it violation of the agreement. Viewing it as consolidation of left alliance, NC reiterated its demands for PM's resignation. UDMF comprising five Terai-based parties also opposed the reshuffle. K.P. Oli of the CPN (UML) also accused the PM of betraying the party. CPN (Maoist) reiterated that they were within their rights to change party representatives in the government. Jhalanath Khanal resigned as PM on 14 August 2011.

Madheashi Janadhikar Forum

It begun as an advocacy movement demanding ethnic self-determination rights with the formation of a Madhesh autonomous region, an election system based on proportional representation and setting up of federal republic of Nepal. When G.P. Koirala was Prime Minister, the country witnessed bloody war between MJF and CPN (Maoist) outfit, Madheshi Rastriya Mukti Morcha. Maost leader Prachanda compared MJF with contras of Nicaragua. Tarai Madhesh Loktantrik Congress led by Mahantha Thakur is another Madhesh formation. Further, there are liberal parties like RPP, RPP (Nepal), RJP (Monarchist), many of them are often termed as royalists.

Elusive Peace and Constitution

United Nations Mission in Nepal (UNMIN)

UN Mission in Nepal was established by the Security Council resolution 1740 passed on 23 January 2007. In September 2010 its term was extended to 15 January 2011 after a political agreement among Nepali forces to finish the remaining task of peace process in four months. UN Mission's mandate included monitoring 19000+ Maoist People's Liberation Army (PLA) combatants and 3000 weapons and 21 camps as well as restricted number of Nepali Army personnel and areas. The UNMIN headed the joint monitoring coordination committee, a dispute resolution mechanism that included representatives from the NA and the PLA. UN Mission term ended on 15 January 2011. Sharp differences emerged among leading political parties over UNMIN's future and arrangements for future. Caretaker Prime Minister Madhav Kumar Nepal held the view that the government would not request another extension, while the CPN (M) vice-chairman Narayan Kaji Shrestha demanded another extension and threatened that they may unilaterally ask for it. He declared that UNMIN's exit before the conclusion of the peace process would create complications as it was an important part of the past agreements. However, Nepali Congress stated that it could support Unmin's extension only with a revised mandate, where monitoring did not extend to

Nepal Army and the Maoists made tangible promises on integration and rehabilitation of their combatants. It was stated by the caretaker government that the task of monitoring was to be performed by the special committee, which was opposed by the Maoists. However, the United Nations Security Council did not extend its term. India as a non-permanent member as well as two permanent members—the USA and the UK were not in favour of the Unmin's extension.

All Party Special Committee for Supervision, Integration and Rehabilitation

The peace process required Maoists to transfer the PLA under the all party special committee for supervision, integration and rehabilitation of Maoist armed personnel. The committee has constituted a 12-member secretariat that had proposed a mechanism consisting of serving and retired state security personnel to be stationed in the in the 28 Maoist camps to monitor arms and the personnel.

Constitution Making

Constituent Assembly on 11 January 2011 unanimously resolved to form CA regulation draft committee. Four major issues in constitution writing that remain unresolved among major political parties are the form of government, electoral system, nature of federalism, and notion of prior rights for ethnic minorities. There exists basic difference between the Nepali Congress and the Maoist party on most of these points.

As regards the form of government, there is no consensus among major political parties. Nepali Congress still claims to stand for a traditional Westminster parliamentary system, while the CPN (Maoist) continue to argue in favour of a directly elected head of the government and the state. The efforts to reach consensus on this item was initiated by the task-force constituted by the sub-committee on dispute redress of the Constitutional Committee of the Constituent Assembly. Headed by a seasoned politician, Laxman Lal Karna, who is the co-chairman of the Sadbhavana Party; the task-force tentatively arrived at a compromise formula based on the French model. It envisaged a directly elected President having responsibility for foreign relations and the army and a Prime Minister elected by the Parliament having charge of the day-to-day administrative matters, budget and governance.[6] However, none of the major parties has given up its original stand. About the future electoral system, the NC pushes for direct first-past-post system, while the Maoists insist on a fully proportional representation based system on the lines of multi-member parliamentary constituency. An emerging consensus in the task force is in favour of the mixed electoral system, similar to one that was used in the

Constituent Assembly elections. Under the scheme, a certain proportion of seats would be based on direct elections, while the rest would be proportional representation based where parties would select candidates based on their vote share. The selection of candidates would be inclusive and proportional, giving place to marginalised communities. Similar divergence subsists on the nature of federalism to be adopted. The CPN (Maoist) dominated committee on state-restructuring constituted by the Constituent Assembly has proposed the formation of 14 states in accordance with the position of their party. However, the Nepali Congress opines that seven states would be appropriate. It reiterates its demand for the constitution of a State Restructuring Committee (SRC) as stipulated in country's Interim Constitution. This suggestion of the NC is being opposed not only by the CPN (Maoist) but by the United Democratic Madhesi Front as well. Maoist leaders insist that it is too late to form an SRC. They state that deciding the number of states is a political question. However, they show their willingness to reduce the number of proposed states to eight or ten based on the criteria of identity and capacity. They suggest constituting a team of specialists to advice on exact boundaries of states. Though the suggestion of the NC is unacceptable to the Madhesi parties, they are not acquiescent to stand of the Maoist party to create many states in the plains as well. The Madhesi parties want a single state in the Terai region neighbouring India. However at the task force level, the division of power between the centre and states has been broadly sorted out.

With regards to the notion of prior rights for ethnic minorities, divergent stand of the political parties halt decision. The CPN (Maoist) and various ethnic groups have demanded that only a person from a dominant ethnic community in a state should be entitled to become the chief minister of that state for two terms as compensation for historic discrimination. The Nepali Congress rejects this demand maintaining it to be violator of individual rights and democratic principles. There is a possibility of convergence among parties on some of the constitutional issues.

Integration and Rehabilitation of PLA

When the term of the CA was extended on 28 May 2011 for three months, political parties had agreed to finish the fundamental task of the peace process and prepare a draft constitution within tree months. However, any advance on these issues would depend on progress in peace process that is integration and rehabilitation of the People's Liberation Army cadres now referred as Maoist combatants. Maoist stand on the issue was summed up by one of its leader, Devkota. He stated their commitment to peace process but linked it to constitution writing and power sharing. The stand of other parties was succinctly put by Sadbhavana party co-chairperson Laxman Lal Karna. He stated that till the Maoists do not move on the peace process, other parties would not cooperate on the constitution writing. He asked as to why should other parties reveal their cards and show flexibility till one party stands on having a private army.

The peace process remains one of the major questions. Divergent stand of parties on the following issues held up progress. These issues are: (a) number of combatants to be integrated, (b) modality of integration, (c) rank harmonisation, (d) norms of entry, and (e) nature of rehabilitation packages and cash handouts. Further, parties differ on questions relating to the leadership or command, mandate, standard norm of the new force. During parleys on government formation in early 2011, just after the exit of the UNMIN, the Maoists had assured the Prime Minister Khanal that they would actively participate in the meetings of the Special Committee for supervision, integration and rehabilitation of the Maoist combatants to find out agreement on the contentious issues. Maoists said that they are willing to regroup the combatants based on those to be integrated, those opting for rehabilitation, and those who wish to voluntarily exit and join political work by the end of August 2011. In April 2011, Prachanda had stated in an interview, "no looking left and right, party would move forward to complete the process of integration and rehabilitation and peace process."[7] Prachanda clarified that his party accepted the modality proposed by the Nepal Army to create a mixed force under an NA directorate. Prachanda assured PLA general staff including commanders and deputy commanders of all the seven divisions of the Maoist army that any deal would be respectable. CPN (Maoist) central committee demanded that leadership of the mixed force under the NA directorate be given to a former PLA commander. The force should have a combat role and entry of combatants be made unit wise. PLA commanders demanded that rank harmonisation should be based on existing position in PLA hierarchy. Kiran's faction demands on integration include their deployment in border security. On the question of dual security of Maoist leaders, PLA soldiers protecting Maoist leaders from Prachanda and Bhattarai factions were sent back to the cantonments. As a gesture of good faith these leaders now relied only on state security personnel. However, Kiran termed Prachanda's action as "sell-out" and continue to maintain dual security.

From the discussion above, crisis facing Nepal's political parties are evident. Party system institutionalisation has not taken place in Nepal. All major parties are badly faction-ridden. Leaders' clamouring for power knows no limit. They lack commitment toward constitution writing and accomplishment of peace process. NC has yet not reconciled to its decay in post-CPN (M) scenario, while the Maoists still speak of people's revolt confirming apprehension of their anti-system properties. CPN (UML) is also wavering. Madheshi groups are anxious about their fate. The term of the CA is coming to an end in August 2011 and national unity government is nowhere in sight. Acting on PM Khanal's resignation on 14 August 2011, President has asked parties to form national unity government by 21 August 2011. Baburam Bhattarai and Sher Bahadur Deoba appear to be candidates. Earlier the NC had indicated that if integration and rehabilitation decisions are consensually taken, then they would not hesitate to accept a Maoist leader as Prime Minister. Intra-party decision making suffers from lack of transparency. Leadership question within CPN (M) and NC remain unsettled. A section whispers that Baburam would lead national unity government, while in case of majoritarian government Prachanda would throw his hat in the ring. So, peace process and constitution making being twin aspects of Nepal's democratic consolidation are passing through a critical phase in which the role played by major political parties are unquestionably faltering. One could only hope that leaders would show statesmanship and take Nepal out of its present predicament.

END NOTES

1. The author is thankful to the Indian Council of World Affairs, New Delhi for organising an international seminar at Muzaffarpur and also to *The Hindu*, Kolkata and its Kathmandu correspondent Prashant Jha on whose news reports he has heavily banked.
2. John Mage, The Nepal Revolution and International Relations, *Economic and Political Weekly*, no. 42:20, May 19, 2007, pp.1834-39
3. Mahendra Lawoti, Nepal: Breakdown of Democracy, *Economic and Political Weekly*, no. 52:50, December 15, 2001, pp.4623-26
4. Interim Constitution of Nepal, 2007, pp.1-96
5. See, for details on Maoist movements and ideology, R K Vishwakarma, ed, *People's Power In Nepal*, Manak Publications, New Delhi, 2006
6. *The Hindu*, Kolkata, 5 August 2011
7. 'We want to strengthen the relationship with India', Interview with Pushpa Kamal Dahal "Prachanda" taken on 26 April 2011 by Prashant Jha for *The Hindu*, New Delhi

11

Constitutional Vacuum in Nepal

SACHIDANAND SINGH

For the conduction of any nation, a constitution is that instructive regulation on the basis of which a nation is directed. It sets the rights and duties for the government and the citizens. Adherence to it and respect towards it is the responsibility of every unit associated with the nation and each citizen. Nepal is a sovereign nation and has a constitution too. But the irony that has occurred with Nepal is that after approximately sixty years of political journey, this nation could not find a binding constitution. The nation found a constitution in VS 2007, 2019 and 2047 but it was ephemeral; despite political turmoil in VS 2062/63, the search continues for a sorely binding constitution. Today, Nepal is being operated by the Interim Constitution—2063. Under it, the nation has been steered from the twin-column political structure of constitutional monarchy and coalition democracy to a 'Federal Democratic Republic'. For the new constitution, election of 601 members for the committee was accomplished. And for the announcement of the new constitution, the committee was given s time of two years which ended on Jyeshtha 14, VS 2067. But this constitutional committee could not achieve its basic target within the given time and took an extension of one year. But the sensitivity that is expected towards the main goal is deficit in the active political parties. Different parties have their own definitions for different sections of the constitution. Within merely two years, the interim constitution has undergone eight modifications. Despite that, it has not been able to cater to the desires of the people, nor is there a desire for it. That is why the common people are disappointed and uncertain.

The committee that is responsible for making the constitution and also for fulfilling the executive liability seems to have gone astray. The various parties responsible for this have forgotten their legislative duties and are working hard to make a government. Virtually this constitutional committee can be called unconstitutional or excessively constitutional because duties are given to them for a specific time period; using the inherent legislative power, the legislature increases its very tenure then this situation can be called illegal and not adhering to democratic value recognition. This constitutional committee had found its character taking a mandate of two years and its tenure was unsuccessful keeping in mind the basic goal. On the midnight of past Jyeshtha 14, VS 2067, the parties looking over it suddenly increased its work tenure by one year. This can virtually be called a consent based on personal interest of the political parties and its leaders. This could be possible because of the interim power of the committee as the common people were not in its favour. The reason is that they saw their leaders' deviant and confused towards the main goal, where the mandate had been given for structuring the constitution. Nilabar Acharya, political thinker of Nepal and head of the draft committee believes that the main reason for the constitution not being completed was the absence of the making of the legislative as one of the priorities of the political parties. Except this, dispute within the parties, dispute between various parties, the non-implementation of agreements made between parties, and their getting involved in power-centred politics are other reasons. Generally, the political parties here are not able to understand the sensitivity of the interim period and they have developed the thinking that they can issue complete guidelines once in power. That is why they have concentrated on power-centred politics and this difficult situation has come up.

After the palace murder case in VS 2057 and during the times of the so called people's war by Maoists, the election of the representative assembly (parliament) could not be done in the set time. Due to this the democratic powers got weakened and the faith of the people towards it kept dwindling. That is the reason why when the then monarch transferred power, the people did not indulge in any retribution programme that is worth mentioning; and after defining the sections and sub-sections of the then constitution 2047, autocracy was forced upon a democratic nation. The political parties here were so helpless and uncertain that it was after one year that programmes of opposition against this action of the Court were made public. Despite that this arrangement went on till Vaishakh 2063. The irony that occurred is that the parties that were creating hue and cry about democracy have become pawns of monarchy and kept leading an unconstitutional government. That was because they neither had the strong politics to bailout the nation out of the Maoist conflict, nor a fixed plan for the nation's development. That was the then monarch's increasing ambitions because of which the democratic powers organised together and paved an ideological platform for the 2062-63 people's movement. The election of the constitutional assembly was made possible after the Maoists' coming into the mainstream, which got legislative as well as executive rights. But even after more than a decade having gone by, the local body elections have not been possible. In a way, local democratic institutions are destitute of representatives. It is true that Nepal is not a country of acute economics, but even if slow, there at least has to be speed. For the development of the state, money is being assigned at various levels. But this amount is managed by those who are either deficient in mandates or those who have lost public trust. Party share comes up predominantly in this entire organisation. All this happens under the care of state employees and officers. In a way, the bureaucracy dominates the whole process which cannot be considered to be analogous to democracy. It can also not be taken that the head of the authority being democratic, the whole structure of the state has become democratic.

The security of its people and their wealth is the responsibility of the state. There is a constitution in Nepal as well according to which the responsibility the people and their wealth is on the state. But the conditions on which the Maoist rebels were brought into the mainstream have backed the trend of violence in the society. In a way the message has gone to the common people that any dream of change in the nation can be accomplished on the basis of power and weapons. That is the reason why various people from neglected communities from various areas have begun armed struggles. Today there are more than a hundred armed groups in the lowlands. Decidedly some of them are going on with the demand of political rights and some are operating criminal activities under its cover. The government is inept to handle such elements both at political and administrative levels. As a result, there is a state of terror funding in the society; there is a state of insecurity around. Institutions and business are operated under the shadows of terror. The industrial development of the country has been affected. This situation cannot be called the situation of constitutional rule.

Maoists have come into the political mainstream. During the time of conflict, the property of common people was forcefully captured in order to establish an equitable society. This is the biggest party in the present constitutional committee. They have led the government for thirteen months and are making efforts to lead the government again. But despite many agreements the acquired property of the common people has not been restored. The government and political parties make agreements on this, but no concrete steps have been taken in this direction. None of the parts of the state is capable of getting justice to the victims. The weapons of consent, conversations and agreements are ineffective. The state is not in the psyche to solve it strictly because there is a possibility of a political earthquake with that. Thus this situation hints towards the lack of a constitution in the country. And the state cannot be operated on the basis of agreement. It is essential to have administrative volition.

Every nation has an army whose objective is to save the borders of the country from foreign infiltration and invasions. Nepal also has an army which was known as 'Royal Nepalese Army' before VS 2063. But after the change in arrangement in the country, giving up 'royal', it became the 'National Army'. But in this arrangement, the nation found another army in the name of people's freedom which was completely run by the ideology of political parties. Its target is more party wellness than the good of the nation. Today this army is maintained by the funds assigned by the nation and considers itself equivalent and with equal duties as a national army but also participates with dignity in party activities. Under the agreement with Maoists this party has to be adjusted, but here this is like the question of the *yaksha* the answer to which is different for different parties: they want to adjust the Maoists guerrilla living in camps and the government and border security forces supporting them, armed sentinel groups, industrial security forces, district sentinels, etc., and make their situation like 'salt in food'. But Maoist leaders do not want their power to be shattered and wish to utilize them in an organised way for the completion of party works. That is why this adjustment has not been possible and its existence remains. It is a burning question that to what extent is it constitutional to have two armies in one country.

The election of the prime minister of Nepal has become a mere joke in the present times and a constitutional problem has arisen. There is a working government in the country for six months. The process of election of a prime minister began under the present constitutional arrangement after the resignation of the present prime minister. This election took place sixteen times with no results. The main reason is not only the clash of the parties, it is also the clash within the parties. The personal ambitions of the leaders have risen over national good and the state government is in a destitute state; the process of staging the resultless drama continues unabated. The Supreme Court has expressed disagreement to this political comedy of a selection process and talked of the meaningful use of the parliamentary manual. Along with it, it laid emphasis on the role of the committee head (Constitutional committee head) in bringing the nation out of this maze; also talked of beginning the process of the election of the prime minister afresh. After this regulation given by the Supreme Court, the head of the assembly Subhash Nemband gave the provision for compulsory voting for members of the assembly for electing the prime minister and till now it does not seem to be a strategy by the members to make neutral votes to make the process without conclusions. Because as per the new regulations, it is not possible to be neutral in the election process but no facility has been provided with respect to being absent from the voting. So the election process can be made conclusion-less using this whip. In this way in the present democracy of Nepal, the age of the working government seems to be endless and this situation is a marker for the country's constitutional vacuum.

The first constitutional difficulty under the present interim constitution came when as Prime Minister Pushpa Kamal Dahal took steps for the dismissal of the then army head Rukmangad Kutwal. At that time those in the government supporting the government and people in the opposition resisted strongly against the then prime minister's decision. There was a state of turmoil against this decision by the government within the army also and national and international politics were also working against it. Despite this the government took this decision but the president cancelled this dismissal and stopped the upcoming earthquake in the nation. To what extent was this step by the president constitutional was a topic for dispute but it got appropriate political and people's support. The long-term effect of this decision was that the government could not bear this stinger of insult and as the head of the government, Pushpa Kamal Dahal resigned as the prime minister. Post this coalition government gave a sort of direction to the country; now the question arises that now when the country is roaming in the process of election of the prime minister, what is his parental role as the head of the nation? The constitution does not give any clear instructions on this point. The role of judiciary is important in a democracy and to do justice is their goal. But along with meting out justice, it is necessary that the message of the institution's reliability reaches the common people. The breach of trust against the judiciary takes the nation towards chaos. Unfortunately, the judiciary of Nepal has been charged time and again owing to its decisions. Virtually, during the oath taking ceremony of the vice president, the way that the Supreme Court gave out quick decisions was a topic for dispute and the interim order that was given recently regarding the compulsion of having a citizenship evidence sheet for having one's name in the electoral list also led to a dispute. This superior institution has been in dispute at either one place or the other.

Today, a state of chaos can be seen in the political, administrative and social condition of Nepal. In the past two financial years the nation has not seen a budget in time and in a way the entire economic set up was standing on the edge of disorderliness and confusion. But on the day of the budget, what happened inside the constitutional assembly was something that the common people had not imagined. In this assembly of respectable people, some inhuman things happened. The assembly hall became a wrestling arena and the nation did not get its Budget. Now the government did not have any option and it brought the budget through the medium of ordinance, which has not got an approval from the house of legislature yet. It is imaginable how the daily political workings in Nepal have become conventional in the form of 'talks' and 'disagreement'. If this situation continues and the budget cannot win the confidence of the house in time, then to what extent will the income and expenditure will be considered constitutional? Also of importance is the fact that no action can be taken against the culprits of the unparliamentary activities that happened in the constituent assembly without the recommendation of the head of the assembly; and the head cannot recommend action against him because it hints towards the danger of political imbalance.

Today, a lot of volunteer organisations are active as NGOs in Nepal. The source of their income is foreign wealth. It is leading to the investment of the government wealth of various nations here. Whatever country is investing here also has its own ambitions as well. Because they do not directly meddle with the workings, but make the citizens their pawns and try to influence the policies in one way or the other. With this, Nepal has become the playground of the diplomacy of various powerful nations that want to shape the government structure as per their ambitions; under their ambitions, the nation's politics seems to have entangled. Institutions like the UNMIN and United Nations human rights active here are also not free from controversy/dispute and have also been accused of creating confusions in preservation of international interests and the internal politics here. All these things help us comprehend the fluid constitutional and political situation here. Today, one can see a conflict between indecision and disagreement in the country and its root is mutual anti-political ideology. The politics here is run by Left, radical Left, South wing and the moderate. The present government is that of the Left democratic alliance which is run by keeping in the centre democratic socialism. That's why it is not simple for it to share a platform with the party like Nepali Congress that follows a moderate ideology. On the other hand are radical Left and radical South wing parties whose basic agenda is nationalism and is against the so-called Indian expansionism. It is for this agenda that they receive feelings and support. One side is a supporter of India, and the other against it.

REFERENCES

1. *www.cscenter.org.np/uploads/.../100524034103_SituationUpdate92...*, accessed on October 13, 2011
2. *www.cscsarchive.org:8081/.../9002166987F6C15E6525731A00286...*, accessed on January 19, 2011
3. *www.everestuncensored.org/.../delay-in-constitution-making-of-nepa...*, accessed on February 1, 2011
4. *www.fesnepal.org/reports/2009/seminar_reports/report_mkmc.htm*, accessed on May 21, 2011
5. *www.groundreport.com/.../A... Constitution... Constitution.../ 2940969*, accessed on February 11, 2011
6. *www.himalmag.com/.../743-confusion-in-constitution-making-nepal...*, accessed on August 10, 2011
7. www.icird.org/files/Abstracts/ICIRD_2011_Abstract43.pdf, accessed on March 1, 2011
8. *www.idea.int/.../Nepal%20-%20workshop%20paper%20-%20Yash%...*, accessed on April 9, 2011
9. *www.ksl.edu.np/.../constituent_assembly_purpose_process_english.p...*, accessed on February 10, 2011
10. *www.liquida.com/article/26736172/nepal-kathmandu-peace/*, accessed on September 30, 2011
11. *www.madhavnepal.com/.../2010-01-18-30PM_Speech__Nepal_Cons...*, accessed on November 30, 2011
12. *www.n-peace.net/sites/default/files/...docs/Curriculum%20Vitae.doc*, accessed on September 15, 2011

12

Constitutional Dilemma in Nepal: Critical Issues and its Implications

C D AMAR

The constitutional crisis in Nepal appears to have begun with the resignation of Prime Minister Madhav Kumar Nepal in June 2010 and thereafter the failure of the Constituent Assembly to elect a Prime Minister by consensus. The antecedents of the crisis, however, are deeply rooted in the very first session of the Constituent Assembly. In contemporary political history, Nepal has witnessed constitutional crisis also in the 1990s. While the constitutional crisis of the 1990s was concerned with the working of the then Constitution of democratic Nepal due to the frequent exit of duly elected governments, the present one is related mainly with the writing of the new Constitution of the Republic of Nepal. This article discusses the implications of the constitutional crisis which plagues Nepal currently.

Various factors are responsible for the present crisis in Nepal. But before a study of these factors it is essential to keep in mind that the framing of the Constitution was the culmination of the last stage of the people's movement launched for the restoration of the democracy in 2005. In 2005 King Gyanendra dissolved the duly elected Parliament and seized power in order to re-establish absolute monarchy. Prince Gyanendra became king after the assassination of his brother in 2001. He desired to bring Nepal once again under absolute Monarchy and for that he suspended/dismissed the duly elected government of Sher Bahadur Deuba in 2002 and subsequently, dissolved Parliament and seized power in February, 2005. Violating the restrictions imposed upon the people's freedom and also on the Press, the people from all walks of life protested the king's nefarious move. Both the common people and the media, in fact, launched a crusade against the king's autocratic move. Without being daunted by the highly repressive measures taken by the king to suppress the movement, the people continued to fight till the end and till the restoration of the democracy in Nepal.

With the success of the movement for the restoration of democracy the next daunting task before the Maoists and Seven-Party Alliance (SPA) has been the drafting of the Constitution of the newly formed Republic of Nepal, and for that purpose the Constituent Assembly was constituted in May 2008. As it was a hung Assembly with the Maoists emerging as the single-largest party, Pushpa Kamal Dahal, popularly known as Prachanda, was elected Prime Minister and headed the coalition government. The Constituent Assembly was entrusted the task of drafting the Constitution for the Republic within two years. It, however, failed to do so, and another year has been given to it for that purpose. Regrettably, it has failed to do so even till now. Various factors are responsible for this, which might be discerned from the differences that surfaced between the Maoists and SPA in the very first session of the Assembly. The differences were of two types. Some of them were issues on which they finally came to agree whereas some of them remained the bone of contention. Whether the Republic of Nepal should have parliamentary form of government or presidential, whether there should be a post of president or not, and what should be the modality of the election of the Chief Judge etc., were among the important issues on which both the Maoists and SPA finally resolved their differences and decided to have a parliamentary form of government with the President as a nominal head.

The most important issue that remains a bone of contention is the issue of the integration of the People's Liberation Army (PLA) into the national army. There are nearly 19,600 PLA combatants who as per the Peace Pact of 2006 would have to be inducted in the Nepalese army. However, the SPA in general and Nepali Congress in particular has not only started opposing the merger but has also demanded the detachment of the Maoists from its own PLA. The SPA fears that if merged/integrated, the PLA would supersede the Nepalese army. The fear became deeper after the leakage of a tape showing Prachanda claiming that his party had inflated the PLA's strength in order to control the army. In addition, some other factors are also responsible for the ongoing constitutional crisis of Nepal. The most important among them is the selfish attitude/behaviour of the Seven-Party Alliance and also of the Maoists. Almost all of them wish to have maximum benefit for themselves and that has led to a lack of trust amongst them which may be one of the most important causes of the failure of the Constituent Assembly to deliver the Constitution.

The existence of the multiparty system is also responsible for the present-day crisis in Nepal. In case of the two-party system the people would have been left with only one choice; to elect one party or another. In a multiparty system people's vote gets divided amongst the various parties, resulting in the failure of single party to get a majority as is the case in Nepal presently. Certainly, the Constituent Assembly, having a single, strong political party, would have been in better position in drafting the Constitution than an Assembly having a fractured verdict. As the parties of Nepal do not have the experience of running a coalition government like India or elsewhere, the crisis has become more critical. Besides the aforesaid domestic factors, some external factors are also responsible for the constitutional crisis in Nepal. Both of Nepal's big neighbours directly or indirectly are responsible for the crisis that Nepal is facing today. China wishes to have an unstable political system in Nepal through the support that it has been extending to the Maoists since the mid-1990s in order to make its presence much stronger. What to talk of direct involvement in sorting out the difference that exist among the SPA and Maoists; India, indeed, as is alleged, is perpetuating the crisis firstly by encouraging the Nepali Congress to continue the stalemate by refusing to accept the merger of PLA in the army; secondly, by encouraging the Madhesi parties not to participate in any move to draft the Constitution in which the Maoists would have an active participation; thirdly, the demand that is being made for making the Tarai region an autonomous region, is also allegedly being also encouraged/instigated by India. Fourthly, by extending support to the forces that wish the Monarchy to survive; finally, by demanding the detachment of Maoist from its own PLA.

While the aforementioned factors are the antecedents of the crisis, the immediate cause is the resignation of Madhav Kumar Nepal from the post of Prime Minister and thereafter the failure of Constituent Assembly to elect the new prime minister even six months after Madhav Nepal's resignation. Madhav Kumar Nepal, it is to be noted, became the Prime Minister after Prachanda's resignation in 2008 from that post owing to his differences with President Ram Baran Yadav on the issue of the removal of the army chief from his post. The difference surfaced when the president reinstated the chief whom Prime Minister Prachanda had removed from his post.

Whatever might have been the causes of the constitutional crisis, the crisis has left very serious implications both for India and Nepal. It has posed a serious threat to the peace and stability in Nepal and that is not only due to the non-availability of stable political system but more particularly due to the way the Maoists have organised strikes, bandhs, demonstrations and blockades of roads after the resignation of Prachanda. The situation has become more serious due to the decision taken by Maoists in November 2010 to convert its movement into the violent movement if they and the Seven Party Alliance failed in achieving consensus on the issue of drafting the Constitution.

Secondly, the crisis has affected the economy of Nepal badly. The backbone of the Nepalese economy is tourism. Nearly half of the population directly or indirectly depends on it for its livelihood. But due to the frequent calls of strikes, bandhs and disruption of road/transport services, Nepal has failed to attract the tourists. Those who were on Nepal's visit either left the country or are planning to leave. Secondly, the strikes, bandhs and disruptions of road communication have also affected trade and business as shops, markets and industries have remained closed. Thirdly, the youth are jobless and that has affected the economy adversely. The economy, affected badly due to the factors mentioned, has forced more than half the population to live in abject poverty as they do not have adequate means of livelihood. The sky-rocketing inflation, has made the situation worse. People have no purchasing capacity. The crisis has proved highly injurious for the socio-religious harmony of the society as it has led to the resurgence of ethnicity particularly among the Madhesis, the people of Indian origin. They have formed their separate political parties/ organisations such as the Madhesi Janadhikar Manch, Tarai Madhesi Loktantric Party and Sadhbhavana Party, etc. and have started demanding their share in the country's politics as well as a separate autonomous province for themselves. What has made the situation more critical are the strategies of Maoists to exploit the ethnic resurgence for their narrow personal gain particularly after the resignation of Prachanda.

The crisis has left serious implications for India, the nearest neighbour of Nepal. China, as seen earlier, has used the unstable political system of Nepal for making its presence much stronger in order to counter India's emergence as a major global power. Despite the efforts of normalization being made, India has precarious relations with China. In such a situation, the ever-growing influence of China in an unstable Nepal is highly critical for the security and integrity of India. Secondly, it's no secret that through the ISI and through the terrorist organisations operating in Pakistan, the latter is sponsoring terrorist activities through Nepal and that has posed serious threats not only to the security and integrity of India but also to the law and order situation; and finally, the threat to the the law and order situation is also coming from the Maoists. In their meeting of November, 2010 the Maoists had decided to convert their peaceful struggle into a violent one in case of the failure of a consensus for drafting the Constitution. As the Indian Maoists have linkages with the Nepalese Maoists, recourse to violence by them would certainly be highly injurious to India's security and integrity and also to the law and order situation in Nepal.

Besides, the crisis has also left serious economic implications for India. India wishes to become a major global power and for that its accelerated economic growth is essential. Stable political systems in its immediate neighbourhood are a prerequisite for that. Secondly, not only due to being an immediate neighbour but more specifically due to its specific location, Nepal's and India's economies are interdependent. The crisis has ruined the economy of Nepal and naturally that has brought heavy burden on India's economy. Thirdly, Nepal is a good market for India's products. The crisis has posed a serious challenge for Indian products and finally, the Nepalese are facing unemployment which has led to the flow of refugees from that country to India. India has to provide for their maintenance on humanitarian grounds which has led to an additional economic burden.

Evidently, what is essential for both countries is to make more effective efforts for diffusing the crisis. While both the SPA and the Maoists must realise the seriousness of the situation and make genuine efforts for drafting the Constitution by sorting out their differences and keeping faith on each other, they also have to extend cooperation amongst each other by giving up their selfish attitudes and behaviour while electing the new prime minister. Being an immediate neighbour and being deeply affected by the crisis it is essential for India to take active part in the process of electing the new prime minister and more particularly in the drafting of the Constitution of Nepal. For that, it has to give up its passive approach or indirect involvement and has to play the role of a mediator and conciliator in sorting out the differences that exist between the SPA and the Maoists and between the various constituents of the SPA itself. The active role on India's part is needed not only due to its commitment for democratic values and ethos being an immediate neighbour, but more particularly because a stable and peaceful political system in its neighbourhood would always be beneficial for it particularly in terms of security and integrity and accelerated economic growth.

REFERENCES

1. B C Upreti, *Nepal: Democracy at Cross Roads*, New Delhi, 2007, pp. 47-79
2. *follesdal.net/projects/ratify/nepal/Ghai-2011-New-Nepal.doc*, accessed on September 4, 2011
3. *idsn.org/.../user.../Nepal/Nepal_UPR_session_-IDSN_analysis.pdf*, accessed on September 25, 2011
4. *indigenouspeoplesissues.com/index.php?...nepal...constitution...*, accessed on August 16, 2011
5. *manjeet.com.np/.../global-climate-talks-and-constitution-making-in-n...*, accessed on February 19, 2011

6. *nepal.usembassy.gov/ep-12-17-2008.html*, accessed on November 1, 2011
7. *nepalicount.com/.../25-america-nepal-society-interaction-program- ...*, accessed on April 10, 2011
8. Prashant Jha, 'Nepal: Republic Now' *Frontline*, Chennai, vol. 25:12, June 7-20, 2008, pp 131-34
9. Prashant Jha, 'Maoists in Nepal: The Differences Within', *The Hindu*, Chennai, December 6, 2010
10. Siddharth Vardarajan, 'The Danger of India's Nepal Policy', *The Hindu*, Chennai, August 16, 2010
11. *www.amazon.com/Constitution-Making-Under.../dp/.../0231143028*, accessed on November 5, 2011
12. *www.andhranews.net/Intl/.../Constitution-making-process-43750*, accessed on April 11, 2011
13. *www.ccd.org.np/*, accessed on February 10, 2011
14. *www.chumlung.org.np/page.php?page=19*, accessed on February 11, 2011
15. *www.crisisgroup.org/.../nepal/128_nepal_s_constitutional_process.pd...*, accessed on September 10, 2011
16. *www.cscenter.org.np/uploads/.../100524034103_SituationUpdate92...*, accessed on October 13, 2011
17. *www.indianexpress.com/news/will-guarantee-security...nepal.../0*, accessed on August 22, 2011

13

Nepal's Constitutional Dilemma and India's Security Concerns

MANJARI VERMA

Nepal is a small, developing country situated on the southern slopes of Mt. Everest. Its northern border lies more or less along the Himalayan watershed and forms a natural border between the Tibetan region of China and Nepal. In the south, Nepal's boundary runs more than five hundred miles along the Gangetic plains of India.[1] As India has no formal boundary treaty with Nepal, it makes both the countries easily accessible to each other. India prefers to maintain an open border because it binds Nepal to it closer, culturally, economically and politically.

Geographically sandwiched between the two big Asian powers—Communist China and Democratic India, the position of landlocked Nepal had been like a pendulum since the end of the monarchy in the region. Both the countries took deep interest in Nepal for promoting their foreign policies. When the Indian President said that "the relations between India and Nepal are not of body but of soul,"[2] the Chinese Prime Minister responded that "Nepal and China are blood brothers and nothing can poison their relationship,"[3] Thus, when India was evolving a theory of "Special Relationship", China put a question mark on its acceptance of inclusion of Nepal in India's defence parameter. In 1950, the Chinese occupation of Tibet alarmed India as her northern border had now been gravely exposed to foreign invasion. The vital importance of Tibet has been observed by a Western scholar in his study on "Communist China and Tibet" in these words:

> "(He) who holds Tibet dominates the Himalayan piedmont, he who dominates the Himalayan piedmont, threatens the Indian subcontinent, and he who threatens the Indian subcontinent, may well have all (of) Southeast Asia within its reach and with it, all of Asia."[4]

> India therefore would like Nepal to be strengthened—neither ignored nor "swallowed."[5]

Impact of Indian National Movement

India's desire for establishment of democracy in Nepal was an extension of its freedom struggle. Many Nepali Congress leaders not only supported but also participated in the Quit India Movement of 1942. Deeply impressed by Indian leaders like Gandhi and Nehru, they also desired democracy in Nepal. They even considered India a safe base for launching a movement against the Rana regime. In January 1947, some Nepalese residing in India formed the "Nepali Rashtriya Congress" in Banaras with the support of Indian socialist leaders Ram Manohar Lohia and Jayaprakash Narayan. King Tribhuwan, who was virtually a prisoner of the Ranas, too was interested in ending their autocratic rule. He sympathized with the democratic forces throughout the struggle against the Rana regime. As Ranas were not hostile towards India at that time, they agreed to introduce people's participation in Government and promulgated a new Constitution for Nepal in 1948. The Constitution envisaged Fundamental Rights, the formation of an independent judiciary, a public service commission and a bicameral legislature.[6] Thus, the democratic movement in Nepal was nurtured under the powerful inspiration of Indian National Movement and its leaders. However, due to strong opposition from the reactionary Ranas, the nascent democratic movement could not gain ground.

Treaties of 1950

Relations between India and Nepal were close but fraught with difficulties stemming from geography, and common cultural, ethnic, linguistic identities that overlapped the two countries' borders. In 1950 both the countries tried to consolidate their complex relationship with the signing of the treaties of "Peace and Friendship" and "Trade and Commerce". The treaties defined the security relations between the two countries and an agreement governing both bilateral trade and trade transiting India. It stated that "neither government shall tolerate any threat to the security of the other by a foreign aggressor" and obligated both sides "to inform each other of any serious friction or misunderstanding with any neighbouring state likely to cause any breach in the friendly relations subsisting between the two governments." These accords cemented a "special relationship" between India and Nepal that granted Nepal preferential economic treatment and provided Nepalese in India the same economic and educational opportunities as Indian citizens.[7]

Limited Democracy in Nepal

During the period of Ranas' rule, the democratic forces had become active in bringing about liberal political reforms in Nepal. But Pandit Nehru was well aware of the fact that unlike India, Nepal did not have any tradition of parliamentary democracy. Besides, the institution of monarchy was greatly respected by the people of Nepal for its symbolism, so it must be retained. He stated in Parliament:

> "We are anxious that there should be peace and stability in Nepal. At the same time we feel that the introduction of substantial political reforms was essential for this purpose."[8]

Hence, in 1950 when a revolt against Rana rule erupted all over Nepal, India played a decisive role in bringing about peace in Nepal. New Delhi brokered a deal and the Sah King after a century of being humiliated by the Ranas was on the ascendant again. The king was to be only a constitutional head and the Rana rule was over. A ten-person interim cabinet with five members from the pro-democracy Nepali Congress and five from the Rana side would take over. The new Government would oversee the transition to democracy.[9]

Failure of Democratic Experiment

The revolution of 1950 brought about a political change in Nepal but its democratic experiments never really took off. Neither the Ranas could reconcile to the loss of their absolute power, nor could the Nepali Congress be satisfied with the new-found "limited democracy". Nepal had been put into an experiment for which it was ill-prepared. Nepalese political parties lacked ideological commitment and there were deep factional cleavages. The army was ill-equipped and unorganized. The country's economy was in deplorable condition. The judicial structure was still feudal in character. The existing bureaucracy lacked the experience and expertise to run the democratic system. Without evolving a concrete infrastructure for running democracy, the old system had been disrupted. Under the circumstances the new experiment was bound to fail.

Anti-Indianism

As the involvement the India in the process of democratization deepened, Nepal started feeling uncomfortable with the "special relationship". King Mahendra strongly believed that pro-Indian democratic forces were responsible for political upheaval in Nepal and that the Monarchy had the crucial role to play in Nepal for restoring stability and dignity. He did not like New Delhi guiding Nepal's future political developments. To give a practical shape to his policy, he rejected all the democratic experiments, turned down the popular demand for constituting a cabinet and introduced a system of Panchayat Government run by an aristocracy of the Shahs and the Ranas.[10] On May 10, 1954, B.P. Koirala remarked:

> "It is a fact that there is a wide spread feeling in Nepal against India and it is the latter's policy of interference in Nepal's internal affairs which is responsible for it."[11]

It is obvious that the growth of anti-Indian sentiments were encouraged at the people's level also. Nepal's discontent against India were targeted on the following logic—

- That India interferes in the internal affairs of Nepal.
- That Kosi embankment was made on Nepal's land.
- That Indian army and technical experts were present in Nepal despite latter's unwillingness.
- That some trade restrictions were introduced for Nepal.

In foreign affairs the King made it clear that Nepal was not a buffer state and evolved a global strategy of playing India off against China. Nepal entered into an agreement with China for building the Kathmandu-Lhasa Road and sharing Mount Everest which was openly criticised by India. China declared that:

> "Neither language differences nor the Himalayas stood in the way of friendship between Nepal and China".[12]

Indian Government in Action

In the Sino-Indian border conflict in 1962, Nepal followed the policy of equi-distance from both the countries and decided to remain scrupulously neutral. But soon the King realized that despite China's friendship, Nepal could not do much without India's support. So he started displaying a soft corner towards India. At the diplomatic level, India too, made special efforts to remove misunderstandings between the two countries, which generated a healthy atmosphere, and opened up new horizons of goodwill and cooperation. The Indian government provided huge economic aid and technical support in infrastructural development related to roads, rivers, electricity, irrigation, etc. in Nepal. Some events took place in the 1970s which included the signing of the Indo-Soviet Treaty of Peace and Friendship, the Indo-Pak war and creation of Bangladesh, merger of Sikkim into India, rise of naxalism in the border areas of West Bengal adjoining the Nepalese border, the Indian Nuclear test, etc., made Nepal apprehensive about the impact of the growing influence of India as a regional power. In 1978, India agreed to separate trade and transit treaties, satisfying a long-term demand of Nepal. Nepal in the meantime, raised its demand for the country to be declared a "zone of peace." India did not respond because it rather preferred the whole of subcontinent be declared so. In 1988 dissatisfied with Nepal's acquisition of Chinese weapons without India's approval, New Delhi insisted on reviewing Indo-Nepal relations as a whole. Following the so-called "Indian blockade" in 1989 Nepal faced devastating consequences. As petrol and other consumer goods disappeared from the market, violent demonstrations took place all over Nepal. The agitating people demanded a return of democracy with a constitutional monarch and they got it. With this began an era of multi-party democracy in Nepal in 1990. Since then till the royal massacre in June 2001, Nepal had 9 Prime Ministers, some of whom lasted only for a few months.[13]

The Return of Democracy

In 2005 after King Gyanendra took over, Nepal's relations with India deteriorated. The King like an absolute despot declared Emergency, dismissed the elected government and grabbed political control of Nepal. The Nepali political parties and the ruling elite, in reaction, joined hands with the Maoist insurgency and started a violent people's war against the monarch. The King was forced to declare the re-establishment of Parliament in April 2006. The new Parliament took away all the royal powers and the Maoists decided to join the interim government. With this, the 240-year long rule of the monarchy came to an end on May 28, 2008, and Nepal was declared a secular, federal, democratic Republic.[14]

Present Political Crisis in Nepal and India's Concern

The emergence of the Communist Party of Nepal (Maoist) as the single largest party in the Constituent Assembly elections in April 2008 came as a big surprise and shock for India, which has sufficient reasons to worry about its security that may not be served with a government led by 'red' forces, closer to China. In Nepal despite a revolutionary transition from Monarchy to a

Republic, the constitutional deadlock is still prevalent. The newly-elected Constituent Assembly, till now, could neither draft a Constitution that would guarantee fundamental rights and rule of law to the citizens of Nepal, nor could it democratize the Nepalese army, both of which were a part of the Comprehensive Peace Agreement of 21 November, 2006.[15] To realize the Assembly's mandate, May 28, 2010 was set as the deadline but nothing concrete could emerge to end the constitutional crisis in the information of the new government. Due to inability of Parliament to choose a Prime Minister, the country is facing a leadership crisis too. The UN mission till January 15, 2011 has been entrusted with the responsibility of looking after the progress of the peace process in Nepal.[16] Till then, India will have to wait and watch. In the present context, the ground realities within Nepal cannot be overlooked. Nearly half of the Nepalese population lives in abject poverty and has no adequate means of livelihood. Inflation and food prices have skyrocked. Nepal's land distribution remains a major concern and the Maoist army is yet to be completely integrated into the country's defence forces. Thus, while officially welcoming election and hoping a democratic Nepal will be established soon, India has viewed all the political developments with concern. China's presence and influence in Nepal is growing day-by-day. Allegations over Chinese assistance to the Maoists and use of the unstable political situation to its own advantage have been levelled. At the moment India should continue to adopt a non-interventionist approach in Nepal.[17] It should rather focus on improving trade, transport and communication ties in an effort to be a key stakeholder in Nepal's development. Mutual respect and cooperation must be given top priority.

END NOTES

1. *beyondheadlines.in/2011/10/many-nepalese-want-kingship-back/*, accessed on August 13, 2011
2. *biz.nepaltrekkinginformation.sajha.com/sajha/html/openthread.cfm?...*, accessed on November 16, 2011
3. Dharamdasani, M D, *Indian Diplomacy in Nepal*, Aalekh Publishers, Jaipur, 1976
4. *hamropalo.com/nepal.../maoists-intensify-works-on-constitutionmaki...*, accessed on October 7, 2011
5. *lawandotherthings.blogspot.com/.../constitution-making-in-nepal.htm...*, accessed on February 10, 2011
6. *lesliechand.blogspot.com/2011/.../citizens-participation-in-nepals.htm...*,accessed on February 6, 2011
7. *Nepal Today*, Kathmandu, no. 5, July, 2009
8. *nesac.org.np/main/publications/democracy_constitution.html*, accessed on November 3, 2011
9. *news.oneindia.in/.../constitution-making-difficult-koirala-121014900...*, accessed on June 19, 2011

10. *tweetmeme.com/.../nepal-national-youth-campaign-for-constitution-...*, accessed on September 12, 2011
11. *unsr.jamesanaya.org/.../22-nepal-alleged-exclusion-of-indigenous-pe...*, accessed on June 17, 2011
12. *video.ezinemark.com/voices-from-below-constitution-m... - United States,* accessed on June 19, 2011
13. *www.apssnepal.org/.../ ...*, accessed on February 6, 2011
14. *www.andhranews.net/Intl/.../Constitution-making-process-43750,* accessed on April 11, 2011
15. *www.campaign.org.np/activity_summary.php,* accessed on June 10, 2011
16. *www.can.gov.np/en/committees/view/14,* accessed on May 10, 2011
17. *www.ccd.org.np/.../constitution.../Robert_Piper_Address_to_Intl_Co...*, accessed on March 10, 2011

14

Constitutional Impasse in Nepal: Critical Issues

KUMARI KIRAN

Ever since the revolutionary overthrow of the monarchical order on April 24, 2006 Nepal has been on an accelerated path of political transformation. The fall of the old regime opened the door for the restoration of the old Parliament, of an interim Constitution, formation of an interim legislature that included the Maoist rebels, and finally the induction of the Maoists in the government. The political transition reached a new stage with the holding of the Constituent Assembly election in April 2008 and the subsequent Maoist accession to power through the parliamentary process. The pace and scale of change since 2006 has turned the erstwhile unitary state into a federal structure and the Hindu Kingdom into a secular republic. However, monarchy was not militarily defeated. The Maoists joined hands with the SPA to defeat the king, through a peaceful Jana Andolan, and joined the government accepting G.P. Koirala, a bourgeois chieftain as an all-powerful Prime Minister and the head of state of 'New Nepal'. The Maoists wished to succeed as the new rulers of the country and saviours of all the oppressed and disadvantaged groups in Nepal, but that did not happen. Therefore, they repeatedly demanded to make Nepal a republic instantly and Koirala to become the first president. The latter refused; he wanted to wait until the CA election. The Maoists began projecting their leader Prachanda as the only viable candidate for the first president of Nepal.

In April 2008 elections for the Constituent Assembly were held in which the CPN (Maoist) emerged as the single largest party in a House of 601 members. The first meeting of CA on 28 May 2008 adopted a resolution abolishing the monarchy and declaring the country a republican state. The provisions for the President followed by a Vice-President, were inserted in the Interim Constitution through amendments, as Head of State of the new republic. The Constituent Assembly (CA) elected Dr. Ram Baran Yadav and Paramananda Jha as the first president and vice-president respectively. Thus the transfer to a Republic from that of the 250-year old Monarchy, despite many speculations, was accomplished peacefully. However, the peace process and the Constitution-making are yet to be accomplished.

The Interim Constitution had allotted two-year term to the CA, beginning from its first meeting, for its work on drafting the Constitution. The first meeting was held on 28 May 2008, which meant it had to complete its work by 28 May 2010. However, the Constituent Assembly having been unable to deliver the Constitution within the specified deadline, has wrested another tenure—May 28 2011. The CA schedule has been changed several times due to the delay in the preparation of the report by some of the thematic committees specially those working for restructuring the state and the form of the government, etc. Three successive administrations have governed Nepal since the monarchy ceded its power to Parliament in 2006. Shortly after Parliament was reinstated that April, the Seven Party Alliance (SPA) elected the Nepali Congress (NC) party president Girja Prasad Koirala as prime minister. Koirala was re-elected in April 2007 to head a coalition government that included representatives from both the SPA and the Maoists. An impressive flurry of legislative activity, as well as partisan bickering, occurred under the interim government. Following the April 2008 CA elections in which they won a plurality of votes, the Maoists formed a coalition government.

In its early months, the Maoist-led government succeeded in passing a budget, holding regular cabinet meetings, and adopting economic policies benefiting poor Nepalese. But it is also showed worrisome signs of a lack of commitment to democratic values, demonstrating intolerance to criticism, a tendency to interfere in the functioning of the judiciary, and a reluctance to punish its cadres for acts of violence and arson. Following a constitutional crisis and conflict with the Nepalese arm, Maoist Prime Minister Pushpa Kamal Dahal (better known as Prachanda) resigned, bringing to power a weak coalition of 22 parties headed by Madhav Kumar Nepal of the Communist Party of Nepal-Unified Marxist Leninist (CPN-UML).

The Maoist tussle with the President began after Prime Minister Pushpa Kumar Dahal, citing insubordination dismissed the then Chief of Army Staff Gen. Rukmangaud Katwal on May 3, 2009 and appointed Gen. Kul Bahadur Khadka as acting Chief. Before the night was over, however, President Ram Baran Yadav dispatched a presidential order quashing the prime minister's decision and asking Gen. Katwal to carry on as Army Chief. Sensing that the internal and external balance of power was not in his favour, Prime Minister Pushpa Kumar Dahal decided to step back from the brink and offered his resignation on May 4th. This brought a premature end to the chequered career of the nine-month-long Maoist-led government that had been formed after the Maoists emerged as the largest party in the Constituent Assembly elections held in April 2008.

The Maoists saw the Army Chief Gen. Rookmangud Katuwal as an aspiring autocrat clinging to the last vestiges of a dormant monarchical system. His first crime was to defy the United Nations Mission in Nepal (UNMIN's) mandate not to recruit new soldiers, which also goes against the 12-point peace agreement signed by the political parties back in 2006. Prime Minister Pushpa Kumar Dahal argued that when an institution within the government fails to submit itself to the rules agreed upon they ought to be punished. The interim Constitution specifically mentions that the army is under the control of the democratically elected government. Thus their mobilization solely rests on the government. Having been subjected to the King's whimsical orders and wishes, the COA found it hard to comply with the government which was elected with overwhelming majority. The political system has changed but the old guards disguising themselves in new clothes carry the age-old superiority complex that has dogged our ruling elites for ages. The government saw the army challenging the authority and the sovereignty of the people. The army's decision to disregard the government orders was a challenge to the new Republic. The sheer force of circumstances which led to the dramatic debacle of the Maoist government over the Army issue begs for a fundamental reappraisal of much of existing theorizing on civil-military relations and the idealized claim of civilian supremacy. One lesson that emerges from the Nepal's case is that despite its normative claim, civilian supremacy is to a large extent a social construction shaped by the balance of interests among the major political constituents. Simply put, unity among the dominant classes establishes civilian supremacy while discord invites its breach. Once the government initiated steps to sack the Army Chief, the political accord between the Maoists, the Nepali Congress, UML, and Madhesi Janadhikar Forum had already begun to unravel on fundamental issues of state. It must be considered the height of political irony that the republican parties were becoming more fearful of the authoritarian trait of the civilian government on the Left than of a potential praetorian army to the Right.

In the absence of a ruling consensus on the nature of the civil-military relationship, the Maoist plea for exercising civilian control over the military failed to find sympathetic hearing within the country or outside, even though some of their claims can be construed as perfectly legitimate within the ambit of the liberal normative, albeit not in the manner presented by the Maoists. Just like the prime minister, the president too is essentially a civilian position, duly elected by the Parliament. The question was not whether too is essentially a civilian, but where the ultimate state power rested, constitutionally. Although Nepal's interim Constitution makes the cabinet the sole executive authority, it has also named the president as the supreme commander of the Army and requires the cabinet to route many of the important military decisions such as the appointment of the Army Chief through the president's office. By not following this procedure in sacking Gen. Katwal and appointing his successor, the Maoist government was seen to have undermined the constitutionally mandated position of the president as well as transgressed the established rules governing civil-military relations.

In the above-mentioned context it is important to point out that with the United Nations Mission to Nepal (UNMIN) now certain to exit by the third week of January, the vexed issue of integration and rehabilitation of the Maoist combatants will remain unresolved. And the Nepal Army, which has been treated as at par with that of the Maoists—in the sense that both armies remained confined to their designated camps and barracks as long as the UNMIN was reverted to pre-UNMIN status. That is sure to invite further tussles between the army and the Maoists. Following the demise of "old" Nepal in 2006, the current phase is proving to be particularly adverse for "new" Nepal. Despite the Comprehensive Peace Agreement in 2006 and the Constituent Assembly elections conducted in 2008, a sufficiently decisive hegemonic bloc is yet to emerge that can pre-empt destabilizing rivalries between competing forces, establish a new order, and articulate a new state identity and purpose. Hampered as it is by substantive differences on the fundamental structure of the state and system of governance, the ruling alliance is unable to articulate a coherent purpose at this point. The degree of cooperation and trust amongst the ruling alliance since the Constituent Assembly election has made it apparent that "the actual writing process is going to be more contentious as the various constituencies fight over each word and clause in the constitution." How can the constitution be drafted when there are such fundamental and substantive differences? How much can one compromise?

In contemporary Nepalese politics, a number of challenges exist in the path of Constitution-making. The activities of the political parties have among other things also created challenges in this direction. The difference in the basic philosophies/ideologies of the political parties regarding the Constitution and reconciliation have further complicated the issue. In fact the political parties in the initial phase intended to make a Constitution to achieve a number of objectives including promotion of perpetual peace, inclusive democracy, state structuring and peace making process. The Interim Constitution, 2007 thus has underlined the basic concept of political parties as the guiding governing principle but soon after the election of the CA, the political parties remained involved in a numbers game, concentrating on the formation of the government or capturing political power.

As the political parties represented in the CA have failed to demonstrate a friendly environment by developing political consensus among themselves the timely drafting of the democratic Constitution according to the spirit, wishes and needs of the people and the country has become a serious issue. These political parties, as mentioned in their election manifestos and party programmes and declared policies, have differences on various issues including the inclusion of the combatants into the government army, state restructuring, federalization (e.g. the number of federal units, the models of federalism, division of power), nature of the political system (e.g. parliamentary, presidential mixed French model), the powers and functions of the executive (Active or nominal), type of the legislature (unicameral or bicameral), type of electoral system (First-post the post system, mixed or proportional representation-PR). In this way, the differences on the content and subject of the Constitution (e.g. federalism, and forms of government) have complicated the process of drafting the Constitution in time. In fact, the major political division is on the subject of federalism. Although Nepal has been declared a 'federal democratic republic', the government is not clear about the federal structure of the state. Major political parties such as the NC and the CPN UML have reluctantly accepted restructuring the country as a federal state but other fringe parties are against such a federal restructuring. Those who are for a federal state, believe that it will enhance harmony among various groups. However, there are conflicting views regarding the acceptance of a federal state amongst parties and Janajatis. Some are of the view that the country should be divided geographically, while others, especially, various Janajati groups insist on division on the basis of ethnic and linguistic lines. The Janajatis' demands for autonomy and self-determination rights are intended to promote their languages and cultures on equal basis, while certain groups in Terai region are insisting on a federal state with rights to secession.

As the country is certain to adopt the federal system, new areas of political conflict also appear. They are basically regarding the ownership of natural resources, delineation of internal boundaries, revenue-sharing and equalization, native-foreigner dichotomy, minority issues, etc. Most federal countries have mechanisms for conflict management. The new Constitution is also expected to devise mechanisms appropriate for Nepal. Various mechanisms are being floated in this regard. They are: political conference, inter-state council, parliament and parliamentary committees, judiciary, Referendum, etc. However, it is yet to be seen whether the CA agrees on them and enshrines them in the Constitution.

To conclude, the existing political instability, intra and inter-party conflicts and their unhealthy competition for sharing power and their low priority towards Constitution making and settling the controversial issues have further complicated the process of constitution drafting. The Maoists have used the peace and democratic process to capture the state. There is a perceived threat to national unity and social and religious accord. Democratic parties have failed to deliver a Constitution and consolidate democracy, and there has been brazen meddling by the outside world. Clearly Constitution drafting and sorting out their differences on fundamental issues are not the first priority of the big three political parties—the Nepali Congress, the Unified Communist Party of Nepal, and the Communist Party of Nepal (Unified Marxist Leninist) even now. If the political parties fail to draft and ratify the Constitution in time they will lose both the people's faith and international recognition.

REFERENCES

1. A P Parajulee, *The Democratic Transition in Nepal,* Rowman and Littlefield Publishers, Inc., New York, 2000
2. Devokota, Grisma Bahadur, Nepalko Ranjitik Darpan Part II, Kathmandu, Dhruba Bahadur Devakota, 1979
3. Election Commission Nepal, Constituent Assembly Members Election Result, 2064 VS Kathmandu, 2008
4. Government of Nepal 2008, The Interim Constitution of Nepal, Ministry of Law, Justice and Parliamentary Affairs, Kathmandu, 2007
5. Joshi, BhuvanLal and Leo Rose, *Democratic Innovations in Nepal,* California Press, Reprinted in Nepal by Mandala Publications, Kathmandu, 2004
6. Khanal, Krishna, "Restructuring of the Nepali State: The Federal Perspective", Lok Raj Baral, ed., *Nepal:New Frontiers of State Restructuring of State,* New Delhi, Adroit Publishers, 2008
7. Mahendra Lawoti, ed., *Contentious Politics and Democratization in Nepal,* Sage Publications, New Delhi, 2007

8. Rishikesh Shaha, *Modern Nepal: A Political History: 1769-1955*, Manohar, Delhi, 1990
9. Shrestha, Chudabahadur, *Nepal Coping with Maoist Insurgency: Conflict Analysis and Resolution*, Kathmandu, Chetana Lokshum, 2004
10. Tamang, Sitaram, ed, *Restructuring of State in Nepal's Context*, Samana Praksan, Kathmandu, 2006
11. Thapa, Deepak, ed, *Understanding the Maoist Movement of Nepal*, Martin Chautari, Centre for Social Research and Development, Kathmandu, 2003
12. Thapa, Surya, *Struggle Between Monarchy and Political Parties in Nepal*, Nawayug Publications, Kathmandu, 2006
13. www.citizenside.com/.../nepal-a-demonstration-for-constitution-by-a- ..., accessed on September 30, 2011
14. www.cocap.org.np/.../citizens'-conference-on-role-of-civil-society-o...,accessed on February 25, 2011

15

Gandhi's Constructive Programmes: An Antidote to Nepal's Constitutional Crisis

VIKAS NARAYAN UPADHYAY

Nepal one of the closest and nearest neighbour of India. Her relation with Nepal is so close that particularly from Bihar, we go their without passport and visa. Being a Hindu Country our mind set is the same. After the collapse of the Kingship, the constitutional crisis has developed. The Communist Party in the Nepal has not created the atmosphere of democracy. We people from the very near visualize day to day affairs of this country from the border area of Raxaul (Bihar). Bandha and Naxal problem really created constitutional crisis in the Nepal. It's effect can be sounded in our country through the adjacent district of Bihar (Raxaul) and Birgunj. The then government of Mr. Kamal Dahal Prachand has created more problem than constitutional solution. Still, we feel here constitutional tremor, which only creates problems in our country and particularly the people of Nepal are facing lot of problems of constitutionalities.

Now, in the time of crisis only Gandhian way can save the country. Still, the effect of Gandhi can be seen in the Nepal and its Tarain area as well. Late Mr. B.P. Koirala, Ex P.M. of Nepal was the real follower of the Gandhi and Jay Prakash Narayan and residents of Nepal are also follower of the Gandhi and Gandhian way of life. So, in this paper I highlighted that only Gandhi's constructive programmes are an Antidote to Nepal's crisis. Nepal as a nation almost remains a silent witness to the appalling fall in values and all round deterioration marked by a disgusting and suffocating atmosphere of self aggrandizement.

The world is passing through the process of globalization. All most all country, voluntarily or involuntarily are involved in this process. The voluntary participants in this process are encouraged, supported and aided and the rest are condemned, criticized, provoked and isolated. Most of the participants and the non-participants are aware of the fact that globalization is natural, a irresistible and long time activities but are not sure about the destination of this exercise, taking into consideration the systems and subsystems of the human life-world in a holistic perspective. In this light, it is important to note that the development paradigm of the present Nepal is guided and determined by two major factors, namely science and technology and ideology. Both these factors are complimentary as well as independent in nature. The one without the other can survive but cannot flourish. Peace and development are not the exclusive property of any one of these factors. Therefore, a holistic and integrated approach is essential.

In the Nepal, only constitutional crisis is not there, the entire system, peace and the process of development is stopped since last two years. People of Nepal tried their best to fled away from their mother land in the search of job as well as peace with dignity. It is important to reconstruct Nepal upon the twin pillars of truth and nonviolence, where socio-politico-economic decentralization and sustainable means of production and distribution would bring forth a developed society. Gandhi a prophetic visionary of the modern time, conceptualized and visualized the idea of Swaraj (Self-rule) and Vasudev Kutumbakam (Global family), preached them experimented with them and disseminated and practical and workable form through his constructive programmes. Due to the king ship in the last phase of the 20th century Nepalese were facing the problem of "God on the Earth". The king can do no wrong concept was alive in the Nepal till the last phase of the king Birendra. Another aspect, which people feel was the lack of development process in the time of globalization. People of Nepal without knowing the benefit of globalization, started praise for the same. The dominance of Communism and Naxalism also damaged the face value of Nepal. Any how, Kingship became the history and communism formed the government in the name of the people. Some how or other the rule of China from the back door was important in forming the Prachand's government. But as a matter of fact china could not get the proper passage to deal the matter. But politically speaking, the Indian government was serious to solve the crisis in Nepal through the Gandhian method. As per the version of Prof. Bimla Prasad, Ex-Ambassador of Nepal and political analyst "Gandhi's thoughts and programmes are still considered and effective alternative to globalization, which is based on mass production, which mainly depends upon, complex and expensive technology, for Gandhi was talking about production by the masses with the appropriate technology, depending upon mere science and technology without values results in equity, exploitation and domination of those who control and use technology as a means to sustain and perpetuate their hegemony. Gandhi's was not against the technological improvement but he wanted it do remain with in the operational limits of every one and be eco-friendly". It is very clear that Prof. Prasad being a political analyst of Nepal's problems also talks about Gandhian way to solve the crisis depending upon technological improvement with values, which is not possible in the present Nepal's situation. So, the advocates of globalization underlined the importance of values, ethics and social responsibilities in humanizing globalization.

Now, in an age Nepal where major concerns of most of those who matter are E-mail, E-commerce and economics where do the principals of Gandhi who emphasized value based development, non-violence, purity of means and ends, non-exploitation, production by the masses instead of mass production, gender equality, non-possession, simple life stand? In Nepal the texture and rhythm of human life have under gone such changes that would make the core of Gandhian teachings outmoded superficial in the eyes of champions and prophets of high tech civilization. As a matter of fact the constitutional crisis in the Nepal which has disturbed the Indian sub continent and its crisis only be solved as I think through the Gandhi's constructive programme. The development models Gandhi suggest and the strategies he adopted for non-violence social transformation and individual emancipation and empowerment are needed to solve the crisis in Nepal. Scholar and activist Prof. Gene Sharp have three main parts to suggest to solve the crisis in the Nepal –

1. Improvement of Individuals in their own lives and ways of living.
2. A constructive programme to begin building a social order even as the old one still exists, and
3. The practice of various forms of non-violent action against specific social evils.

Gene Sharp, after careful analysis of the various programmes talked about above noted three main parts which may solved the crisis of Nepal's constitutional problems. Being a political strategist he clearly said about the specific social evils which has crated the constitutional problems. Constitution is just like a mirror in which one can see the face of the country. The very mirror is missing due to various short of problems crop up after the removal of the Kingship. Being theoretician his directions may be criticized but the above noted three points are comprehensive and holistic to solve the problem of Nepal known as constructive programmes.

At last, Gandhi's constructive programme which he has used 21 years in South Africa is now understood as crusade for achieving largely in the crisis of Nepal to solve the problems. A well thought out programme of action in which every one should take part to solve the crisis in Nepal is must through democratic method. In well ordered society the citizens know and observe the laws to solve the problems, which I feel necessary for the benefit of Nepal. The constructive programme of Gandhi in the context of Nepal is "The blue print" for a new social order there "The constructive programme is an attempt to build the beginning of the new social order while the old society still exists. The relevance of constructive work programme for societal transformation and end of constitutional crisis appears to be greater in the emerging national and global scenario. When concerned humanity agonizingly looks for constitutional crisis in Nepal, the Gandhian vision and practice and sustainable social order which ensures justice to all is being recognized. It is important to mention here that even political revolution is valid only to the extent that, it brings about a moral transformation in the character of human society.

But then, Gandhi was innovative and he developed credible and durable alternatives without compromising on core values. Do we have that realism? The need of the hour in the context of Nepal is not to get stuck up with Gandhi. But go forward with the Revolutionary Gandhi who had courage to imbibe, innovate and adapt. It is probably this ability of Gandhi that we require today as an antidote to Nepal's crisis.

REFERENCES

1. A D Khetri, *Political News*, Research Paper, Dept. of Politics, Tribhuwan University, Kathmandu, Nepal, 2004
2. Bimla Prasad, "As I have seen Nepal", *Political Scientist*, Research Journal of Ranchi University, Ranchi, vol. 3, 1995
3. Gene Sharp, *Gandhi: A Political Strategies*, Gandhi Media Company, New Delhi, 1999, pg.80
4. V N Upadhyaya, "Gandhism Reconsidered", published in *Democracies, The Journal of Jag Jiwan Ram Institute of Parliamentary Studies and Political Research*, Patna, vol. 7, no. 1&2, January-March,1987
5. V N Upadhyay, National Seminar on *Gandhian Liberation Techniques for National Regeneration Movement*, 2nd Freedom Struggle in SAARC Countries, Organized at Gandhi Gram Rural Univeristy, Dindigul, Tamil Nadu, 1-3 Feb, 2008
6. *www.gorkhapatra.org.np/gopa.detail.php?article_id=51673&cat...*, accessed on September 19, 2011
7. *www.groundreport.com/.../A...Constitution...Constitution.../ 2940969*, accessed on February 11, 2011
8. *www.himalmag.com/.../743-confusion-in-constitution-making-nepal...*, accessed on August 10, 2011

9. *www.hindu.com/2010/06/23/stories/2010062353731200.htm*, accessed on April 1, 2011
10. *www.ibanet.org/Document/Default.aspx?DocumentUid...9BEF...*, accessed on September 1, 2011
11. *www.igd.org.np/pages.php?section=pages&page_id=96*, accessed on September 20, 2011
12. *www.indianexpress.com/news/will-guarantee-security...nepal...*, accessed on August 22, 2011
13. *www.indigenousportal.com/.../Nepal-Failure-to-Comply-with-the- ...*, accessed on April 30, 2011
14. *www.international-alert.org/.../consolidating-peace-nepali-constitution...*, accessed on February 1, 2011

16

Nepal: A Vibrant Journey from Dominion to a Political Democracy and its Connotation for India

SADHANA THAKUR

The year 2008 was a red-letter year in the history of Nepal. It marked the collapse of the 240-years old monarchical system, paving the way for the proclamation of a Republican Democracy. As a flow of events demonstrated the transition in Nepal, on 28th May, was newly declared a Federal Democratic Republic, and the newly elected 575 member constituent assembly (CA). Unanimously passed a proposal tabled by then Prime Minister, Girija Prasad Koirala, which gave the order to King Gyanendra 15 days to vacate the Narayanhiti Royal Palace. In this perspective, it is cognizable that the people's faith in monarchy had already been dilapidated in the wake of the 1st June 2001 Royal Palace massacre, which was made historic by the assassination of King Birendra and his entire kinship. However, it was King Gyanendra's seizure of power on 1 February, 2005 that triggered a sequence of events, which reached the crescendo in the declaration of the Republic.

The Kingdom of Napal was consolidated in the late 18th Century by Prithvi Narayan Shah, ruler of the Gorkha principality (in present day West Nepal), who occupied Kathmandu in 1768. In terms of geography, Nepal is a roughly rectangular landmass of 147,000 sq. km, bordered on three sides by India along a perimeter of 1,46 km, and along its mountainous northern length of 1,100 km by the more inaccessible Tibetan Plateau. Its demographic statistics of 28 million has a population density of 144 per sq. km, which is overwhelmingly. Only about a meager 15 per cent is towndwellers, while around 75 per cent of the population earns its living through subsistence framing. With the capita Gross National Product (GNP) of approximately US$ 226, Nepal is among the world's most poverty stricken countries. The economy is predominantly agricultural, accounting for 40 per cent of GNP and 80 per cent of the labour force. Moreover, Nepal's Industrial Sector is small in which manufacturing activity provides employment to about 1 per cent of the total labour strength.

Ethnically, Nepal is a "salad-bowl" of multicaste/ethnic, multilingual, multi-religious and multi-cultural people. In terms of the 1991 Census, there are more than 50 dialects spoken by various ethnic or tribal groups in Nepal. According to the census of 2001, the Hindu constituted 80.6 per cent Buddhists 10.7 per cent, Muslims 4.2 per cent and Kirants 3.6 per cent. However the post-1990 political and economic development gave rise to the 'democratic' elite, which today constitute the leadership of all the mainstream 'democratic' forces in the country. Thus, the socio-political conditions in Nepal are contaminated with a massive rural/urban divide. Democracy, which in true sense means a system of the people, for the critic principles, which include popular legitimacy, accountability, participation of common masses in the way of functioning of the system, equity and equality are universal means to measure the performance of a democratic norms the lack of a stable democratic order was prompted by the sterility of the parties and their leaders and the class often visualized between the politicians and the traditional monarchy for their respective space within the Political system. Moreover, the practice of conducting periodic elections, under the auspices of the Monarch with different political parties loyal to king, without paying any performance of the elected government, had dismally failed to fullfil the minimum requirements to the democratic tenets. It is important to note that in Nepal both party-less Panchayat or Panchayati Raj, involving three tier systems of village, district and zonal assemblies which indirectly elected a national assembly with only advisory capacity to the kind and multi party Political system have been present side by side. This system actually emerged in the social fabric of Napal in the aftermath of the Royal coup of 15 December 1960. Consequently, after thirty years of its implementation under the patronage of the king in 1990, the Panchayat System finally crumpled with the support of various political parties and the common people. And this paves the ways to re-introduce multi-party democracy. In may 1991 fresh elections were held and the new Prime Minister, Krishna Prasad Bhattarai heralded a smooth transition from absolute monarchy to constitutional monarchy incorporating the framework of a multiparty system. On the whole, the taste of democracy which Nepal had experienced during these three decades was "exclusionary democracy". Marked by frequent government changes, untimely elections, etc., which in contrast to the concept of "inclusive democracy", prevented the distribution of political power to the minorities, and full participation by all citizens, thereby undermining the universality of democracy in letter and spirit.

The history of Indo-Nepal relations over the years has been structured on a framework of co-operation in the regional as well as in the security spheres Nepal Treaty of Peace and Friendship in 1950 established the scaffolding for the unique ties between the two countries and remains the main bone of contention of mistrust and acuity. There main components of this treaty was security, cooperation, economic benefits and privileges to accrue to the citizens of both countries and people-to-people relations, as was evident in the free movement of people across the border. India as a responsible neighbour, has always rendered economic assistance through formal trade after the Treaty of Trade was inked between them in 1951. According to this treaty, India provides on a non-reciprocal basis, duty free access, without quantitative restrictions, to the Indian market for all Nepalese-manufactured articles, barring a sort negative list, Besides this, since the early 1950's India has contributed immensely to the development of Nepal's economy and infrastructure, as exhibited by major irrigation project and the construction of the Kosi and Gandak barrages. There is a huge dependence of Nepal on India for economic needs. India is Nepal's largest trading partner, accounting for more than 60 per cent of its trade. About 12 of the 13 trade routes of Nepal are via India. New Delhi has transactions, India has been the main supplier of weapons, surveillance and communications equipment, helicopters and training personnel to the RNA, which increased significantly since the Maoist People's War began in 1996.

With the gap of time, both India and Nepal have realized the importance and mutual inevitability of each other, as testified by the former Indian Ambassador to Nepal, Shyam Saran, who said, "Nepal is not India-locked but India open". Cooperation in the security realm is yet another critical feature of their bilateral relations, as both the countries countenance in the security realm is yet another critical feature of their bilateral relations, as both the countries countenance grave threats to the their individual national security. Nepal has often proclaimed its unwillingness to allow and promote anti-Indian activities from its soil and has made sincere efforts to curb such clandestine movements as well. Likewise, India has assisted Nepal in different spheres, including internal security, especially during the period of domestic turmoil.

In an interview to the Hindu, the Maoist Chairman Prachanda observed that it is more or less impossible for Nepal to maintain stability and prosperity without increasing the level of its cooperation with India. Since India and China are fast-growing economies in the neighbourhood, they acknowledged the significance of forging cordial relations with both. Describing his stand on equi-distance policy with India and China, Prachanda said in an interview to the CNN-IBN on 18th May, 2008. "…we will not side up with one country against the other. We will maintain equi-distance in political sense and not in terms of co-operation and other things." The unprecedented victory of the Maoist in Nepal elections places the Indian Policy makers in a serious dilemma. First, having helped the Maoists to their electoral triumph, will India now help them transform into a democratic polity? Secondly, India, which has invested political capital in the democratization process in Nepal, must realize that any subversion of the people's mandate will have deep-rooted negative implications for both Kathmandu and New Delhi. Former Indian Ambassador to Nepal, Shiv Shanker Mukherjee, while focusing on the changed political landscape, asserted that, he had contracted the Maoists and both sides were willing to work together in the context of the new global ambience. While Pranab Mukherjee the India Foreign Minister Said that he Poll results signaled a positive turn for Nepal, the leader of the Communist Party of India (Marxist), Sitaram Yechurty, emphasized the necessity of a close working relationship between the two governments.

The former Indian Ambassador to Nepal said that India will have to deal differently with the next government and accept that Prachanda represents the sensitivities and aspirations of the Majority of Nepalese. It now needs be one of equals. As India's government is getting ready to work together with the Maoists, this line of thinking is highly disliked by the country's opposition Parties led by right wing Bharatiya Janta Party (BJP), who warned New Delhi that a 'Red' Nepal could embolden Maoist and Naxalite rebels in various parts of India. One of the party's leaders from Uttar Pradesh, Yogi Adityanath said that "If Indian government could declare Indian Maoists and Naxalites as terrorists, why Maoists in Nepal are not declared Nepal's a terrorist outfit? He further held that accepting Nepal's Maoists as a legitimate political organization would send mixed signal to India's rebels and weaken the government actions against them.

India currently faces an unprecedented Maoist campaign in many parts, where poverty and weaken in federal structure are prominently prevalent. This weakness led the Naxalites to extend their political influence also into the cities on the one and, especially in working class and industrial areas and rural areas, on the other. The other implications of Maoist victory in Nepal is that it would have a demonstration effect on the Maoists to give up their armed struggle and take part in elections like their Nepali counterparts, it will have to rely on more that political percolation and display a more responsive and pragmatic role towards the grassroots. Thus, Nepal's future success of democracy is clearly linked with effective functioning of Institution of governance, public resource management, effective delivery of services to the people mainly to the lowest rung of the social order, greater emphasis on economic and development agenda based on caste determinants India, being a responsible member of SAARC and believer of the principle of democracy, should follow a more pragmatic and responsible role, unlilke the past years. There is no reason to think that the Maoist group in Nepal will behave or act like its part thinking, since they are already in the parliamentary process as well as the people's recent verdict on this party, it is expected than ideologically, in order to sustain themselves in power. The Maoist will not act in such a manner which might antagonize the Indian foreign policy makers, since they hone that their economic prosperity to a large extent depends on India's good offices. For Nepal, India will remain the nearest market for its surplus goods, services and power, the source of know-how, technology, opportunities for higher education, sophisticated health services etc. Thus it is necessary for both the government of New Delhi and Kathmandu to keep in close touch and formulate their individual agenda, on the premise of the policy of Inclusion, Both the countries should think pragmatically and act rationally, not locally but regionally, based on present realities.

REFERENCES

1. *www.ipcs.org/.../nepal/constitutional-rumblings-in-nepal-three-scenar...*, accessed on September 18, 2011
2. *www.karunacenter.org/prog-nepal.html*, accessed on June 19, 2011
3. *www.ksl.edu.np/ca/.../cocas/constituent_assembly_concept_purna.ppt*, accessed on November 1, 2011
4. *www.ksl.edu.np/.../constituent_assembly_purpose_process_english.p...*, accessed on February 10, 2011
5. *www.liquida.com/article/26736172/nepal-kathmandu-peace/*, accessed on September 30, 2011
6. *www.madhavnepal.com/.../2010-01-18-30PM_Speech__Nepal_Cons...*, accessed on November 30, 2011
7. *www.mediahubsouthasia.com/.../nepal-constitution-making-at-stake-i...*, accessed on May 20, 2011
8. *www.minorityrights.org/.../minorities-and-the-constitution-building-...*, accessed on February 1, 2011
9. *www.mirestnepal.org.np/upload/files/Tool%20kit%20-english.PDF...*, accessed on July 11, 2011
10. *www.mirestnepal.org.np/news/detail.php?id=325*, accessed on February 18, 2011

17

Constitutional Deadlock in Nepal

MADHU SINGH

Nepal a small landlock country situated in the North of India, has a lengthy border with India. Apart from that we share cultural, religious and historical ties. The ruling elite (till recently) i.e. the Thakuri's are originally from Rajasthan. The Madhesis people living on the border have a shared culture with the states of Bihar and UP. A peaceful and stable Nepal is necessary for India and the world. For quite some time there has been political strife in Nepal. A country which is famous for its scenic beauty, peace and friendly people has passed through very difficult times and lost its earlier identity. There was a spate of lawlessness, no security for life and property of the people. Presently Nepal is going through a period of transition. The old structures and institutions are giving way to new. The political future of Nepal has great implications for India. Nepal is going through difficult times. Presently the situation of Nepal can be described as bordering on a constitutional deadlock. This is not the first time in the history of Nepal that such a political and constitutional crisis has occurred: The deadline for enacting the new constitute is on May 28, 2010. This is a Herculean task in the face of the fact that the wants and aspiration of the people as regarding the type of constitution they want is varied. Some want a democratic constitution and others want it in line with communism.

All political parties across the nation have joined hands to draft a constitution which will address the problems of the people comprehensively. There has been a problem in meeting the deadline. The politically divided opinions has created confusion on major subjects of the constitution. There is a tussal between the Maoists and the other parties like Nepali Congress on many subjects such as state restructuring, forms of governance, modality of federation, constitutional bodies, state organs and fundamental rights. Many people feel that it is technically impossible to meet the deadline.

History of Earlier Constitutions

The earlier constitutions of Nepal failed to establish rapport with the people. The Interim Constitution of 1961 established the Supreme Court and independent Public Service Commission. Within two years king Tribhuvan started violating the constitutional provisions. The impartial election of a Constituent Assembly was blocked. The King did not hold the Constituent Assembly elections and the Parliamentary elections. The next process of Constitution-Making was started by King Mahendra in 1962 he proclaimed partyless democracy, which is known as the Panchayati System. The Panchayati System functioned for almost 30 years. All powers were still in the hands of the Monarch. Slowly, there was progress among the people. People were dissatisfied and critical of the rulers. This led to a great political upspring under the communists in 1990 with the support of the Nepali Congress. This uprising is popularly known as the First Jana Andolan. Nepal got a new constitution. It turned into a multi-party democracy by the proclamation by the King of Nepal. According to this constitution the people of Nepal were identified as the source of political legitimacy and they were guaranteed basic rights. The first decade under the New Constitution was marked by frequent elections and unstable governments. Experiments of all forms of government were being made. But democratic system failed to make inroads into Nepals politics. The politics of Nepal was trapped in a vicious circle with political bickering within the political parties. The Maoist forces tried to defame the parliamentary system. All this finally culminated in the palace coup in February 2005. This polarised the political system of Nepal completely and led to the formation of the 7 party alliance against the Kings autocratic regime, thus started the 2nd Jana Andolan.

The success of the 2nd Jana Andolan resulted in a radical change in the country. It ended the Monarchical rule and restored the people's power and parliament. Later on the interim parliament and interim government were formed jointly by the SPA (Seven Party Alliance) and the Maoists. Both Parties agreed to introduce a "peace accord". This accord led to the election of the Constituent Assembly, the elections was held in 2008. The elected Constituent Assembly had dual responsibility—to make the constitution and help the Constituent Assembly function as a parliament.

Nepal's Constitutional Aspirations

The Constituent Assembly has been tasked with writing a new constitution and fundamentally reshaping the government as part of the peace process. The Constituent Assembly has 601 members, it is the most representative assembly that Nepal has ever had. It represents most of the country's political forces from the revolutionary communist party of Nepal to the Madheshi Janadhikar Forum, as well as a variety of Fringe parties. There is hope among the people of Nepal that this time the Constitution will reshape the economic and social fabric of the country. The constitutional committee has been given the responsibility for formulating the final draft. The report must consist of thematic and subsequent recommendations, which will be followed by debates at different levels. The important steps of the process are first, the discussion of the first draft in a full session of the Constituent Assembly. The second step will be taking the draft constitution to the public and thirdly, interacting with experts.

Political Impasse

However the situation has come to a standstill both constitutionally and politically after the resignation of the Prime Minister on May 4, 2009 protesting the direct unconstitutional intervention of the president in the firing of the Chief of Army Staff. The Prime Minister said in his address to the nation that the interim constitution of Nepal has no provision for the president to do anything without the recommendation of the government. So, the presidents order violates the interim constitution. They have also said that the presidential direct order to the commander of the Army staff to stay on the job is a constitutional coup. They said that the president has not quoted any clause of the interim constitution to write a letter to the CoAS, as the interim constitution does not permit the president to do anything independently, so his writing a letter was an attempt to be an authoritarian rulers. They also blame the presidents distribution of videotapes of Prachanda instructing the trainees of the Peoples Liberation Army in 2008 to justify the presidential coup.

Since their departure from the government Maoists have been holding demonstration in the assembly and in the streets of Kathmandu protesting the presidents move which they say undermined "Civilian Supremacy" President Ram Baran Yadav has denied the accusation and other political parties backed him. Earlier this year the Maoists called an indefinite national general strike demanding the resignation of the Prime Minister Mr. Nepal and the formation of national unity government under the leadership of their chairman Pushpa Kamal Dahal. They halted the strike six days latter after the prime minister said he would not yield to street protests and the general public started defying the strike amid shortage of necessities. Baburam Bhattarai, a senior Maoist leader demanded the Prime Minister's resignation to reach a political consensus on the constitutional issues. However Nepals press adviser blamed the deadlock on the Maoists and said the Prime Minister would not resign because he has the majority support of 22 parties in the Parliament. Thus Nepal still does not have a new government, Ram Chander Pondel of Nepali Congress and Pushpa Kamal Dahal of the Unified CPN Maoists have been unsuccessful to get elected even after 16 trails. This dead lock helped to strengthen the life of the caretaker government of Mr. Nepal.

Major Constraints in Constitution Making

The political deadlock has lead to a constitutional deadlock as member of the Constituent Assembly have been working since their election in 2008 with little progress to draft a new constitution. The major constraints are firstly, lack of trust among the political parties and also within the differences parties. Large sections of the Nepali Congress, the Communist Party of Nepal UML (Unified Marxist-Lennist) and Madhesi parties do not trust the Maoists, as the Maoists themselves claim they want to establish a special democracy. They feel that they want to establish an authoritarian type of government in line with China. They are also scared of the strength of the Maoists and their stand on the Peoples Liberation Army. The Maoists on the other had have grievances, they feel that the other parties along with Nepal Army and external powers have kept them out of power. They say that they are committed to democracy as can be seen by their participation in the elections and keeping their army in the barracks.

Then there are intra party dissensions and the Maoists are also divided with Baburam Bhattarai who is pragmatic and advocates closer ties with India and Pushpa Kamal Dahal along with Mohan Vaidya adopting a more conservative line and alleigning towards China. They feel that India is enemy number one. This is one major factor which has stalled the constitutional process. There are differences in the Nepali Congress and UML. The UML Chairman Jhalanath Khanal is closer to the Maoists other leaders like K.P. Oli and Madhav Nepal are closer to the Nepali Congress. The second major constraint is the demand of the Madhesis for federalism with autonomy. They want the whole Terai region to be one state in the federation. They want proportional representation in the legislature, executive, judiciary and in the public services. One of their main demands is the recognition of Hindi. They also want economic resources and revenue to be re-allocated. The third stumbling block is India's role in Nepal. India is very suspicious of the Maoists and want to isolated them politically. The relationship worsened during Prachanda's term as Prime Minister, with Pracnahda playing the China card. India feels her security interest will be compromised by the Maoists effort to reshape the Nepal army. India played an active role in blocking the Maoists move to dismiss the then army Chief. They want the ending of anti-India activities and rhetoric. The Role of the UNMIN was also looked at suspiciously by India, USA, UK and also the non-Maoist parties and the Nepal Army. They all felt that the UNMIN was pro-Maoist. A special Committee headed by the Prime Minister has taken over the UNMIN's task of monitoring of the management of arms and armies. There are also problems with the exhausted list of Fundamental Rights and Directive Principles. The report of the committee on the Rights of Minority and Marginalised communities has also created controversies by putting forth ambiguous provisions as to the compensation to be paid by the state to certain communities for past abuses against them.

However, despite all these problems. The democratic process in Nepal has been streamlined. People have elected their constituent Assembly to draft a constitution which will highlight the needs of all sections of the people. The 240 years long deep rooted institution of monarchy has been outdone by the constituent assembly. Despite differences it is commendable that the Maoist have joined the mainstream political process along with the other parties. After the UN's exit from Nepal's peace process the opposition Maoist Party handed over the second division of its Peoples Liberation Army to the government in a symbolic gesture that indicated that now nearly 20,000 combatants stand disassociated from the mother party and are ready to start a new life. The Prime Minister Madhav Kumar Nepal who heads the Special Committee and the Maoist Chief Pushpa Kamal Dahal signed an agreement that the PLA was passing into the formal control of the Special Committee for the Supervision, integration and rehabilitation of the Maoists. The handover has marked an important and new stage in the peace process. Now the Maoist combatants do not belong to any party and would work to build a new Nepal. They still have a long way to go. They have to reach an agreement on how to empty the 28 camps. While the Maoists are demanding that all the PLA fighters be included in the army and be allowed to keep this ranks, the parties have been insisting that about 5,000 PLA combatants be inducted. The rest should be rehabilitated, preferably given business training and sent abroad if they wanted. Thus a major obstacle that has brought the peace process to a standstill since the fall of the Maoist govt. in 2008 has been partially dealt with. Now all out effort is being made to overcome the deadlock. Nepals President Ram Baran Yadav directed parliament to hold fresh elections to choose a new Prime Minister on the basis of majority as two deadlines given by him to the battling political parties to form a consensus government has failed. The Business Advisory committee of the house that regulates elections has announced the dates for the new polls. Because of the earlier failure of the political parties to form a government. The committee has readied for three elections in quick succession on February 3, 5 and 6, 2011.

Public anger is growing against the three major parties for their unbridled power lust, that has held the nation hostage for nearly seven months. This time, to pre-empt abortive elections, parliament has amended poll regulations so that only three rounds of vote can be held at a time. Till now the Maoists, the communists as well as the centrist Nepali Congress—the three largest parties in parliament are seeking to lead the new government. Unless one of them decide to support any other. These elections will also be doomed so will the new constitution which has to be promulgated by May 28, 2011. The constitutional deadlock has created a crisis in Nepal. There is need for consensus among the various parties. They will have to sideline their personal interest for the greater interest of the Nation. Then only will they be able to overcome all the obstacles in the path of constitution making. It is imperative that the new constitution is made according to the wishes and aspirations of the People of Nepal and they get the type of political system best suited for the development of the country. A peaceful and stable Nepal is the interest of India's security. So an all out effort must be made to overcome the constitutional deadlock.

REFERENCES

1. "Dawn and Epochal Change in Nepal", *Mainstream*, vol. XLVI, no:18, New Delhi, April 19, 2008
2. Krishna Khanal, "Democracy and Federation of the Nepali State", *Sangam Journal*, vol.1, no.1, December 2009, pg.8
3. Sanbhagyan Shah, "The Nepali Post-Conflict Prospects for Conflict Transformation and Democratic Consolidation," *Journal of International Affairs*, Washington, vol.1, 2009
4. Yubraj Ghimire, "Nepal: Impact of Internal Conflict on Security", *CSA-Intra State Conflicts and Effects*, Delhi, September 30, 2010
5. Subhas Kapila, "Nepal: Political Turbulence from a New Quarte", 17 February 2007
6. Nepal Govt. takes Formal Control of Maoist army, *Times News Network*, Delhi, January 23, 2010
8. Siddhi B Ranjitkar, "Current Constitutional Crisis in Nepal", *Mainstream*, vol.19, Delhi, 10 May 2009

9. *The Times of India*, Patna, 28 January 2011
10. *www.nepaldemocracy.org/media/nepali_media_at_crossroad.htm*, accessed on March 18, 2011
11. *www.nepalhumanrightsnews.com/news.asp?id=1144*, accessed on September 19, 2011
12. *www.nepalmountaintrek.com/nepal/current-political-situation-in-nep...*, accessed on August 18, 2011
13. *www.nepalsamuha.com/component/option,com.../id.../view,details/...*, accessed on July 19, 2011
14. *www.nepalitimes.com/issue/2009/11/.../ConstitutionSupplement/1648...*, accessed on September 25, 2011

18

Development of State-Society Relations in Modern Nepal

RAJKUMAR SINGH

In present-day Nepal the centuries-old system of monarchy ceased to exist abruptly in May 2008 when the Himalayan Kingdom became a Federal Democratic Republic through a democratic revolution. Although this was done through a popular mandate and people within and outside the country saw it as the end of decade-old dominance of anarchy and insurgency, yet it was not the end but the beginning of a new type of political uncertainty which the country is witnessing today. Factionalism in the form of different interest groups has raised its ugly head in mainstream national politics and has stranded the normal political development of the country in recent years. In the prevailing situation, every representative group claims to have a lion's share in national political power and is far from any hope of compromise to end the ongoing impasse. This deadlock has necessitated once again an in-depth study of State-Society relations in Nepal and it is hoped that this article would help understand its nature in the larger interest of the country, the region and the world.

Initiation and Impact

The foundation of modern Nepal as a nation-state was laid by Prithvi Narayan Shah in 1768 when he conquered 60 small principalities and the Kathmandu Valley. The new king was shrewd, strategic in his thinking, meticulous in his planning and ruthless in obtaining his military objectives. He gave the country a single name and a strong central government and his emergence as a strong monarch out of the prevailing chaos and uncertainty, made the Kingdom state-centric and not society-centric. The state-centric approach is described as the perception that operators of the state system play the most decisive roles in the determination of public policies. In the system even the state is defined as all those individuals who occupy political offices that authorise them and alone to make and apply decisions.[1] The system so established, checked the development of political consciousness and a clear sense of identity with the symbol of nationalism. The new-born state of the time remained far from the process of political modernisation in which major clusters of old social, economic and psychological commitments are eroded or broken down and the people become available for new patterns of socialization and behaviour.[2] The political elite in this system consisted primarily of high-caste Indo-Aryan Hindus who migrated to Nepal during the Muslim invasions of India in 12th–16th century and gradually assumed a dominant role throughout the sub-Himalayan areas. The first state system of Nepal in the form established by Prithvi Narayan Shah did not even qualify the minimum basic criteria of a state. From the time of Plato the state has captured the imagination of political theorists because it is central to many of the questions that are asked by many regarding justice, institutional arrangements, good life, dignity and the self-respect of human beings. Even the classical political theory has been preoccupied with the nature of the good life, it has sought to realise that vision in institutional arrangements with the state being at the core of these arrangements which are necessary for human being to flourish, for their needs to be met, and for their capacities to be realised.[3] The state without exception emerges as the principal corporate actor in political, cultural, social and economic narratives of societies. The major theories of economic development which emerged in the late 1940s and early 1950s also envisaged the state as the most important agent of growth and modernization and called for centrally conceived plans for industrialization and physical infrastructure development.[4]

In the period of Prithvi Narayan Shah and following his death in 1775 the nature of Nepalese state remained almost the same. Soon after the demise his successors established an absolute political system in which the monarch was the centre of power. The words and commands of the king constituted the rules and regulations of the country and these took the shape of laws. In the highly segmented pyramidal structure of the political system that evolved, the king was advised by a number of prominent Brahmin families which came to occupy dominant positions in quick succession. The subsequent periods witnessed the direct rule of the king with authority and under the circumstances a political system was evolved which relied for its effectiveness on intrigues and rumour mongering, and primarily on manoeuvres and counter manoeuvres.[5] For hundreds of years, the central government in Nepal was run by a number of interrelated families, with the most influential and powerful of them keeping the Prime Ministership or the position of chief executive to themselves.[6] Centrally-appointed governors provided the link between Kathmandu and the rest of the country. Thus, the modern Kingdom of Nepal began to be ruled by kings and regents who were either insane, inept, profligate or promiscuous, or all four. It was the primary obligation of the common people or the masses to support the elite in the government and in the landed aristocracy. The government existed for the elite rather than for the people. The organs of the government were used largely for personal gain and the masses were exploited rather than benefitted.

As a result of the state system the social system of Nepal is included in the highly backward social systems of the world where traditional responses, custom and rituals carry the authority with them. Authority remains where it has been and no serious effort is made in the direction of political mobilisation, socialisation and recruitment. The right to participate in deciding both in the institutions of government and in the limited number of voluntary associations is largely confined to members of particular kinship and lineage groups, or to those belonging to religious or caste communities. This hierarchical structure of authority results in either excessive submissiveness among the people at large, or adherence to extremist egalitarian ideals as a reaction against the established system.[7] In this category of the social system in which the Himalayan Kingdom falls, primitive norms and values are dominant. The high offices of the state are shared by the men of the same family or tribe or by the elites who enjoyed a sort of charismatic hold over the destiny of their simple and innocent people.

Thus, the people of Nepal have a fairly low level of political consciousness. They neither have a clear sense of identity with the symbol of nationalism nor strong attitudes regarding the proper limits of political activity.[8] The system was feudal in nature and to promote one's status, it was necessary to become part of the ruling hierarchy or to undertake some activity with its favour and sanction. For those who could not belong to the ruling hierarchy, the landed aristocracy was the second best choice as long as opportunities for reclaiming new land in the Terai and the hills existed. Under the circumstances the principal functions of the government were to maintain law and order and a semblance of justice within the territory to protect it against encroachment from outside, and to raise revenue from the inhabitants of the territory for the services of order and protection.[9] The political culture of Nepal has always been characterised by authoritarian tendencies. Both religion and general societal norms have reinforced the authoritarian tradition by encouraging blind obedience to autocratic authority. Just as the will of the head of the family had to be obeyed under all circumstances, the ruler's wish was a law and command to the people. Nepal was ruled for centuries by the personal fiat of one strong man or the other. Considerations of the common people seldom figured in the calculations of the rulers.

Landmarks in State-Society Relations

A significant shift in State-Society relations took place when a century of Rana-rule ended and Nepal entered the era of democracy in 1951. The Rana rule established in 1846 was counting its days and as the time passed it became hostile to and incompatible with the modern concepts of power, authority and legitimacy which in a nutshell, required the broadening of the regime's base by making it people-oriented.[10] At the time the Rana rule was faced with the greatest crisis in its history particularly after the withdrawal of the British from India. The hereditary Rana Prime Ministers of Nepal on the one hand proved incapable of the courage, foresight and statesmanship demanded by the circumstances. On the other, people were impatient for a change in Nepal. Initially, protests against the Ranas were made in the form of condemnation of the regime's activities. In the 1930s two clandestine anti-Rana organisations were formed in Nepal—the Prachanda Gurkha in 1931, and the Praja Parishad in 1935. It was the time when the Nepalese leaders began to think of founding an organisation to carry on the struggle for democracy in the Himalayan Kingdom. The result was the founding of the All India Nepali National Congress at Varanasi on 31 October 1946 who later in January 1947 dropped the word All India but the aim of the party was proclaimed to be the achievement of a constitutional monarchy in Nepal.[11] Following its independence in August 1947 India was engaged in planting the institutions of democracy in its own land and desired that these be planted and may take firm roots and flourish in all the newly emerging states of Asia and Africa.

Changes occurred in politics and society of the Himalayan Kingdom paved the way further in the democratic direction with the help of New Delhi. As a result of the compromise plan provided in February 1951 a coalition government was formed in Nepal whose constituents were the king, the Ranas and the political leaders who had all committed themselves to the ideals of modernisation.[12] The compromise plan provided for an amnesty for insurgents, the restoration of King Tribhuvan, the inclusion of popular representatives in the cabinet on the basis of parity with the Ranas and the holding of elections to a Constituent Assembly by 1952. King Tribhuvan through a declaration resolved that his people would be governed according to the provisions of a democratic Constitution framed by a Constituent

Assembly elected by the people on the basis of universal adult suffrage.[13] This was an interim arrangement in the transition from authoritarianism to democracy. It was a synthesis of the forces of tradition and modernity. It was a net result of Nepalese youth and exiled politicians and their Indian supporters who expressed the desire to overthrow the autocratic Rana rule and unleashed a struggle against them that was in power for more than a century.

The downfall of the Rana regime in Nepal was a revolutionary step in the direction of the fall of autocracy and beginning of the constitutional government. A political system exists and performs functions in and around its environment. Properties of environment being both friendly and inimical to the system invariably influence and strain it. The post-revolution periods in Nepal witnessed a steady broadening of the popular base of government and on March 30, 1951, the Council of Ministers adopted the interim Government of Nepal Act which was also known as the interim Constitution of Nepal. As a further step on February 12, 1959, a new Constitution was adopted which envisaged responsible self-government on the British pattern with the king retaining all powers, acting with the aid and advice of the Council of Ministers. This was the beginning of constitutional monarchy in Nepal. According to the new Constitution Parliament was to be made of two Houses—the House of Representatives (Pratinidhi Sabha) and the Senate (Maha Sabha). The election process for the election of Pratinidhi Sabha started on 18 February and ended on April 13, 1959. The Nepali Congress which commanded a mass base won 74 seats out of 109 and B.P. Koirala, its leader, became the Prime Minister on May 27, 1959. The new Constitution was come into force on 30 June and Parliament was inaugurated by the king on 4 July 1959.

Even the political system established by the Constitution of 1959, although in name was Parliamentary, but simultaneously several provisions were made that undermined Parliamentary sovereignty. In it, the king was empowered to reject the recommendation of the Prime Minister to summon or dissolve Parliament. Another infringement related to the post of the Prime Minister in which the king was given a discretion to appoint even an outsider to the office of the Prime Minister if he found no person commanding the confidence of the majority in the House. The king was given power to dismiss the Prime Minister after consulting the Rashtra Parishad.[15] But above all the Constitution itself was the result of the king's promulgation. The first elected government of Nepal under the premiership of B.P. Koirala was allowed to function being sandwiched between people's aspirations and king's uncontrolled powers.

Nepal having a duly elected democratic government headed by B.P. Koirala and its growing power and prestige both inside and outside the country had pained King Mahendra, and he feared the end of royal power in Nepal. A power rivalry between the king and the Prime Minister did not last long and the former by a Royal Proclamation on December 15, 1960, dismissed the popular government and assumed direct administrative charge of the state. Although the Parliamentary system was not abolished immediately, it was suspended for the time being and in 1962 a new Constitution was promulgated which emphasised on a partyless democratic Panchayat system. In the official version of the Royal Proclamation the Parliamentary system was blamed for the sorry state of affairs in the country and an attempt was made to convince the people in favour of the Panchayat system that became essential in the national interest.[16]

After the Parliamentary system, with new innovation King Mahendra seemed to have expected three dimensions—to recognize the king's direct leadership, to create a front to meet oppositional politics and to generate public opinion in favour of the system.[17] However, at the heart of the matter remained the fact that King Mahendra was opposed to political parties because he viewed every kind of organised popular force as a threat to his absolute power. Even in the new Panchayat system the king was in the centre and the whole structure revolved round him. By taking over the government, the king had virtually imposed dictatorial rule in Nepal. Unfortunately the changeover from democracy to dictatorship continued in Nepal for decades. King Mahendra ruled till his death in January 1972 and his demise followed the coronation of his son King Birendra during whose dispensation, the agitation for restoration of democracy was hastened. The age-old system of absolute monarchy in Nepal was replaced by constitutional monarchy on April 8, 1990, when King Birendra agreed to the demands of the people for putting an end to the partyless panchayat system. Though over the period of time Constitutions had been framed and suspended for political reasons of monarchy, it was in 1990 when Nepal got its first ever systematic, Constitution based on the multi-party system. Before 1990 Nepal was under the Panchayat Constitution of 1962 that defined the social objective of the new scheme. In Part 4 of this Constitution it was clearly mentioned that the social objective of the Panchayat System shall be to establish a harmonious social life based on morality, by eliminating the obstacles that may arise in the process of mobilising the general public for setting up of a society as envisaged by Clause (1) and to maintain national unity with due regard to the existing mutual harmonious tolerance and the cultural and traditional values of Nepal adhered to by the Nepalese citizen from time immemorial as the prosperity and glory of Nepal as well as their national character.[18] Through this system the political development of Nepal was also hoped as it was an important source of political communication between the king and the people. The National Panchayat fulfilled this need and connected the people and the king through different ways. With this aim in view, King Mahendra also promulgated the new civil code to remove legal disparities prevailing in Nepal based on caste, tribe, class and area.

However, despite constitutional provisions and administrative efforts for the social development of Nepal, the Panchayat system was dominated by traditional elites mainly drawn from the three major upper castes. These elites benefited from the ban on political parties and autonomous trade unions and other organisations, because these bans effectively constrained the organising abilities of most non-elite groups in the country while the traditional elites could exploit their elaborate social networks and their formal political and administrative positions, especially through the *afno manchhe* and the tradition of *Chakari*.[19] The term *afno manchhe* literally means 'one's own people'. It refers to the predominant form of social interaction and organisation in Nepal whereby people act on the basis of strong attachment to each other within a particular group while at the same time treating other citizens as outsiders. The practice encouraged factionalism, nepotism and corruption and discouraged cooperation between different groups.[20] The practice of *Chakari* (sycophancy) implied that people less well off and less powerful tend to spend a lot of time and energy just showing their obedience and dependence on high class elites and persons in powerful positions. Thus, under the national Panchayat system both elite groups and poorer people of society gradually emerged as strong opponents to the partyless Panchayat system. The extreme concentration of political power under that system provoked protests on several occasions from 1979 onwards. In November 1990 a new Constitution was promulgated which guaranteed the multi-party system and changed the King's position to that of a constitutional monarch; he retained his position as the commander of the armed forces. Elections were held on 12 May 1991 and resulted in a victory for the Nepali Congress Party, which secured a narrow majority of 110 seats in Parliament; the second position was won by the Nepali Communist Party with 69 seats. On 29 May, G.P. Koirala became the first Prime Minister of Nepal in the restored multi-party system. However, the fully democratic set up could not deter the monarchy from exercising its autocratic rule. Nepal's political scenario also became prone to monarchical autocracy as no government could provide political stability because of the lack of understanding among its fragmented and avaricious political parties.

The State of Nepal has a long history of Monarchy leading the democratic institutions like the Government in trouble. The monarchy has been loath to stay as a rubber stamp in the pursuit of power. Rather, it had always been keen to capture power and rule the country at will. To grab power it had taken all possible steps to damage the institutions, thereby leading the kingdom into state of considerable insecurity. The intention of monarchy was to rule over the Kingdom arbitrarily like the Monarchs in medieval France before the French Revolution or autocratic Russian Czars before the Russian Revolution.[21] However, with the implementation of the 1991 Constitution which provided a multi-party system in Nepal, the whole history of politics and society in the Himalayan Kingdom appeared to be fast changing/growing. Ever since the first election the Maoist forces have become a deciding player in national politics and even formed the government with intervals.

The Present Impasse

With the entry of the Maoists as a potent force, the State-Society relations in the country began to change rapidly. Especially from 1996, when the Maoists presented their 40-Point demand before the Nepali Congress Government, a serious internal problem erupted in the country as the rebels intensified their armed struggle. It became the biggest challenge to Nepal's democracy and to its internal security. Over the decade of 1990s Nepal witnessed grave political crises arising out of the armed intensification of the rebels followed by the fall of the governments one after another. The Maoists in Nepal had demanded several basic changes in Nepalese political system including the abolition of monarchy which had continued for centuries and establishment of a federal democratic republic. Despite the fact that Nepal had a constitutional monarchy it lacked political stability on account of dissension among the leaders of the Nepali Congress and the rising power of the Maoists. Economic and social backwardness of Nepal added fuel to the fire and a large section of the people began to lean towards the Marxist ideology. Gradually, Nepal was moving towards a phase of lawlessness. It gave birth to Maoist insurgency which disliked the king and the political system alike. The Parliamentary system has failed miserably in managing popular aspirations of economic well-being and social justice. Political leaders and elected representatives of the people gave priority to their preoccupations with power and self rather than to the concerns of their wider social constituencies.[22] In a calculated move for a long time (1996–2001) the monarchy of Nepal quietly patronized the unfolding Maoist rebellion. With the democratic politics in Nepal being extremely factionalised, successive governments in Nepal found it difficult to implement governmental policies and programmes.

The key social problem of Nepal is the absence of linkage between the people at large and their government. Consequently, the formation of a healthy civil society has been held in check. The conflicts in Nepal have been the outcome of incongruence between societal aspirations and state institutions. In the context of Nepal, democratisation could mean expanding and deepening democracy by reforming the polity to include traditionally excluded groups and extending civil liberties and political rights to them. It could also mean making public officials accountable and responsive to people's aspirations. In the words of Robert Dahl, "democratization occurs as more people participate in the polity." According to an estimate about more than two-thirds of the population is excluded from the influential realms of governance in Nepal. They include indigenous nationalities, (Adibasi Janajati), Dalits (traditional untouchables) and Madhesis (plains people). In the *Nepal Human Development Report, 1998*, the elite caste group occupied 98 per cent of the top positions in the civil administration in 1854 and in the mid-1990s they occupied about 92 per cent. In addition, historical exclusion and discrimination have contributed to the contemporary exclusion.

In the circumstances, the People's movement launched at the end of April 2006 was the result of King Gyanendra's autocratic Emergency imposed on 1 February 2005. It compelled the democratic and Maoist forces to come closer to each other and form a common platform against the King. In the struggle of the Seven Party Alliance (SPA) against the king the former won and the latter had agreed to give up executive powers and work with an interim government. The interim government would also have to administer the country till the formation of a new government elected on the basis of the Constitution which will emerge from the Assembly's deliberations.[23] The election to the members of the Constituent Assembly was held on April 10, 2008, in which the Maoists emerged as the single largest party. Under the rules of Nepal's interim Constitution a two-thirds majority was needed for any major decision including the election of Prime Minister and President. By giving the Maoists a little more than one-third of the seats, the electorate said that it wanted the Maoists to keep alive the principle of consensus that had served Nepal's parties so well in the struggle against the monarchy.[24] In August 2008 a Maoist-led coalition with the support of the Communist Party of Nepal (UML) and the Madhesi Janadhikar Forum (MJF) formed the government and Pushpa Kamal Dahal 'Prachanda' became the first Prime Minister of the new Federal Republic of Nepal. These developments in Nepal's politics and society had ushered the Himalayan Kingdom into an era of hope and despair which the land is bound to face in future.

To conclude, Nepal was brought together territorially by the Gorkha conquest. It has not been unified psychologically and economically even after more than two centuries. This is partly because the Nepali state was captured and exploited by a small elite class ever since its formation. The ruling group defined the rights and duties of citizens towards the state to promote its own interests. This disjunction between the state and society has been the underlying cause for the eruption of many contentious activities in present-day Nepal, which have directly or indirectly adversely affected the recent trend towards democratisation. The existing fractured and fragmented dispensation bears the responsibility for mismanaging the contradictions and faultlines which lie at the base of Nepalese society.

REFERENCES

1. J W Bjorkman, 'Changing State-Society Relations: Broad-Brush Approaches and Analytical Models', *Administrative Change*, vol. XXVIII, no.1, Jaipur, January-December 2001, pp.12-13
2. John Martinusen, *Democracy, Competition and Choice: Emerging Local Self-Government in Nepal,* Sage, New Delhi, 1995, pp.17-18
3. Karl Deutsch, 'Social Mobilisation and Political Development', *American Political Science Review*, vol.5, September 1961, pg.496
4. Morton Davies and Vaughan Lewis, *Models of Political Systems*, Vikas Pulishing House, Delhi, 1971, pg.97
5. Neera Chandhoke, *State and Civil Society, Explorations in Political Theory*, Sage Publications, New Delhi, 1995, pg.8
6. Rajkumar Singh, *Less Tasty Indo-Nepal Political Relations: 1947-1997*, Novelty & Co, Patna, 1998, pg.18
7. Rishikesh Shaha, *Nepali Politics: Retrospect and Prospect*, Oxford University Press, Delhi, 1978, pg.26
8. *www.cocap.org.np/.../citizens'-conference-on-role-of-civil-society-o...*, accessed on February 25, 2011
9. www.constitutionnet.org/.../The-CA-of-Nepal-An-Agenda-for-Wome..., accessed on November 2, 2011

19

Making of the Constitution in Nepal: Problems and Solution

NARESH KUMAR

The present geographical map of Nepal as one nation in the political sense is the result of the integration done by the Gorkha King Shri Prithvi Narayan Shah V in 1669. The political setup of Nepal as a nation began with the establishment of a democratic regime by Prithvi Narayan Shah. Sometime later, during the reign of Surendra Vikram Shah, Jang Bahadur Rana captured the then king in the palace and declaring himself the third maharaja prime minister forced all to sign on the stamp papers giving him complete political governance rights. Jang BahadurRana obtained recognition of his political ruling rights from the then Governor General of British India Warren Hastings. Post this, Jang Bahadur Rana's autocratic political rule continued in its all authoritarian nature for 104 years. In this way, the political structure of Nepal can be clearly viewed from monarchical arrangement in 1769 to the century long autocratic rule of Jang Bahadur Rana till 1949. In the last leg of the Rana rule after the Delhi agreement of the Opposition, Shamsher Jang Bahadur Rana stayed as the last Rana prime minister. From then on began the enterprise of political rule following a written constitution in the presence of the king and his crown. There was a return of the political power of Raja Tribhuvan Veer Vikram Shah Dev. Almost after a decade of political surge and ups and downs, the constitution was made in VS 2015 (1958); keeping the entity of the king located as the head of the democratic organisation intact, the juristic situation with the prime minister as the user of political power—selected by the house of legislatives elected by the public—was established.

In this way, the prime minister being appointed as a people's representative, keeping the king's power within a limit, was a major step towards a democratic arrangement. Within the landscape of the entire set of aforementioned events constitutional problems also started rising. As the successor of Raja Tribhuvan, Raja Mahendra sat on the throne. He held an acute ambition of becoming an actual ruler.

Although the political situation of Nepal was established as a constitutional democracy, two power centres were made in it. First, the power centre of a hereditary king, second the power centre of the prime minister elected by the people. The clash of two political people was clearly visible. The constitutional distress of Nepal also began from here. The 96-month old infant called democracy died an instant death. Dissolving the parliament of VS 2015 (1958), Raja Mahendra Singh took control over complete political power. All political activities were forbidden. Whoever was caught in this political chase was sent to jail. Prime Minister Vishveshwar Prasad Koirala was also sent to jail. Those who went underground took shelter in India. Now under the guidance of the king, a face of the revised constitution was seen in the independent Panchayati system established in VS 2017 (1960). This situation continued uninterrupted for three decades. On the other hand, the struggle for getting the democratic arrangement back also kept working in and out of Nepal in some form or other. Thus the coming and disruption of the constitution continued.

Raja Mahendra's son Raja Birendra took over the royal throne in 1972. He tried to root the independent Panchayati system that he received as inheritance as much as possible. But he was a little more liberal as compared to his father Raja Mahendra. He took the courage to take liberal steps for this Panchayati system. He made possible the collective public opinion in the movement of independent versus coalition in VS 2063 (2008). Although the independent side came out victorious in this people's opinion, but the public inclination towards coalition was also reflected in the very minute difference in votes (approximately four-and-a-half lakh). Probably it was sensing this that Raja Birendra gave the freedom for direct elections. Supporting the crown, people were given the opportunity of participating in the election process. In the local body, chief and deputy officers along with the members of the ward were being selected directly by the people. The Member of Parliament with 25 per cent supporters could become candidates for prime minister and the ones with 60 per cent votes they could become the prime minister. In reality the supporters of the king were always the prime ministers but the provision of nomination was nonetheless established. The king could criticize the prime minister and the royal family. In about ten to twelve years, the movement for the restoration of the democratic setup became intense. Former Prime Minister Vishveshwar Prasad Koirala was permitted to enter Nepal, was arrested, a case was run on him, and he was released. A landscape kept coming up for a movement. The movement was touching its zenith in VS 2048. The masses were not only ready, but eager to get a constitutional rule. King Birendra understood the seriousness of the situation and announced the transformation of monarchical rule into democratic rule. Amending the sections in the previous constitution to suit a democratic nature, the rights of the king were deduced keeping the provision of a king as the constitutional head. The constitution of VS 2048 became the constitution of Nepal. This constitution was formulated by experts, including people like Lakshmimal Singhvi from India.

Political structuring began analogous to provisions in the constitution. As a result of various types of events, movements and upsurges, democracy began in Nepal in place of monarchy in VS 2048. In this entire political environment, various seeds for hazards were also sown. The germ of Maoism began to grow. Its formation, power and effect became ubiquitous. The orgy of violent movements was also expanding. The government take it too seriously in the beginning. Further on it led to an environment of terrorism in Nepal. Not only the government, but the people's struggle with it also gained ground. Internal discord within political parties, factionalism, clash of personalities in the leading class, over ambitiousness, etc., were important reasons that led to problems in the constitutional governing period in Nepal's political system. The second reason worth mentioning is that the Leftist parties kept conspiring against the democratic constitution. This continued to happen in an indirect as well as visible manner. Before the constitution in VS 2048, when the constitution in VS 2015 was dismissed, the Leftists supporting the throne had given full support to the king. To keep Nepal away from a becoming a democratic state, the Leftists opposed the democracy-supporting Nepali Congress. It was accused as being a broker for India and supporting its expansionist policies; many more abusive terms were used for it. Those Left groups were openly China supporters and worked on its strategy; China also kept building up a situation through its strategy with the Leftist followers in the context of not having a democratic constitution in Nepal.

When the constitution of VS 2048 was implemented, the opposition to it began with the reason that it had not been made by the constitution assembly; and that it was a constitution inspired by a particular party. In the beginning the sound of this resistance was a little less detailed. When the Maoist group of the Left was formed and expanded its power, the resistance also became sharper. The Maoists kept protesting in the form of an armed group collectively at various places in Nepal. It is said that this protest against a constitutional order kept happening at a violent level and within a time span of 10-12 years, about twenty thousand innocent people were killed in some way or the other. Many families were forced to flee from Nepal and take shelter in India. The main goal of the Maoists was to establish their domination over the state rule in Nepal on the basis of terrorism and expansion of their power. Thus they are a deterrent in the formation of a constitution because a democratic constitution stops the establishment of autocracy. Maoists advocate a republic constitution only to establish autocratic rule, just like China. Their conviction towards democracy or democratic order is clearly doubtful. After a decade of violent movement and the court murder, designated King Gyanendra submitted to the people's movement and transferred authority; in the history of Nepal, this led to the exit of the dynasty rule from the politics of Nepal. They were committed to now select a representative chosen by the people and formulate the constitution within a span of two years. It was required that an interim government works on a temporary basis to manage governance and trade. In this context, a president and vice-president were designated as the head of the nation. The government was formed under the leadership of Maoist Pushp Kamal Daham 'Prachand'.

Post this began the work of the constitution assembly with 601 members. And from here also began the stretch of difficulties in constitution-formation. The speed of formulating the constitution could not be as intense as it should have been. When the term of two years was coming to an end, a one year extension was given. It would be expedient to understand the problems in framing a constitution both thematically and objectively. It would be fact oriented and accurate to clearly mention the problems and barriers in the formulation of a constitution in two forms: (i) the problems created due to the provisions listed for making the constitution; (ii) the analysis of factors causing obstacles in the process of its construction. Firstly, we should view the problems within the constituent assembly. The tenure of the constituent assembly was increased by a year; half the time is about to finish. Serious discussions have taken place on some of the issues. On the basis of ideas presented by 601 assembly members and 25 political parties, there has been a discussion on 220 topics based on the differences between three major parties and Maoist groups. Now it is a subject of responsibility on how this is solved. Based on the decision taken by all members from parties of the constituent assembly, a committee was formed under the leadership of Pushp Kamal Dahal 'Prachand' on Ashwin 24, VS 2067 to take forward the efforts of consent. It had the following members: A group including seven people—N.K. party head Jhalnath Khanal; Ramchandra Podel from Nepali Congress; the head of Madheshi Janadhikar Forum, Upendra Yadav; Nepal Mazdoor Kisan Party head Narayan Man Bijukchhe; members Prem Bhadur Singh and Rukmini Chaudhary—was formed. To help this group, a six member cooperation committee was also formed including Bharat Mohan Adhikari, Ramesh Lekhak, Dev Gurung, Ratneshwar, Sunil Prajapati and Vasudev Chaudhary. They have to present recommendations for various questions. A decision will be taken on those on the basis of the constituent assembly. But the constituent assembly head Nilambar Acharya found this to be an intervention in the working of the assembly. The group tried to bring consent on any one out of the 220 topics after a discussion for thirty days. The following are the major ones: 1. Laying foundation for socio-cultural unity: there was difference on ten questions in this context. The question on language was the major one. For this, there was consent on the formation of a language commission. Along with it sanction was given to Nepali language written in the devanagri script; it was agreed to decide a regional language by provincial legislative and all government work to be done in that language. Conservation of national interest: there were seven questions in the committee associated with this. Under this the right to enter into agreements and treaties with nations was given to the Centre. But in doing so, permission will have to be taken from the province on the subject coming under regional list. Taking permission from the Centre, the state can enter into an agreement with a foreign company for industrialisation. Regarding managing the army, the president will appoint or dismiss the supreme commander on the insistence of the council of ministers. A consensus has been reached on this. There is still dispute on the point of giving army training to an eighteen-year-old youth.

There were quite a few points of discord in the committee for fundamental rights and guiding principles. The committee has accepted the idea of solo citizenship, keeping the regional identity intact. Under this, provision has been given for three types of citizenship: to the descendant, to one who is adopted, and non-resident. There were ten questions of dispute under the committee on judicial system. Maoists (integrated) were of the opinion that the legislative should be appointed and dismissed by a special committee; but there has been agreement on the independent and impartial nature of the judiciary. Agreement was made on the provision of the theory on control and balance in distribution of power. The chief of the constitutional body and chief justice of the Supreme Court to be appointed by the recommendation of the constitutional council or a similar independent body and other judges also to be appointed by independent bodies. But there is still dispute over the formation of an independent body. There are eleven questions concerning the nature of governance in the nation. Dispute on these continues. The major points of discord include direct election of the president, president elected by the parliament, prime minister either elected by the parliament or appointed directly. There is also contention over the election process. Multi-member direct election process, proportional and mixed process and completely proportional process are subjects of discord. Union, province and local level organisation is also under dispute. The legislature, executive and judiciary of Centre and province are also subjects of dispute. Differences are intact on questions of geography and population of the constituency.

After the Madhesh movement, the madheshi elements have become an important political landscape on the political horizon of Nepal. No party can ignore it and walk ahead. Almost all prominent political parties have established a madheshi cell. The Madhesh movement has struck on the psyche of keeping the madheshi population subordinate and keeping them as followers for long term politically. They do not want to let the madheshi elements gain prominence through conspiracy. Thus these states keep creating obstacles in restructuring. In this case the main cause of the deadlock is in this way of thinking. It can easily be understood what this restructuring committee still having not been made hints towards. The committee of the constituent assembly has put forward a proposal for fourteen states on the basis of majority and minority. This also is under acute dispute. The present constitutional hazard in Nepal in reality is due to the difference in the fundamental thinking of various political parties and authoritarian attitude, and due to the internal factionalism. A particular party is incapable of reaching upon any conclusion because of their hegemonic, totalitarian and authoritarian attitude. First of all, it is necessary to analyse the internal discord, factionalism and power politics of political parties, mainly three major political parties and the madheshi groups. Nepali Congress, Nepali Maoists, and Madheshi parties—comparatively speaking, these are the main causal factors for politics in Nepal. Girija Prasad Koirala from the Nepali Congress kept his monopoly rule intact on his party and rule. His personality kept him the chairman of the Nepali Congress for his lifetime; despite groups and sub-groups being formed within the party, he never let them dominate the party interest and he used them for the benefit of the party. Dissatisfied, Narhati Acharya and Ganan Thapa put their attention to organisation. There was always a competition between the SushilKoirala group, BahadurDeuwa group and RamchandraPadol group. The tendency to defeat each other to move ahead can be clearly seen in them. The prime ministerial candidature is being opposed by these two groups only. There is factionalism from the level of Centre to the village within the Nepal Communist Party between Madhav Kumar Nepal (prime minister), head Jhalnath Khalal and K.P. Oli as competitors. Jhalnath Khalal is the core opponent of Madhav Nepal. Nepal can never come with two groups; he can fulfil his interests by making any sort of agreement. To make one's group reach power is the sole purpose/goal.

The situation of madheshi groups is also such due to internal factionalism. The founder RamjanmTiwari who has been fighting for the rights of the madheshis ever since the time of the monarchy has bided his time in jail. He established the Nepal Sadbhavana Party along with his supporters. This was a landscape achievement in the institutional sense for the madheshi wakening. But clash of personalities and factionalism began in his term. Hridyesh Tripathi took Anandi Devi, wife of the madheshi leader Gajendra Narayan Singh, who was the sharp speaker of the Sadbhavna party and was the backbone of the Hindi-speaking party in the parliament, and formed another group. In a similar way, Bhagyanath Gupta made a separate group. But now Amar Yadav has separated from Upendra Yadav and has made the Madheshi Janadhikar Forum. There is a situation of division in the Tarai Madhes party. Mahanth Thakur and Vijay Gachhdar have come from Congress and worked on breaking the madheshi solidarity by forming a separate madheshi group. If all of them had put their voices together on one platform, it would have given some speed to the formation of the constitution.

The public has chosen constituent assembly to frame the constitution. Till the next constitutional order, there had to be a working government so that the regular daily workings of the nation can work smoothly. But this has been turned into a haunt dominated by party interest. Democratic constitution stops autocratic rule. Thus the Maoist head Prachand wants to make a government under his leadership and establish his own domination. But he does not want to follow the terms that he was supposed to follow as per in the agreement in the past. If in a democracy a party keeps armed forces separately, then the democracy can never be successful. If they wish to be a part of the democratic stream with honesty, then they will have to create a democratic psyche and will have to dissolve their armed force. Otherwise it would be dishonesty to talk about democracy. How will the constitution and rebellion go hand in hand? The election of a prime minister has been without a result for seventeen times. The danger of possession of power is clearly visible in the thoughts and actions of the Maoists. The problem of faith is also seen between the various parties. Madhav Kumar Nepal resigned from his post as prime minister on VS 2067 in order to pave way for the formation of a government by national agreement. It has since been four-and-a-half months but a government of national agreement seems far-fetched. Maoists leader Prachand had said that a government with national agreement would be made within two hours of Madhav Kumar Nepal's resignation; he considered Nepal as a deterrent to the formation of a constitution. But it could not happen even in seventeen chances. During the meeting of the three major parties held at the Hathipan Resort at Ferwing on Kartik 19 VS 2067 and at the Gokarna meeting (Kartik 24), agreement could not take any concrete shape. The Maoists consider the Nepali Congress their enemy. Because the Nepali Congress is acting as a deterrent in its policies of self-interest and will always be. Both of them are at two poles. Arjun Nat Singh K.C. says that no reliable step has been taken in the process of constitution formation and peace process. Maoists Dev Gurang says that the constitutional parties have become of the nature of national self-surrender. Especially Nepali Congress according to him does not have thoughts of national independence. Here, it is a thing worth understanding that if the construction of the constitution will be done together, then there will be ideological solutions. But this question in itself hints at national self-surrender and does not hold very well. The agreement that the Maoists talk of are on their conditions. After all, what is independence for—to give all power to Maoists? For single party arrangement? Can we ignore this? It is not at all inappropriate for the Maoists to talk of stopping violence because this is happening at various places. It would not be wrong to believe that there is clash between single party leadership on the one hand and multi-party democracy on the other.

When there is talk of the construction of a constitution, they do not carry out a positive role in it, and after the constitution not having been made for fourteen ashadhas, they threaten with an armed rebellion by the people. This is said by those people who have come into the constituent assembly members with maximum number of votes. These people want the construction process of the constitution to attain salvation. It seems they want to kill the very foetus of a democratic constitution in the womb. This sad question is worth consideration and disturbing. It is very easy to understand the psyche of the Maoists behind scuffle with the finance minister and the minister of energy resources on 19 November, the day the budget was presented for the economic working.

In the name of making the Nepali people sovereign, the Maoists indulged in a violent rebellion. Sixteen thousand people died in these. Fifty-eight thousand people were handicapped. Seventy-one thousand were displaced. Many public places were destroyed. To overcome this, a twelve-point agreement was made in Delhi. It is to be noted that in VS 2007 as well there had been an attempt to look for a political solution through the Delhi Agreement. There was a revolution again with seven political parties in April 2006. A larger peace agreement was made on 21 November 2006. Late Girija Prasad Koirala and Maoist Prachand signed this on the part of Nepal government. The constitutional assembly was made as a result of this. Federal republic became another order in the rule of Nepal. The Madhesh Movement had a consequential role in it. The adjustment of Maoist combative and their relocation was included in the agreement. Two billion rupees have been spent on Maoists living in camps in 2009-10. 560 million rupees have been spent to set up camps. These participate in the Maoist political programmes; this is unfair. Maoists do not realise their social duties. They do not want to change the trend of self-serving through terrorism. The complexity in Nepal today have arisen due to this reason. This is an impediment in the proper establishment of a political system in Nepal.

It is an important task to establish a new political system after sacrifices and struggle. It is not essential to only change the system, it is more important to establish an alternative system. It is a big challenge to hold a democratic system. It is essential to have a cautious, honest and democratic intent for the same. A system devoid of political organisation will give rise to disturbance in Nepal. Peace process cannot be just on the basis of verbal compaign. Peace should be visible on the surface. Willy Brandt has said, "Peace is not everything, but without peace everything is nothing." Usually it is alleged that there is obstruction due to India. This is away from truth. The peace agreement was possible in Delhi with the support of India. It collaborated in the transfer of power as well. India cannot see Nepal boiling because its own good is also involved therein. No nation can take a step sacrificing its own good. The Indo-Chinese diplomatic competition in Nepal is a reality. Frankly China has come into the forefront. Thus in keeping into account all the circumstances, Indian diplomatic steps cannot be called inappropriate. India has always been helping in various ways and it always will. There is no doubt in it.

REFERENCES

1. *nepalaawaz.com/index.php?option=com...nepal...*, accessed on June 8, 2011
2. *nepalnews.com.np/contents/2011/englishweekly/.../face2face.php*, accessed on October 17, 2011
3. *nepal.usembassy.gov/ep-12-17-2008.html*, accessed on November 1, 2011
4. *nepalicount.com/.../25-america-nepal-society-interaction-program- ...*, accessed on April 10, 2011
5. *southasiamonitor.org/detail.php?type=n&nid=418*, accessed on November 5, 2011
6. *story.nepalnational.com/index.php/ct/9/cid/.../id/16378389/*, accessed on November 4, 2011
7. *swiss-nepal.ch/downloads/newsletters/nl_FinalN97-p04.pdf*, accessed on February 16, 2011
8. *www.albanytribune.com/15082011-nepal-deadline-for-... - United States*, accessed on April 12, 2011
9. *www.apssnepal.org/.../ ...*, accessed on February 6, 2011
10. *www.andhranews.net/Intl/.../Constitution-making-process-43750*, accessed on April 11, 2011
11. *www.asiaviews.org/index.php?option=com_content.*, accessed on July 13, 2011
12. *www.beta.undp.org/undp/en/.../nepal_peoples_constitution html*, accessed on February 8, 2011

20

Peace Process in Nepal and Role of UNMIN

NAM SEONG MUN

United Nations has adopted the resolution 1939(2010) for the extension of UN Mission in Nepal (UNMIN) till January 15, 2011. It is important to note that UNMIN was established under resolution 1740 (2007) and this is its seventh extension. Earlier, in the wake of wide criticism of UNMIN's role in Nepal's peace process amid differences among the political parties, UN Secretary General Ban Ki-moon said that he was not in favor of repeated extensions of UNMIN's mandate in an atmosphere of 'persistent and unfounded' criticism that complicates its ability to function. However, he had maintained that the UN wants to see its body's mandated tasks completed. Ban Ki-moon added that commitments made by the Nepalese political parties have become unrealistic in the absence of a consensual approach and parties of Nepal are paying more attention to the formation of a new government than the peace process itself.

UN has adopted the resolution to extend the UNMIN's tenure after the Prime Minister Madhav Kumar Nepal and UCPN(M) Chairman Pushpa Kamal Dahal, signed the four point agreement on September 13, 2010, renewing the peace deal and agreeing upon UNMIN's extenstion for four months. Both the leaders committed to give a final shape to all documents prepared by the Special Committee for forwarding the peace process by reaching agreement on them as soon as possible and implementing them. They also agreed to finish all remaining tasks of the peace process by January 14,

2011, when UNMIN's mandate will finally expire. UN Security Council has requested Mr Ban Ki-moon to report back to it by October 15, 2010 on the implementation of the agreement, following high-level discussions among the United Nations, the government of Nepal and the political parties. Prior to the decision, there were signs of clear division among members of the Council whether to accept Nepal's request for the extension or go for a short rollover of the current mandate. United Kingdom was in favor of technical rollover by a month, while China argued for acting upon the request of Nepal. EU, led by the United Kingdom, wanted to send a strong signal to Nepal that the failure of the local actors couldn't be passed on to the world body. The grace period of one month was intended for Nepali parties to come clean on their words and deeds.

India and UNMIN

India has consistently supported the peace process in Nepal. It should be noted that India also welcomed the establishment of the UNMIN in 2007. In fact, India provided more than 80 vehicles and 50 wireless sets to UNMIN to help its activities get going and even today, the containers in which the weapons are stored are provided by India. India is of the view that extension of UNMIN's mandate is a decision taken by concerned Nepali authorities. India believes that the peace process in Nepal, in order to have legitimacy, must be Nepali-led and Nepali-driven.

UNMIN's Arms Monitoring Office continued to monitor the compliance of the Nepal Army and the Maoist army with the Agreement on the Monitoring of the Management of Arms and Armies. Arms monitors also visited the satellite cantonment sites on a regular basis. Again, the Child Protection Unit of UNMIN continued to provide advisory support to UNICEF and UNDP in the implementation of rehabilitation programmes for former Maoist army personnel disqualified as minors. UNMIN's political affairs officers have maintained regular contacts with a broad range of Government officials, political party representatives, civil society organizations and international actors.

UNMIN is being accused by several sections that it has been working against its mandate and favoring particular political powers and ideologies. The Special Committee to supervise, integrate and rehabilitate Maoist army personnel has not achieved a quorum in its meetings during the reporting period because of the non-attendance of some members, principally UCPN-M, which has not participated for several months. Serious disagreements persist on key issues such as the number of Maoist personnel to be integrated into the Nepal Army and other security forces, their eligibility criteria, whether they integrate individually or in groups, and the sequencing and time frame for the implementation process. UNMIN is also criticized for failing to recognize even the existing and potential actors of reintegration and to coordinate with the various stakeholders in different layers.

Nepal's peace process remains stalled, with few signs of a consensual way forward. The major parties are preoccupied by profound internal fissures and the question of power-sharing. While the extension of the Constituent Assembly by one year averted a grave political vacuum, almost four months have passed without notable headway in the peace process. Despite the sustained efforts of the UNMIN, little progress has been made towards the conditions for its departure. Therefore, the UNMIN must relook its activities regarding the reintegration of ex-combatants in Nepal; otherwise, such plans could add more political tension and confusion over the peace process in coming days in Nepal. The ill-designed reintegration plan may push the nation into further conflict and political polarization. UNMIN should have worked more closely with other UN agencies and bilateral development partners, aiming to transform the current peace mandate to a broader peace, development and reconciliation platform. UNMIN must work more closely with the Nepali people and civil society and not just politicians to foster a permanent peace that can contribute overall sense of peace, security and happiness.

REFERENCES

Deb Mukharji, "Elusive Horizon", *Frontline*, Chennai, September 2010, pg.53

Prashant Jha, "Vacuum as UNMIN Prepares for Exit", *The Hindu*, December 31, 2010

www.n-peace.net/sites/default/files/...docs/Curriculum%20Vitae.doc, accessed on September 25, 2011

www.norway.org.np/.../Norway-supports-public-debate-on-the-const..., accessed on September 29, 2011

www.nytimes.com/.../nepal-party-chief-warns-king-to-turn-over-pow..., accessed on November 15, 2011

www.silobreaker.com/peace-process-constitutionmaking-to-complete..., accessed on June 19, 2011

www.slideshare.net/.../struggle-of-people-in-nepal-for-ri... - United States, accessed on October 29, 2011

www.telegraphnepal.com/.../constitution-making-process-facing-chal..., accessed on November 11, 2011

www.thehimalayantimes.com/fullNews.php?...Nepal... – Nepal, accessed on June 19, 2011

www.unicef.org/worldfitforchildren/files/Nepal_WFFC5_Report.pdf, accessed on January19, 2011

www.uni-bielefeld.de/midea/pdf/Keshab.pdf, accessed on February 12, 2011

21

Constitutional Progress in Nepal

B K L Das

The Crisis in Nepal's political System lies in the inter-party clashes, rivalry, and dominance over other fraction. The Personality cult of leaders of political parties creates problems in setting up a political system smoothly. The leftist fractions suspect the constitutional rule to be established in Nepal. They gradually began to increase their organizational strength in whole Nepal from Hill area to Terai area. They opposed the VS 2048 Constitution on the basis that it has not been made by the Constitution Assembly. Therefore, it is not people's Constitution. About twenty thousand people were killed in the civil war. No popular government can flourish having an armed group. This Situation has badly developed a road with thorns in way to making a constitution. Maoist clearly wants to dominate the political system and to keep political power in their clutch. It is the main obstacle and crisis of the political system and constitution making. The struggle for democratic system was gaining ground very deeply and widely. 601 members of all political parties expressed their divergent views but no solution was agreed unanimously. After thirty days discussion committee tried to reach for agreement on the following issues:

(i) To make basses for social cultural unity—in this issue there were disagreement on ten points. The language was main issue of concern. They agreed to make a language commission. The committee also gave their assent to use provincial language in government affairs.

(ii) Protection of National Interest—Seven points were included in this head such as—Right to make treaty and agreement with other nation was given to the centre. They agreed on the appointment of Chief of the Army staff with the recommendation of the Cabinet by the President. But no agreement was shown on the military training of 18 years old youth.

(iii) Judicial System Committee—It included ten points for discussion. But differences were clearly shown on those points. Maoists expressed their view that special committee of legislature should appoint and dismiss judges and Chief justice. But, committee gave assent on independent and impartial judiciary.
On provision of separation of power and check and Balance positive views were shown. The agreed on that head of constitutional body and chief justice should be appointed by an independent body's recommendation. But, deference lies on the organization of independent body issues.

(iv) Form of State Administration—There are eleven points kept in this head for consideration but a lot of differences are seen in these issues. Direct election of the President, Parliament elected President, Parliament elected Prime minister or direct elected Prime Minister are the bone of contention before the committee. Election system is also in dispute. Multimember direct election system proportional election system mixed system and full proportional system are such issues carrying more disputes among members. Federation, Province and local level system are also disputed subject.

(vi) There are thirty eight questions are lying in dispute regarding organs of the legislature age for adult franchise is waiting for assent of members. No consensus has been reached on uni-cameral system. There are many issues on which discussion has not been done in the constitutional committee. There are forty seven questions regarding preamble are waiting for discussion. The most important issue is the structure of state government in the future federal structure. This issue is facing a very difficult condition for reaching any conclusion.

It will be essential to understand the root cause of the crisis in Nepal. Paharia groups always dominated and ruled the present Nepal since Prithwi Narayan Shah to till now. They made Madheshi Population always their slaves and subordinate under their rule. They have had a superiority complex over Madheshi. Madheshi were never given equal treatment. It can be clearly said that political dominance and hegemony over Madheshi People has been systematically established by Paharis in Nepal. Whatever we see the turmoil's and events in Nepal is the result of the under-current of anti-Madheshi mantelity. The problem comes in the way of constitution-making is seen in two types of crisis, one crisis is Inter-party rivalry and making them a dominant role in the government. Another is the crisis within the party itself. Ambitious leaders are pulling legs of their own colleagues for one's own dominance. Another important factor is the rise of Madheshi group as a political force. They are more conscious politically now. In the above background, the political development of Nepal can be analysed.

REFERENCES

A Hotter, *The Caste Hierarchy and the State in Nepal, A Study of the Mulki Ain of 1854*, Wegner, California, 1979

Bhuwan Lal Joshi & Leo E Rose, *Democratic Innovations in Nepal: A Case Study of Political Acculturation*, California University Press, Clifornia, 1966; Mandala Book Point, Kathmandu, 2004

John Whelpton, "Political Identity in Nepal: State, Nation and Community", in David N Gellner E et al., eds., *Nationalism and Ethnicity in a Himalayan Kingdom, the Politics of Culture in Contemporary Nepal*, Harvard Academic Publishers, Amsterdam, 1997

Khanal, Krishna, "Restructuring of the Nepali State: The Federal Perspective", Lok Raj Baral, ed., *Nepal:New Frontiers of State Restructuring of State*, New Delhi, Adroit Publishers, 2008

Prayag Raj Sharma, *The State and Society in Nepal, Historical Foundations and Contemporary Trends*, Himal Books, Lalitpur, Nepal, 2004

Mahendra Lawoti, ed., *Contentious Politics and Democratization in Nepal*, Sage Publications, New Delhi, 2007

Richard Burghart, ed., *The Conditions of Listening: Essays on Religion, History and Political in South Asia*, Oxford University Press, Delhi, 1976

Siddharth Varadarajan,"The Danger in India's Nepal policy", *The Hindu*, 16 August 2010

www.bipinadhikari.com.np/.../Slogan%20of%20Constitution%20ma..., accessed on January 2, 2011

www.ccd.org.np/new/index.php?action=resources, accessed on February 10, 2011

www.mof.gov.np/economic_policy/pdf_2/sSocial_Inclusion.pdf, accessed on January 3, 2011

22

Dilemmas of Constitution Drafting in Nepal

DILIP KUMAR

Nepal has undergone dramatic changes in recent years, transitioning from an absolute monarchy to a fledging democratic republic. A series of events in 2006, including nationwide popular protests, led to the tumbling of the antiquated monarchy, the passage of a democratically oriented interim constitution, election for a constituent assembly, and an end to a decade long Maoist insurgency. The mandate of the constituent assembly's 601 members from 27 political parties was to rewrite the constitution completed in 1990. Each of the big three political parties—the Nepali Congress, the Unified Communist Party of Nepal (Maoists),[1] and the Communist Party of Nepal—Unified Marxist Leninist—has led a coalition government and governed Nepal since the monarchy ceded its power to Parliament in 2006. However, the peace process and the constitution-making are yet to be accomplished. Factors such as absence of an understanding among the political parties on the fundamental structure of state and system of governance, their failure to agree to a common minimum agenda, polarisation and intra-elite conflict, and the lack of clarity on their part to take the peace and constitution-making process towards a logical end, a *mantra* chanted by all of them so many times, have only increased political uncertainty in Nepal.

Hence, in this situation of political uncertainty/political stalemate in Nepal a few important questions are in the realm of speculation: Does the failure of the major political parties to deliver the constitution mean the collective end of their political legitimacy to either rule or exist? How have the developments in Nepal since 2006 affected the wider scope of the state-restructuring agenda? Will this agenda remain fragmentary and ineffective? What has been the behaviour pattern of the CPN-Maoists and how have the pattern differed? What will be the price of the UCPN-Maoists refusing to toe the democratic line? This article attempts a foray into these questions to find those critical issues that are likely to create a constitutional crisis in Nepal.

Orchestrated Politics of Consensus

At the outset it seems sensible to note that Nepal finds itself in a political crisis today because democratic parties have failed to give the country a constitution and a legitimate government. The decision to extend the tenure of the Constituent Assembly (CA) by a year when it failed to deliver the constitution on May 28, 2010 deadline shows that Nepal's polity has yet to mature to the point of being able to run a republic. And worse, it is almost certain that the constituent assembly will fail yet another deadline—May 28, 2011—for drafting a new constitution. This likely scenario, consistent with Nepali politics of the past, will create a constructional crisis—a failure that would naturally bring the legitimacy of the state into question, at home and abroad. Is this lingering uncertainty the result of the demise of politics of consensus? To what extent are the Nepali Congress, Maoists and the Communist Party of Nepal–Unified Marxist Leninist (CPN–UML) and the Terai groups responsible for the lack of progress on the constitution drafting? The answer to these questions are of relevance to the theme of this article; it is important that we get the right.

Interestingly, when Nepal ushered in an age of radicalism four years ago, the target was the authoritarian monarchy.[2] What is often ignored in some of the Nepali intellectual debate is that given the unpopularity of the king then, it was not the Maoists but Girija Prasad Koirala, President of the Nepali Congress, who was a cementing force who brought together diverse political parties united only by animosity towards the king. And this led to the formation of the Seven Party Alliance (SPA)[3] against the King's autocratic regime. The Maoist joined the SPA to bring down the king. This broad coalition/political accord of the pro-democratic forces and the Maoist ultimately forced the king to reinstate parliament and cede his powers. However, what is notable is that herein lies the seeds of the inherent contradiction of politics of consensus.

Infact, the major paradox dotting the Nepali political landscape was that the pro-democracy forces and the Maoists had come together only to axe the monarchy and seize power without working out how the void Left by that 250 years-old-institution would be failed. The result was that this orchestrated politics of consensus tumbled soon after the monarchy was gone and the fear of royal comeback diminished. The Unified Communist Party of Nepal-Maoists which emerged as the single largest party in the April 2008 constituent assembly elections, refused to continue with G.P. Koirala's leadership[4] and instead its Chairman Pushpa Kamal Dahal (better known as Prachanda) became the Prime Minister. The Nepali Congress, the party that led the movement for democracy, refused to Join Prachanda. This was the beginning of the end of the politics of consensus. The Maoist-led government, however, proved to be shortlived and collapsed in May 2009 following a conflict with the Nepalese army, bringing to power a fragile coalition of 22 parties headed by Madhav Kumar Nepal of the CPN-UML. This premature end of the Maoist-led government has repolarised the Nepali political landscape into an uncertain future. Once the new coalition government was formed under the CPN-UML leadership the Maoist Party waged a vigorous political campaign against the new coalition government and demanded the resignation of Prime Minister Madhav Kumar Nepal. Ultimately, Madhav Kumar Nepal had to resign on 30 June 2010. In a bizarre record, political parties have failed to elect a new Prime Minister after Madhav Kumar Nepal resigned as Prime Minister and the country is being ruled by an unaccountable government. Actually, due to the acrimonious rift and rivalries between competing political forces the peace process and the writing of the new constitution appears to be stalling. Infact, since the elections of the CA, the political parties have remained involved in numerical game concentrating on the formation of the government or capturing power. As the political parties represented in the constituent assembly have failed to demonstrate friendly environment by developing political consensus among themselves the making of the democratic constitution in time according to the spirit, wishes and needs of the people and the country has become a serious issue.

Political Consensus Drifts Away

In between, the model of federalism and the inclusion of the Maoist combatants into the government army have triggered speculation about the integrity of the nation, perhaps for the first time in its modern history. Actually, Nepal is being dragged into federalism without enough preparation and homework. The decision to federalize Nepal in March 2008 was taken for short-sighted political expediency rather than with a commitment for real reform. The result has been that in Nepal where political parties operate in a highly centralised structure and the political culture lack federal republican contents, the political discourse on federalism currently has no content and no agreed-upon model. The Maoists' version of autonomy[5] did not have democratic contents but a party controlled command structure which hardly corroborates with federal values. The other major political parties have failed to effectively challenge the Maoist concept of federalism. So far as the question of the integration of the Maoist combatants in the army or their rehabilitation in the police and other forces is concerned, this has been the most controversial and contested structural change initiated by the Maoist government headed by Prachanda. Here it seems important to note that for a decade, the two sides—the Nepalese Army and the People's Liberation Army controlled by the country's Maoist forces—fought a savage guerrilla war. Now the peace plan, stemming from the 2006 accord, calls for blending them together. Here it needs reiteration that the Maoist leader, Pushpa Kamal Dahal had to resign as Prime Minister two years ago following his differences with the army chief over the integration of the Maoist combatants.

Actually as long as the broad-based consensus lasted among the pro-democratic parties and the Maoists on the form and direction of changes, the Maoist regime was able to push through major structural reforms without opposition. But once the Maoist government began to implement its plan to integrate its combatants into the army, the move misfired and resistance surfaced not only from the army which was never happy about being treated at par with the Maoists combatants,[6] but also from its closest political allies. However, it was the Maoists' biggest scoring point, not just over the Nepal army but also over all other political parties. Infact, the Nepal's Maoists have been slow to realise and accept this political truth that giving up gun in favour of democratic politics is not a matter of strategy. It calls for an ideological shift and a new approach to politics and power. That is why they retained their People's Liberation Army even after joining mainstream politics.

Lingering Uncertainty

As the main protagonists of the decade-long armed conflict, there was no love lost between the Maoist Party and the Nepal Army. Rather than helping to bridge the low level of trust between the Maoist Party and the Army, activities of various actors and agencies appear to have actually increased the mutual suspicion of the two sides. With the departure of the United Nations Mission in Nepal (UNMIN), on January 15, 2011 winding up its four-year long operation—monitoring the arms and armies of the Maoists and the state, both confined to the barracks—the vexed issue of integration and rehabilitation of the Maoist combatants remain unresolved. This is the most critical deadline buster. Although a high level special committee under the joint command of three major political parties–the UCPN-M, the Nepali Congress, and the CPN-UML has swiftly come into birth to fill the vacuum that the UNMIN's departure had created. It has at least for now erased the fear that in the absence of a more credible and effective instrument, the mission's departure could derail the limited efforts towards rehabilitation and integration of 19,000 Maoist combatants. However, the major political parties, wracked by internal and as well as intra-party conflicts, are nowhere near deciding a clear mechanism on this vexed issue. That is sure to invite future tussle between the state army and the Maoists. The above narrative clearly leads us to state that in the current political context in Nepal, the chances of the constituent assembly delivering the new constitution on the extended deadline seems more uncertain than ever before because there is no commitment yet from the three major political parties that they would sort out their differences on major contentious issues, and above all, due to the obstructionist strategies adopted by the UCPN-M, which have nearly paralysed the constituent assembly.

The Maoists' Obstructionist Strategies

While saying this, it must also be pointed out that if the peace process and constitution-writing in Nepal remain incomplete and its stability faces yet another threat, the Maoists themselves are to blame. Actually the trouble lies squarely with the United Communist Party of Nepal-Maoists—they can not be fitted into a scheme that they are dead against. They themselves known their problem, but how can they change themselves and their ideology? There is not an iota of doubt that the Maoists have used the peace and democratic process to capture the state and moreover they have been able to exploit the situation mainly because of the lust of power among major political parties in Nepal. The major pro-democracy parties like the Nepali Congress and the CPN-UML have grasped the situation now. These parties have said in so many words that Maoists do not want the peace process and the process of writing a constitution to proceed and that a decisive battle is inevitable.[7] This is evident from a Prachanda-sponsored political document at the central committee meeting of the Unified Communist Party of Nepal-Maoists, in the first week of January 2011. The document identifies "domestic reactionary forces" as their principal enemy and signals a call for a people's revolt, if need be, to defeat these forces.[8] The underlying message is loud and clear, that Maoists may anytime change tack, and that their joining the peace and democratic process five years ago is just a tactical one. Obviously, creating a political and constitutional vacuum has been the method that Maoists have been pursuing.

In fact, the United Communist Party of Nepal-Maoists (UCPN-M) has taken the maximum advantage of the situation. The Party is left with limited options: either to declare that the peaceful, democratic platform it chose was only tactical, or to prove with matching action that the idea of armed battle and their dreams of capturing power have been abandoned for ever. Any ambiguity would mean that the Maoists have no faith in the democratic order. But, as the Maoists know they are discredited in the people's esteem and that of their own party cadres, mainly over the lavish lifestyle and corruption-infected public life they led in the past five years, they would bank more on the growing differences among the other political parties. In such a scenario, if at all, the non-Maoist political parties decide to work with the UCPN-M to finish the task of writing the Constitution, that will be on Maoists' terms—to use the hung constituent assembly to endorse their "people's republic constitution", in essence, a communist dictatorship. And current trends show they have not budged an inch from their ultimate goal to establish a people's republic.

It is not surprising that the current phase speculation about the future of the peace process and the unity and integrity of the nation, and peoples frustration and anger that the Nepali Congress, Maoists and the Communist Party of Nepal–Unified Marxist Leninist (CPN-UML) and the Terai groups are responsible for delay in the constitution drafting, do not augur well for the success of a fledging democracy like the one in Nepal. The height of the political irony is that the rise of radical identity politics and the complete collapse of the state's legitimacy have already created a deep malaise in Nepal. Thus considered from each and every angle, four month from now a constitutional crisis/constitutional vacuum over the lack of progress on constitution drafting is very likely in Nepal.

Three-way Polarisation: Potential Deadline Buster

Certainty, with the peace and constitution-making process more uncertain than ever before Nepal's politics is showing early signs of a three-way polarisation. First, the political isolation of the UCPN-M, the underground outfit that led the insurgency to subvert the Nepali state, appears almost complete. The Party appears on the verge of a split and is left with limited options; either to declare that the peaceful, democratic platform it chose was only tactical, or to prove with matching action that the idea of armed battle and their dreams of capturing power have been abandoned for ever. Any ambiguity would mean that the Maoists have no faith in the democratic order. Second, ultra-left groups from various communist parties, mainly the Maoists, are preparing to regroup with the plea "Give us power or we will snatch it anyway". Third, as the post-2006 politics has failed and chances of the new constitution being delivered within the extended deadline of May 28, 2011, appear impossible and the coalition for peace and the new constitution stands almost fragmented, conventional forces are fast regrouping to seek a revival of the constitution of 1991 that favoured constitutional monarchy and multi-party democracy.

Balance-sheet

All this may not be pleasant scenario for Nepal's political future. Of course, such a tussle among different political forces, if sorted out democratically with people's mandate, could consolidate democracy. But that would be a premature conclusion. Hence, it is imperative that the political parties set aside their differences and expedite the process of writing a new constitution. Ultimately, the kind of brinkmanship practiced in Nepali politics, as ironic as it may sound, remains the only source of hope. Otherwise, it would be a terrible price to pay if Nepal slips back into chaos.

END NOTES

1. In January 2009 CPN (Maoist) and CPN (Unity Centre-Masal) were united. The term united is added before its name. So, now the party is known as United Communist Party of Nepal (Maoist): UCPN-M
2. Michael Hutt, *Nepal's Maoist Rebellion*, Hurst and Company, London, 2004, pg.92
3. The SPA was comprised of the Nepali Congress (NC), Communist Party of Nepal–Unified Marxist Leninist (CPN-UML), CPN-Marxist Leninist (CPN-ML), People's Front Nepal (PFN), Nepal Workers Peasants Party (NWPP), Nepal Sadbhavana Party–Anandi Devi (NSP-A) and the Communist Party of India-Maoist (Maoists). These parties have divergent agendas and were not a real alliance *per se*, but served as the face of the Government after King Gyanendra was removed from power.
4. Koirala was re-elected in April 2007 to head a coalition government and the Maoists joined the government accepting Koirala as the Prime Minister and the head of the 'New Nepal'.
5. Maoists have suggested creation of federal units on caste and ethnic lines with right to self-determination.
6. In the sense that both armies remained confined to their designated camps and barracks as long as the UNMIN was in Nepal. For details also see, Shova Gautam "Nepal Senako Loktantrikaran", Kantipur Daily, Kathmandu, 2 August 2009, pg.7
7. Yubraj Ghimire, "Not by fiery rhetoric alone", *The Indian Express*, New Delhi, 18 December, 2010, pg.12
8. Pranab Dhal Samanta, 'The other K-word", *The Indian Express*, New Delhi, 7 January, 2011, pg.12

23

Contentious Issues in Nepal's Constitutional Evolution

ANJANA JHA

Introduction

The present paper comprises three parts. The first part briefly traces the origin and development of Nepal's chaotic political conditions from 1990 to the present. The second part analyses the main contentious issues which have given rise to the present constitutional crisis in Nepal. In the concluding third part, the paper makes certain observations about the prospects of the constitutional crisis in Nepal.

Political Development from 1990 to 2008

Until 1990, Nepal was an absolute monarchy under the executive control of the king. Faced with a people's movement against absolute monarchy, King Birendra, in 1990, agreed to a large-scale political Referendum by creating a parliamentary monarchy with the King as the head of the state and a prime minister as the head of the government. Nepal's legislature was bicameral consisting of a House of Representatives and a National Council. The House of Representatives consists of 205 members directly elected by the people. The National Council had 60 members: 10 nominated by the king, 35 elected by the House of Representatives and the remaining 15 elected by an electoral college made up of chairs of villages and towns. The Legislature had a five year term, but was dissolved by the king before its term could end. All Nepalese citizens of 18 years and above became eligible to vote. The executive comprised the king and the Council of Ministers. The leader of the coalition or party securing the maximum seats in an election was appointed as the prime minister. The Ministers of the cabinet were appointed by the king on the recommendation of the Prime Minister. However, governments in Nepal were highly unstable; no government could survive for more than two years since 1991, either due to internal strife or dissolution of Parliament by the monarch.[1] The Judiciary was composed of the Supreme Court of Nepal, appellate courts and various trial courts. The Chief Justice of the Supreme Court was appointed by the monarch on the recommendations of the constitutional council; the other judges were appointed by the monarch on the recommendation of the judicial council. Nepal's judiciary was legally separate from the executive and legislative branches and had the power of judicial review under the Constitution.

1996: Maoist Insurgency

In February 1996, the Communist Party of Nepal (Maoist) began a violent insurgency in more than 50 of the country's 75 districts. From February 1996, the phase that witnessed the birth and rapid expansion of Maoist insurgency, up to April 2006 when it gave up violence, the Maoist conflict resulted in the loss of more than 15,000 lives including those of the police, civilians and insurgents; causing widespread devastation worth billions of rupees, and leading to internal displacement of more than 60,000 people.[2] In July 2001 Prime Minister Deuba announced a ceasefire, which the Maoist pledged to observe. Although Maoist-instigated intimidation and extortion continued, the killings had largely subsided since the ceasefire was announced. The government and Maoists held talks an August and September 2001.

Political parties agreed in 1991 that the monarchy would continue, to enhance political stability and provide an important symbol of national identity for the culturally diverse Nepali people. The king exercised limited powers, including the right to declare a state of Emergency in the event of war or armed revolt on the advice of the council of ministers and the prime minister. According to the Constitution, the king's declaration of a state of Emergency must be approved by a two-third majority of the House of Representatives.

Royal Massacre

On 1 June 2001, crown Prince Dipendra was officially reported to have shot and killed his father, King Birendra, his mother, Queen Aishwarya, his brother, his sister, his father's brother, Prince Dhirendra, and several aunts, before turning the gun on himself. Although he never regained consciousness before dying, Crown Prince Dipdendra was nonetheless the king under the laws of Nepalese royal succession. After his death two days later, the late king's surviving brother Gyanendra was proclaimed king.

Suspension of Parliament and Loktantra Andolan

On 1 February, 2005 King Gyanendra suspended the Parliament, appointed a government led by himself, and enforced martial law. The king argued that civilian politicians were unfit to handle the Maoist insurgency. Telephone lines were cut and several high profile political leaders were detained. Other opposition leaders fled to India and regrouped there. A broad coalition called the Seven Party Alliance (SPA) was formed in opposition to the royal takeover, encompassing the seven parliamentary parties that held about 90 per cent of the seats in the dissolved Parliament. In response to events in Nepal, the United Nations set up a monitoring programme in 2005 to assess and observe the human rights situation there. On 22 November 2005, the Seven Party Alliance of parliamentary parties and the Communist Party of Nepal (Maoist) agreed on a historic and unprecedented 12-point Memorandum of Understanding (MOU) for peace and democracy. Nepalese from various walks of life and the international community regarded the MOU as an appropriate political response to the crisis that was developing in Nepal. Against the backdrop of the sufferings of the Nepalese people and the enormous human cost of the last ten years of violent conflict, the MOU, which proposed a peaceful transition through an elected Constituent Assembly, created an acceptable formula for a united movement for democracy. As per the 12-point MOU, the SPA called for a protest movement, and the Communist Party of Nepal (Maoist) supported it. This led to a countrywide uprising that started in April 2006. All political forces including civil society and professional organizations actively organized the people. This resulted in massive and spontaneous demonstrations and rallies held across Nepal against King Gyanendra's autocratic rule.

The people's participation was so broad, momentous and pervasive that the king feared being overthrown. On 21 April 2006, King Gyanendra declared that "power would be returned to the people". This had little effect on the people, who continued to occupy the streets of Kathmandu and other towns, openly defying the daytime curfew. Finally king Gyanendra announced the restatement of the House of Representatives, thereby conceding one of the major demands of the SPA, at midnight on 24 April 2006. Following this action the coalition of political forces decided to call off the protests. On 19 May 2006, the Parliament assumed total legislative power and gave executive power to the government of Nepal (previously known as His

Majesty's government). Names of many institutions including the army, were stripped of the "royal" adjective and the Raj Parishad (a Council's of the king's advisers) was abolished. The activities of the King became subject to parliamentary scrutiny and the king's properties were subjected to taxation. Moreover, Nepal was declared a secular state abrogating the previous status of a Hindu Kingdom. In July 2006, the Prime Minister, G.P. Koirala sent a letter to the United Nations announcing the intention of the Nepalese government to hold elections to a constituent assembly by April 2007.

Abolition of the Monarchy

On 23 December, 2007, an agreement was made for the monarchy to be abolished and the country to become a federal republic with the Prime Minister becoming Head of State.[3] In May 2008 democratic elections for the 601-seat Constituent Assembly, the Communist Party of Nepal (Maoist) got the largest 220 seats amidst a general atmosphere of fear and intimidation from all sides.[4] A federal republic was established in May 2008, with the only four members of the 601-seat Constituent Assembly voting against the change;[5] which ended 240 years of royal rule in Nepal. The government announced a public holiday for three days from 28 May to 30 May 2008 to celebrate the country becoming a federal republic.

Events 2008 Onwards

Major parties such or the United Communist Party of Nepal (Maoist), Community Party of Nepal (United Marxist-Leninist) and the Nepali Congress agreed to write a Constitution that would replace the interim one with the time limit of two years. However, non-cooperative behaviour of the political parties has been cited as the major cause behind the derailing of the peace process. The Maoist, as the largest party of the country, took power immediately after the elections were held and named Pushpa Kumar Dahal or Prachanda as the Prime Minister of the country. The CPN(UML) also joined the government, but the Nepali Congress decided to play the role of the main opposition party. People soon saw that the country's situation deteriorated and political turmoil were in store Prachanda soon fell into a dispute with the then Army Chief, Rookmangud Katwal, and decided to remove him. But the President of Nepal, Ram Baran Yadav, as the Supreme Commander of the Amed Forces, in the country, revoked this decision and gave the Army Chief an extension. An angry Prachanda and his party quit the government, mainly citing this reason and decided to be the main opposition to the government headed by CPN (UML) and co-partner Nepali Congress. Madhav Kumar Nepal was named the Prime Minister. The Maoists have been to this date demanding civilian supremacy to that of the army. This created turmoil in the country and showed vividly that development was a pipe dream and the political leaders were just wrangling for power. The Maoists have been forcing closures (bandhs) in the country and have also named autonomous states for almost all the ethnic groups in the country, which is seen as a part of revenge against the action that foiled their bid to remove the Army Chief. Political leaders are discussing plans to end this turmoil, but all steps taken so far have failed. Many observers opine that this freedom has brought anarchy to the country. Many do not even believe that the political parties will succeed in writing a Constitution.

On 2 May 2010 the Maoists started an indefinite general strike, demanding the resignation of Prime Minister Madhav Kumar Nepal, who headed an alliance of ten parties and had the support of a dozen more. "This is the most corrupt and ineffectual government in the history of Nepal," Prachanda is reported to have said. "It was ready to enter into a clandestine agreement with the Indian government and barter away national security. Any other government would have resigned on moral grounds after the deal was scrapped by Parliament. The Prime Minister is a man who lost the election from two constituencies. Only the Prime Minister's resignation can create an atmosphere for dialogue."[6] On 28 May 2010, the Nepali lawmakers extended the tenure of the Constituent Assembly by one year which served to keep hopes for a democratic constitutional republic and stable nation alive and Prime Minister Madhav Kumar Nepal resigned on 30 June 2010.[7]

Contentious Issues in Constitutional Crisis

Though the political crisis has been defused by extending the tenure of the Constituent Assembly and resignation of Madhav Kumar Nepal, yet the constitutional crisis remains real and dangerous. While a political crisis was averted on 28 May 2010, the drafting of the new Constitution still remains the most contentious issue for more reasons than one. The three big political parties—United Communist Party of Nepal-Maoists (UCPN-M), the Nepali Congress and the Communist Party of Nepal-United Marxist-Leninist (CPN-UML)—which together form more than two-third majority in the House which is required to frame the new Constitution—reached an understanding to complete the assigned role within the new time-frame. The accord signed by three mainstream parties on 28 May 2010, also stated that the Maoist would agree to honour the past commitments like returning the property the party had confiscated from political opponents and ordinary people during the decade-long insurgency. In addition, they also agreed to transform the Young Communist League (YCL) into a civilian outfit and work earnestly for rehabilitation and integration of the Maoist combatants in the Society and Security agencies of the state. However, the ink had barely dried on the signing of the accord before the three parties began squabbling over the last minute, three-point political agreement. The State and politics of Nepal are guided and dictated by the confusion and uncertainty because each top political leader wants to become Prime Minister and therefore, each uses the leverage on other parties to bargain and weaken the opponents within the same party. Yet, the three parties agreed to extend the tenure of the Constituent Assembly for two important reasons: First, they preferred collective survival to joint death. Second, people were feeling betrayed by the inability of the House to frame the Constitution and there was tremendous international pressure from the United Nations, the United States and the European Union to have the term extended so that a legitimate institution of the people does not disappear suddenly. They felt that its absence would aggravate the existing political authority vacuum. Now the question arises: What are the contentious issues that have come in the way of writing the Constitution and given rise to constitutional crisis in Nepal?

The three parties have major differences on at least twenty contentious issues that range from the model of governance to federalism to the independence of the judiciary. Some of the important contentious issues may be mentioned as follows:

First, there is no unanimity among the parties about the form of government—whether presidential or parliamentary or hybrid. Second, they have also failed to agree on the type of federalism to be adopted. Neither the number of states to be formed nor the basis of state formation has been agreed upon. While the Maoists want Nepal split into 12 provinces—mostly on the basis of ethnicity—with the right to self-determination, the two other parties fearing its consequences on national unity, are still not clear about the basis of federalism. Third, the Maoists want a judiciary accountable and servile to the legislature with the provision that judges could be hand-picked by the people's representative body, but the Nepali Congress is in favour of an impartial and independent judiciary. Fourth, while the Maoists want an executive president and UML wants a directly elected Prime Minister, the Nepali Congress continues to harp on parliamentary democracy which is detested most by the Maoists. Fifth, the Maoists have been insisting that they would want a People's Republic in Nepal in which the competing parties would need the endorsement of only one national party i.e., the UCPN-M to operate legally. Their intermittent cry that they would capture state power only makes politics and future of Nepal uncertain as a democracy besides forcing pro-democracy parties to rely more on the security agencies of the state—mainly the Nepal Army—to defeat such a move if and when it comes.

Sixth, the Maoists' guerrilla army—the People's Liberation Army (PLA)—has proved to be one of the most serious obstacles to a negotiated settlement. There are nearly 19,600 PLA Combatants, who, as per the peace pact of 2006, were to have been inducted into the national army. However, the army as well as the ruling parties are now against the merger after a leaked video tape showed Prachanda claiming that his party had inflated the PLA's strength in order to control the army.[8] The ruling parties have insisted that the Maoists must empty their guerilla cantonments first and dismantle the Young Communist League (YCL) which is actually paramilitary in nature, before PLA fighters are inducted into the army. The ruling parties also maintain that no more than 3500 PLA fighters would be taken into the army. The generals of the Nepali army, who waged the war against the Maoist guerillas and backed the monarchy are deeply hostile to the integration of their former foes into the army's ranks. The Maoists have refused to discharge the PLA, though they had pledged to do so when they signed a peace pact in 2006, using their parallel army as a bargaining tool to return to power.[9] The army and the government claim that the PLA has only 3000 former fighters, while the Maoists put the figure at 19000. The numbers are crucial for both sides. The UCPN-M confronts growing discontent from its cadres, who have been languishing in squalid cantonments for nearly four years. The government which wants to keep the army on the side, is intent on minimising the numbers. Army Chief of Nepal, Chhtraman Singh Gurung is reported to have said that the Maoists combatants could not be admitted to the army as a group and their entry would be considered on individual basis provided they fulfill other qualifications. The issue of integrating the Maoist combatants in the security agencies is the single most contentious issue that has the potential to spoil the ongoing peace process. The fact that the two rivals who fought for almost half a decade do not trust each other is understandable.

Seventh, the United Nations Mission in Nepal (UNMIN) was invited for a limited role in the peace process. With UNMIN's arrival in June 2006, the Nepal army was forced to confine itself in the barracks and this may continue until the Maoist combatants are integrated and rehabilitated. There is discomfiture in the army which feels humiliated in being "equated with rebels". UNMIN's initial one year term is being extended continuously for an additional sixth months. Though from 15 January 2011, the UN stops being directly involved in the peace process, it will continue to monitor the state of Nepal's peace process for three further years.[10] However quite often UNMIN is branded as carrying a "pro-Maoist bias" by the non-Maoist parties as well as the Nepal Army. In March 2010, Army Chief Chhatraman Singh Gurung told Lynn B. Pascoe, the UN's envoy to Nepal and UN Undersecretary for Political Affairs that Nepal army is not going to be confined in the barracks indefinitely.

Eighth, another serious situation has developed over fresh recruitment in the Nepalese Army that has been planned by the government. On the 27 July 2010, the Supreme Court quashed the writ filed against recruitment initiated by the Army over filling up of technical posts. The court said that the issue was one that should be resolved by the joint Monitoring Committee set up specifically for the purpose and that court would not intervene. Following the verdict, the Nepal Army has taken steps to fill up vacancies of 3464 personnel in the infantry. The contention of the Army and the defence ministry is that it is only filling up the vacancies that have occurred since signing of the accord and the total strength is well within the ceiling of 95000—a number that was the strength of the Army at the time of the signing of the Peace Accord.

The Maoists have been protesting over the recruitment as a clear violation of the accord. They have declared that they would also be recruiting to fill up the vacancy in the PLA. Their contention is that their present strength is only 19000 against the strength of 31000 they had at the time of Peace Accord. UNMIN has appealed the government and the Maoist to respect the post agreement and act in good faith. The steps that are being taken by both the parties are retrograde ones that will have an adverse impact on the peace process and eventually the stability of the country.[11] Ninth, the Maoists insisted right from the beginning that the Nepal Army must be downsized. "Why should we need this army that is full of rapists and corrupted officers,"[12] Prachanda, is reported to have said during his maiden press conference that marked the end of underground politics at the official residence of the then Prime Minister G.P. Koirala on 2 June 2006. The Nepal Army continued to be his target after he became the Prime Minister in July 2008. He stopped recruitment in the army against regular vacancies and removed General Rookmangud Kotwal as Army Chief on 3 May 2009 which was vetoed by President Ram Baran Yadav under pressure from 18 major political parties. These political parties were of the opinion that Prachanda wanted to divide and destroy the Nepal Army and spread a psychological message that once the army was weak, "the state can be captured.[13] The competition for Security among rival parties made it difficult for the negotiated settlement of the task of framing the Constitution. Tenth, the Comprehensive Peace Agreement (CPA) signed on 21 November 2006—that forms the basis of the peace process—refers to democratization of the Nepal Army, but does not make any mention the model of Disarmament, Demobilization and Reintegration (DDR) and Security Sector Reform (SSR) to be followed. The European Union (EU), particularly the United Kingdom is in favour of SSR, a model that the Maoists have lent their weight behind. The EU is keenly interested, for the first time, in the two crucial areas of formulating Nepal's defence policy and restructuring the Army.

Eleventh, the question of the nature of secularism is another contentious issue which poses serious problem. Nepal's identity as Unitary Hindu Kingdom suddenly changed into a Secular and Federal Democratic Republic. The EU is openly asserting that the secular Nepal must guarantee in its future Constitution the right to religious conversion. The issue has far serious connotation and is now being objected to by several groups of Hindus—both moderate and hardliners—who together constitute more than 80 per cent of the total population. Thus the issues of security and faith are getting linked, closely and this development may lead to serious consequences. The Hindus in Terai are seething with discontent and demanding the reservation of Hindu identity of Nepal. Twelfth, the issue of arms supply by India is also a debatable question. The EU is against arms supply being resumed because it feels that it goes against the spirit of the peace process, while India is keen to lift the embargo it had imposed during the Royal takeover. According to some Nepalese people this is against the 1950 treaty of peace and Friendship and subsequent exchange of Letters (1965) on arms supply.

Thirteenth, by hijacking the political movement through the tactics of political bickering, regular strikes, protests and clashes to cripple the movement towards democracy and forcing the exit of the king of Nepal, the Maoists claim that they alone have spearheaded the democratic movement in Nepal. Prachanda also asserted that he would like to be the first president of Nepal. He ignored the fact that there were many other political leaders who had struggled along the political path for long years. Moreover, they were far more deserving candidates than Prachanda whose sole claim to prominence was notoriety as a leader of the Maoist armed insurgency in Nepal.[14] Fourteenth, the Terai region of Nepal is also seething with discontent. In February 2007, political disturbances and violence broke out in Nepal's Terai region. The Terai region is the long strip of the plains of Nepal adjoining Indian Territory and is inhabited by the Madhesias: an ethnic group of Awadhi, Maithili and Bhojpuri descent. They form 35 per cent of Nepali's total population. Despite their sizeable proportion in the total population they have long been discriminated as second class citizens of Nepal in terms of job opportunities in administration and in representation in the political set up of the country. This, despite the fact that the Madhesias of the Terai region make an overwhelming contribution to the Nepalese economy, both agriculture and industry.[15]

At present, the entire Terai region is in a state of massive unrest and violence has already claimed twenty lives. The spark that ignited the latest unrest among the Medhesias was the killing of their political activist by the Nepalese Maoists' cadres. It was also due to the arrest of their activists in Kathmandu who were protesting against the draft constitution which seemed to have ignored their political concerns and aspirations. Their main demands include proportional political representation and federal structure. The Maoists blame India for generating the Madhesia political turbulence. This political movement poses a serious challenge to the Nepalese Maoists because their call for proportional political representation would thwart the political hold of the Maoist in Nepal. Moreover, the Maoists would be well aware that even if they acquire full political control over Nepal, the Madhesias would continue to have a stranglehold over the Nepalese. Lifelines as all the arteries that run from India to the landlocked Mountain Kingdom of Nepal pass through Madhesia districts and that Nepal depends heavily on the Terai region for its food production. The political turbulence in Madhesia can be said to be a spillover of the new political dynamics that the Nepalese Maoists imposed on Nepal through their armed insurgency and their backdoor entry into the Nepalese political space. The Madhesias too seem to be calling for a change of status-quo in the discrimination that they have suffered so far.[16]

Finally, and above all, constitutional crisis goes hand-in-hand with economic crisis. Nepal today is facing "Shortages of the four basic agricultural sources—land, water, energy and fertilizer. No nation can isolate itself from these scarcities or their economic and political consequences."[17] Climate change has also led to scarcity of water. Issues like terrorism, globalization, and transnational social movements are weakening the capacity of state to create public order, provide service delivery and settle problems and conflicts. Around 3.5 million people are officially declared as hit by food scarcity. Around 35 glaciers out of 2000 in the country are listed as being close to danger point of bursting. This could have disastrous consequences with its effect spilled beyond the border of the country. All these do not augur well for a country known in the past for its social and religions amity as well as land of peace. The nature of economic crisis becomes quite clear by the official statistics which indicate: over 13 per cent inflation accompanied by excessive high price of food; famine like situation in far West Nepal, particularly in Mugu and Humla areas; balance of payment deficit standing at 22.1 billion rupees and remittance growth rate falling to 9.6 per cent from 60.3 per cent in a year; and government's inability to spend more than 26.7 per cent of budget estimate on capital expenditure.[18] Various factors such as financial indiscipline, NRB's failure to appropriately supervise the financial and banking sector, liquidity crunch, unproductive and uncommercialized farming, power outage, labour problems in industrial yards and business fronts, scarcity of water for people and their farms, excessive import, diminishing export, wasteful use of resources, inability to utilize existing roads properly for transporting people and goods have contributed in their own way to building up the crisis.[19]

Conclusion

These contentious issues are the stumbling blocks in current negotiations. Confronted with above-mentioned contentious issues, Nepal is stepping uncertainly into what will now be its seventh Constitution-making exercise, but with two differences from before: the absence of an authoritarian monarch and the involvement of the erstwhile Maoist rebels. Unfortunately there is nothing to indicate that the performance of the Assembly during the 12 month extension will be any different from that of the preceding 24 months. The question is naturally asked: if two years were not enough for elected representatives to draft the Constitution, what difference does an additional year make? Peace becomes artificial and temporary, only to be threatened intermittently by the parties themselves. To build a country from scratch is no light business. Nepal is a poor country with adult literacy rate at 57.9 per cent and an infant mortality rate of 85.5 deaths for every 1000 children under the age of five. There is a lot at stake. Nearly half of the country's population live in abject poverty and have no adequate means of livelihood. Inflation has skyrocketed and food prices have gone through the roof. Given the looming spectra of famine in many districts, massive unemployment, and a domestic economy brought to its knees by power shortages and labour stoppages, a shared sense of history and compassion towards the public is required rather than platitudes to party ideology.

After all, constitution making can be a deeply divisive and avidly political process. But if the process is to succeed this time, the year ahead must be different from the past in the following ways:

(i) The relationship between 601 constituent Assembly members and the body politic needs to be enriched and made more transparent to enable a consistent and cordial dialogue.

(ii) The process, needs to be clearly explained to ensure public knowledge of and requisite participation in drafting the legal framework that will define the country's collective future.

(iii) Progress made and areas where there is still conflict between the drafters needs to be shared publicly.

(iv) A civility of dialogue and disagreement needs to characterize the discourse that exists among the various political parties, within and outside the Assembly.

If managed well, the present year can mark the beginning of the maturation of Nepal's democratic culture. However, unlike other Constituent Assemblies that led countries such as South Africa or India through successful transitions to progressive constitutional democracies, no one political party in Nepal holds even a simple majority of seats in the House. This means that from its inception, Nepal's Constituent Assembly lacks a cohesive political and historical vision that such a process requires. The people of Nepal have neither the benefit of politicians who display a sense of history, nor a political party that can push through its brand of constitutionalism by virtue of Sheer majority. Sadly for Nepal, a leader who projects a moral force and enjoys national credibility like a compassionate, dignified Nelson Mandela or an adroit legal mind Like India's Ambedkar is nowhere to be found. Thus, Nepal is facing the most severe constitutional Crisis it has ever known in a turbulent history marked by massacres, coups, two pro-democracy protests and the overthrow of the royal family. So the answer of the question of "What does the future hold?" is still uncertain.

END NOTES

1. In the first free and fair general elections in Nepal in 1991, the Nepali Congress got the maximum seats and formed the government. In 1994 election, defeat of the Nepali Congress Party by the Communist Party of Nepal (United Marxist-Leninist) CPN, (UML) made Nepal the first Communist monarchy in Asia, with Man Mohan Adhikari as Prime Minister. In mid 1994, parliament was dissolved due to dissension within the Nepali Congress. The subsequent general election, held on 15 November 1994, gave no party a majority and led to several years of unstable coalition governments. In May, 1999 general elections, the Nepali Congress Party once again headed a majority government. There have been three Nepali Congress Prime Minister since 1999 elections: K P Bhattarai (31 May, 1999-17 March, 2000); Girija Prasad Koirala (20 March, 2000-19 July, 2001); and Sher Bahadur Deuba (23 July 2001-03). King Gyanendra discharged Sher Bahadur Deuba and appointed Surya Bahadur Thapa as Prime Minister on 4 June, 2003. "Politics of Nepal", *Wikipedia*, The Free Encyclopedia, pg.1
2. Yubraj Ghimire, *"Nepal: Impact of Internal Conflict on Security"*, CSA-Intra-state Conflicts and Effects, Delhi, 30 September, 2010
3. Binaj Gurubacharya, "Nepal to Abolish Monarchy", *Time*, London, 24 December, 2007
4. *www.international-alert.org/sites/.../Consolidating_Peace_Nepal.pdf*, accessed on February 10, 2011
5. "Nepal votes to abolish Monarchy", *BBC News*, 28 May, 2008
6. Sudeshna Sarkar, *ISN Security Watch*, 22 July, 2010
7. *BBC NEWS*, 30 June, 2010

8. *Op. cit.,* no.1
9. *TNN,* 4 December, 2010
10. *www.international-alert.org/.../consolidating-peace-nepali-constitution...,* accessed on February 1, 2011
11. S Chandrashekharan, *Nepal: Political Stalemate* Continues no. 229, South Asia Analysis Group, 5 August, 2010
12. *www.indigenousportal.com/.../Nepal-Failure-to-Comply-with-the- ...,* accessed on April 30, 2011
13. *www.himalmag.com/.../743-confusion-in-constitution-making-nepal...,* accessed on August 10, 2011
14. *www.ibanet.org/Document/Default.aspx?DocumentUid...9BEF...,* accessed on September 1, 2011
15. Subhas Kapila, "Nepal: Political Turbulence from a New Quarter", 17 February, 2007
16. *www.idea.int/publications/creating_the_new_constitution/np.cfm,* accessed on February 27, 2011
17. *www.indianexpress.com/news/will-guarantee-security...nepal.../,* accessed on August 22, 2011
18. *www.gorkhapatra.org.np/gopa.detail.php?article_id=51673&cat...,* accessed on September 19, 2011
19. *www.groundreport.com/.../A...Constitution...Constitution.../2940969,* accessed on February 11, 2011

24

Constitutional Development in Nepal: Need to Forge Consensus

BIPIN KUMAR RAI

Nepal at the moment is passing through the most crucial phase of history ever since its foundation in the late 18th century. With the enactment of the Interim Constitution (IC) in January 2007 the CPN (Maoist) became a legitimate political force and had seats both in the interim Parliament and the government. The preparation for the Constituent Assembly (CA) elections and the peace process had taken place simultaneously. In April 2008, elections for the Constituent Assembly were held in which the CPN (Maoist) emerged as the single largest party in a house of 601 members. However, following a conflict with the Nepalese army, Maoist Prime Minister Pushpa Kamal Dahal 'Prachanda' resigned in May 2009, bringing to power a fragile coalition of 22 parties headed by Madhav Kumar Nepal of the Communist party of Nepal—Unified Marxist Leninist (CPN-UML). Since its abrupt resignation from the government, the Maoists have been using civilian supremacy as a potent battle cry to wage a vigorous political campaign in Parliament as well as in the street. The major parties, all internally divided, have failed to come together and settle critical issues, including the model of federalism and governance that the future Constitution must put forth. In fact, the existing political instability, intra and inter-party conflicts and their unhealthy competition for sharing power and their low priority towards Constitution making and settling the controversial issues, have further complicated the process of Constitution-making and reconciliation. Against this background, this article seeks to explain and analyse the critical issues that Nepal is likely to face in the drafting of the Constitution in time. In this context, it is important to note that the political parties have to demonstrate strong political will and dedication for completion of their task according to the people's mandate. If the political parties fail to draft the Constitution in time they will loose both the people's faith and international recognition. It is a well-known fact that the people of Nepal have been misled many a time in the name of the Constitution. But earlier attempts at democracy were being made by monarchs. This time all the political parties across the nation have joined hands to draft a Constitution which will address the problems of the people.[1] There has been a problem in meeting the deadline; the divided opinions among the political parties have created confusion on the major issues vis-à-vis the Constitution. There is a stiff tussle between the Maoists and Nepali Congress on many issues: state restructuring, forms of governance, modality of federalism, constitutional bodies, state organs, and fundamental rights, among others.

The earlier Constitutions of Nepal failed to establish rapport with the people. The beginning of the Interim Constitution of 1951 established the Supreme Court and independent Public Service Commission. Within two years, the then King Tribhuvan started violating the Constitutional provisions. The impartial election of a Constituent Assembly was blocked. The King disallowed holding of the CA as well as parliamentary elections. The next attempt at Constitution-making was started by his son, King Mahendra. In 1955, with the death of King Tribhuvan, his eldest son, Mahendra became the new king. On 12 February 1957, he promulgated a Constitution and held the first parliamentary election in 1959. The Nepali Congress (NC) won the election and formed its government. On 15 December 1960, however, Mahendra staged a *coup d'etat,* dismissed the elected government, banned political parties, and imprisoned all prominent political leaders.[2] King Mahendra introduced the Panchayat system under his dictatorship, which lasted for thirty years. The Panchayat system tried to homogenize the country by adopting one religion (Hindu), one language Khas as Nepali, one culture and one-nation policy under the pretext of 'Nepali nationalism'. It systematically suppressed the ethnic languages and cultures.[3]

In 1971, with the death of King Mahendra, his eldest son Birendra inherited the throne and the Panchayat system. In 1979, a spontaneous students' protest movement forced King Birendra to proclaim a Referendum seeking people's opinion whether to retain the Panchayat system with reforms or to reintroduce multi-party democracy in Nepal. The Referendum in 1980 gave victory to the Panchayat with reforms, so all the political parties had to suffer prohibition once again. However, they continued their struggle for restoration of the multi-party system. Finally, a People's Movement (Jan Andolan), succeeded in forcing the king to lift the ban on the political parties on 8 April 1990.[4] King Birendra reluctantly transferred sovereign power to the people with the promulgation of the Constitution in 1990.[5] The Constitution, however, failed to address the problems of the neglected communities and ethnic nationalities, the Madhesis, the non-Hindu population, the Dalits, socially disadvantaged low castes, and women.[6] It also maintained Nepal as a Hindu kingdom and reasserted a single Khas language as Nepali, the official language of Nepal, as the Panchayat Constitution had done. According to this Constitution, the people of Nepal were identified as the source of political legitimacy and they were guaranteed basic rights.

The first decade under the new Constitution was marked by frequent elections and unstable governments. Experiments with all forms of government were being carried out. But the democratic system failed to make deeper inroads into Nepal's politics. With the introduction of the 1990 Constitution, powers of the king had been considerably reduced. The king and other members of the royal family, however, could not adjust to the change easily. In general, King Birendra behaved as a constitutional monarch and acted as a stabilizing factor, but one faction in the palace led by his brother, Gyanendra and queen mother, Ratna Rajya always opposed the loss of royal power and it is believed that they played an active role in weakening political parties, so as to regain the lost power of the palace.[7] Soon after the palace massacre, the game of toppling Prime Minister Girija Prasad Koirala began within his own party—this time none other than his own protégé, Sher Bahadur Deuba, was on the warpath and succeeded in bringing him down. On 22 May 2002, Prime Minister Deuba dissolved the elected Parliament as he failed to gain support from his own party to extend the state of emergency for the third time. On 4 October 2002, however, King Gyanendra abruptly removed Deuba and took over executive power by overstepping the Constitution.[8] The politics of Nepal was trapped in a vicious cycle with political bickering within the political parties. Against the King's authoritarian move, five major political parties, though remaining loyal to constitutional monarchy, intensified their agitations. Amidst increasing anti-king agitations, Gyanendra reluctantly reinstated Deuba whom he had sacked two years ago as the Prime Minister, on 5 July 2004. However, on 1 February 2005 King Gyanendra suddenly staged a *coup d'etat*, which further damaged the already unpopular monarchy in Nepal. This polarized the political system of Nepal completely, and led to the formation of seven-party alliance (SPA) against the King's autocratic regime. With the formation of the SPA, the second Jan Andolan began. The SPA with active support from the Maoists launched their decisive agitations from 6 April 2006, which drew huge support of the people from various walks of life. On 18 May 2006, the reinstated Parliament revoked all the powers of the King and declared Nepal a secular state. It also declared nationalization of all properties he had obtained by virtue of being king. Furthermore, Nepal received its interim Constitution on 15 January 2007,[9] which completely deprived King Gyanendra of any executive rights. With the success of the second Jan Andolan many radical steps were initiated. It ended the monarchy and restored the people's power and the Parliament. Later, the interim Parliament and interim government were formed jointly by the SPA and the Maoists. Both parties agreed to introduce a "peace accord". This accord led to the election of the Constitutional Assembly in April 2008.[10] With the election of the CA, it has been vested with dual responsibility—to draft the Constitution and to help the CA function as the Parliament. It must be stated that the Constituent Assembly has been tasked with drafting a new Constitution and fundamentally reshaping the government as part of the peace process. A body of 601 members, the most representative assembly that Nepal has ever had, has been formed. It represents most of the country's political forces, from the revolutionary Communist Party of Nepal (Maoist) to the regionalist Madhesi Janadhikar Forum as well as a variety of fringe parties. There is considerable hope among the people of Nepal that this time the Constitution will reshape the economic and social fabric of the country.[11] It is the Constitutional Committee that has the responsibility for formulating the final draft. The report must consist of thematic and other recommendations. Thereafter, a proper debate at different levels has to follow. The fundamental steps of the process are: discussing the first draft in a full session of the CA, taking the draft Constitution to the public, interacting with experts on the draft, distributing it to the CA members to study, and discussing each article and passing it by two-thirds in majority in the CA. Yet the job seems ominously difficult, given that the committees have resolved little on matters where there are major differences, particularly between the Maoists and the rest. Instead, the committees have helped to further polarize the political parties.

The major political division is on the subject of federalism, integration of the Nepalese Army and linguistic and ethnic division of the state. The logic for federalism in Nepal has three major grounds: (i) the plural and diverse composition of Nepali society, (ii) strengthening democracy from the bottom, and (iii) speeding up development process in a more equitable and efficient manner. For the second and third reasons, federalism may not be an essential criterion and can be achieved even under a unitary state. However, Nepal's experience with decentralization and development efforts for more than half a century did not yield such results. But the aspirations for identity and autonomy can be best assured under federalism. Nepali society is so diverse and plural that it requires multi-layer polity to maintain unity. Federal polity is considered as an accepted solution to this problem.[12] It is therefore a new process of reordering the state-society relations based on democratic principles and community rights.

With the successful election of the CA, the emotional phase of federalism has slowed down. Now is the time to translate federalism into political reality with objectivity. The Constituent Assembly is expected to chalk out the constitutional structure of federalism. But there is more to it than that. Before the formal draft is announced, political leaders require engaging in a series of consultations, negotiations and compromises. Nepal's process of federalization as elsewhere involves three major but interrelated dimensions—identification of territorial units that corroborate with the ethno-regional setting of the population; multi-level division of power and distribution of jurisdictional authority; and maintenance of unity and stability consistent with federal values and culture. This requires immense homework with sound technical backup.[13] It is the foremost challenge. Another issue is related to the Nepalese Army. In fact, of the entire gamut of structural changes initiated by the post-monarchical regime, none has been more contested as controversial than the one to alter the form and structure of the Nepali military. Indeed, the Maoist government collapsed in 2009 precisely after its handling of the Nepali Army. The People's Liberation Army is controlled by the country's Maoist forces. For a decade, the two sides fought a savage guerrilla war. Now the peace plan, stemming from the 2006 accord, calls for blending them together. But the problem is: how to do it?

There are also problems with the exhaustive list of Fundamental Rights and Directive Principles of State Policy released by the Committee on Fundamental Rights and Directive Principles. The report of the Committee on the Rights of Minority and Marginalised Communities has also created controversies by putting forth ambiguous provisions as to the compensation to be paid by the state to certain communities for past abuses against them. In the same vein, the Committee on Determination of Structure of Constitutional Bodies has proposed 11 independent commissions to deal with issues specific to Madhesis, Dalits, indigenous peoples and others, substantially limiting the role of the elected government in the affairs of the state.

Last but not the least, the Unified Communist Party of Nepal (Maoists) wants a presidential system, with direct elections and a limited-role legislature. The Maoists feel that the promises of their revolution cannot be delivered through a parliamentary system with all the density of checks and balances it entails. In 1996, the Maoists walked away from the Parliament to start their 'people's war' calling the Parliament a 'butcher shop that hangs goat heads to sell dog meat.' A return to the parliamentary system makes the Maoists' 'sacrifices' futile. On the other hand, the Nepali Congress (NC), the second largest party, vehemently opposes the presidential system. NC has a 60-year history of fighting for the parliamentary system and having had the opportunity to rule over Nepal for seven of the nine years in which there was a functioning Parliament in Nepal. For them, giving up on the parliamentary system would amount to a complete defeat of their ideology and political prospects.[14] Until a meaningful middle ground is found on these two stances, moving forward on the rest of the Constitution will be difficult. There are other challenges. It is questionable how a country can preserve its national interest without a clear concept on how to deal with the internal security challenges.

To conclude, today the major challenge before the political parties is to fulfill the commitment of 2006 under the historic peace accord. It was expected that the political parties will draft a new Constitution and bring forth qualitative and social transformation under the Constitution. Members of the Constituent Assembly have been working since their election in 2008 with little progress to draft a new Constitution. The demise of consensual politics has been largely responsible for missing the May 28, 2010 deadline for delivering a new Constitution. The chances of the Constituent Assembly delivering the new Constitution within the extended deadline—May 28, 2011—seem remote as there is no commitment yet from the three big political parties (Nepali Congress, UCPN-Maoist and CPN-UML) that they would sort out their differences on major contentious issues. Clearly, Constitution drafting and sorting out their differences on fundamental issues like the model of governance, federalism, the independence of the Judiciary etc., are not the first priority, even now. In fact, there is reason to believe that because vested political interests have replaced more pressing considerations such as Constitution formation that Nepal finds itself in a political/constitutional crisis today. Unless the current trend is reversed, there is a real possibility that the fruits of a comprehensive peace agreement that brought the decade-long civil war in Nepal to an end, will be frittered away.

END NOTES

1. Baral, Lok Raj, ed., *Nepal: New Frontiers of State Restructuring of State*, Adroit Publishers, New Delhi, 2008, pp. 81-99
2. Joshi, Bhuwanlal and Leo Rose, *Democratic Innovations in Nepal: A case study of Political Acculturation,* Berkeley, University of California Press, Reprinted by Mandala Book Point, Kathmandu, 2004, pg.384
3. *www.myrepublica.com/portal/index.php?action=news_details*, accessed on February 8, 2011
4. *www.mof.gov.np/economic_policy/pdf_2/sSocial_Inclusion.pdf,* accessed on January 31, 2011
5. Bal Gopal Shrestha, "The Question of Sovereignty in the Constitution of Nepal 1990," *Malah,* Kathmandu, vol. 12:19, 1991, pp. 13-16
6. Lawoti, Mahendra, *Towards a democratic Nepal: Inclusive Political Institutions for a Multicultural Society,* Sage Publications, New Delhi, 2005
7. *www.mocs.gov.np/.../2_Journal_Trade%20and%20Development%2...*, accessed on September 13, 2011
8. *www.nepaldemocracy.org/media/nepali_media_at_crossroad.htm,* accessed on March 18, 2011
9. Government of Nepal, *The Interim Constitution of Nepal* of 2007, Ministry of Law, Justice and Parliamentary Affairs, Kathmandu, 2008
10. Election Commission of Nepal, Constituent Assembly Members Elections Result, 2064 VS, Kathmandu, 2008
11. "New Dawn and Epochal Change in Nepal", *Mainstream,* vol. XLVI, no. 18, April 19, 2008, New Delhi, pp.2-3
12. *www.mirestnepal.org.np/news/detail.php?id=325,* accessed on February 18, 2011
13. Khanal, Krishna P, "Democracy and Federalization of the Nepali State", *Sangam Journal,* Kathmandu, vol.1, no.1, December 2009, pg.8
14. *www.mirestnepal.org.np/upload/files/Tool%20kit%20-english.PDF...*, accessed on July 11, 2011

25

Power Games in Nepal: Implications for India

RAJESH KUMAR

Introduction

As close neighbours, India and Nepal share a unique relationship of friendship and cooperation characterized by open borders and deep-rooted people-to-people contacts of kinship and culture. There has been a long tradition of free movement of people across the open borders. As per the 2001 Census Nepal has an area of 147,181 sq. kms. and a population of 29 million. The country has historical, civilisational and cultural links with India. It shares a border of over 1850 kms to the south-east and west with five Indian States—Sikkim, West Bengal, Bihar, Uttar Pradesh and Uttarakhand and in the north with the Tibet autonomous region of the People's Republic of China. Nepal also shares 1400 kms of land boundary with China. Nepal is home to more than 35000 Tibetans whose presence in Nepal raises fears of Chinese retaliation. Since the culmination of elections for setting up of the Constituent Assembly in Nepal and formation of the government there, followed by abolishing more than 238 years old Monarchy and then declaring Nepal to be Federal Democratic and Secular Republic has attracted the attention of not only nearby countries, rather it has also generated enormous interest on part of countries like US, UK, China and international organizations like the UN the involvement of powers in this region has compelled India to reorient as well as restructure its foreign policy towards Nepal in the 21st century. This paper looks at the role of US, China and the United Nations in creating conditions for smooth transition of Nepal into a democratic-secular-republic country of the world and their implications for India's relations with new government in Nepal. The paper examines the support and obstruction created by the ongoing power game in Nepal for its transition to new political and economic arrangements. It also analyses the likely steps India is expected to take vis-à-vis its neighbour and the way these moves and maneuvers are opposed or even blocked by powers like China, guided by its own goals and strategic objectives towards Nepal, most often they are antagonistic to India's policy and perceptions. Lastly it analyses the challenges India is likely to be faced in case of prolonged constitutional crisis in Nepal because of the non-formation of the government and the delay in writing of the Constitution for the people of Nepal.

The US Factor

US foreign policy towards Nepal has provided development and security assistance while seeking to promote democracy and human rights. Prior to the king's takeover, the Kathmandu government faced serious political opposition and increasing pressure to end a Maoist insurgency that since 1996 has caused widespread violence and crippled the Nepali economy. By January 2006, approximately 12,000 people were reportedly killed as a result of the conflict. The Nepali Maoist rebels' continuing violent campaign to overthrow the Kathmandu government has heightened concerns about the government's ability to effectively counter the insurgency. There exists fear on US part that further deterioration of Nepal's security circumstances could lead to further human rights abuses, destabilize the region, spur new tensions between India and China, and potentially create a failed state in South Asia which could become a source of regional instability. The Maoists were listed as an "other terrorist group" by the State Department.[1] There was a time when under US and UK pressure India was made to support the king so as to help him in controlling the menace of Maoist uprisings in Nepal. The US policy makers have not been convinced by the rise of Maoist forces in Nepal and their swearing by the ideology after the name of Mao-Tse-Tung in 21st century when Communism has waned from most part of the world. Even India is genuinely concerned about the linkage between Nepalese Maoist groups and Indian Naxal groups.

New Delhi, Washington, Tokyo, and the European Union each expressed their concern with the king's actions while China and Pakistan offered some support. India and the United States suspended the sale of military equipment to Nepal. It has been reported that China and Pakistan have made military sales, including grenades and ammunition to Nepal. China's motive for doing so was to gain influence in a region bordering Tibet. The European Union has warned that the situation appears to be "moving towards an ever more severe confrontation and polarization, thus increasing the risk of deepening the political crisis."[2] US attention to Nepal has focused on issues related to the Maoist insurgency in recent years though non-military assistance has been far greater. The United States has in the past provided Nepal with light weaponry and other military assistance to assist Nepal in its fight against the Maoists. As of February 2006, lethal military assistance to Nepal remained suspended. It is not anticipated that such assistance will resume until the domestic political situation improves. The United States views the Maoists' plans to institute a one party republic, collectivize agriculture, reeducate class enemies and export revolution as undermining regional stability as well as the promotion of democracy and development for Nepal.[3] Thus, US approach towards the ongoing political turmoil in Nepal is largely guided by disdain for Maoist ideology in present era, support for smooth transition of Nepal into a pluralistic and democratic society, respect for human rights and an early end to political instability and the end of competition between China and India.

India's relations with the USA and Russia have not only been strengthened but also transformed qualitatively with new areas of strategic cooperation added specially the culmination of Indo-US Nuclear Agreement between them. India's engagement with the US has risen to new heights. Visit by Prime Minister Dr. Manmohan Singh to the US in November 2009 and President Barack Obama's visit to India in November 2010 has helped both the countries to embark on a new phase in the global strategic partnership between them. Today the US has emerged as one of India's largest trading partners. The total volume of Indo-US bilateral trade in goods and services stood at US$ 59.8 billion[4] during the period January-October 2009. Today there is a greater US appreciation of India's democratic credentials in the world. US values India's ability to meet the aspirations of 1.2 billion people and remaining free of any political upheavals so far. It is in light of above, US has convergence of interests with India on the issue of Nepal's transition to a new political arrangement. The United States has been supporting India's constructive engagement with Nepal as it would like another South Asian country to turn fully democratic and emulate the democratic values of India and US both. US also has been tacitly supporting India to keep a check on growing Chinese influence in the region. Growing convergence of interests between US and India in recent decades has been resented by China and it often sees such moves for containing its influence in the region and the world. China's policy towards Nepal in present times is an outcome of likely politico-strategic alignment between India and the USA. So far India's policy towards Nepal has received complete support of US.

The United Nations Factor

The Department of Political Affairs provides oversight and support to the United Nations Mission in Nepal (UNMIN), established in January 2007 with a mandate from the Security Council to assist Nepal in its transition to peace following a decade of armed conflict. UNMIN played an important support role in the successful holding, in April 2008, of an historic Constituent Assembly election that constituted a major milestone in the peace process. Based in Kathmandu UNMIN, is headed by the Representative of the Secretary General in Nepal, Karin Landgren. UNMIN, as a special political mission, continues to provide support and confidence to the process, including through its ongoing arms monitoring responsibilities under Security Council Resolution 1864 (2009). Unarmed UN arms monitors are deployed in the 28 Maoist cantonment and satellite sites around the country and one Nepal Army arms storage depot in Kathmandu. Human rights aspects of the peace process are monitored by the office in Nepal of the United Nations High Commissioner for Human Rights (OHCHR).[5]

For several years prior to the establishment of UNMIN, the Department of Political Affairs worked with the parties to help them move in the direction of a politically negotiated settlement. The signing of the Comprehensive Peace Agreement on 22 November 2006 signaled the end of a conflict which had claimed over 16,000 lives, displaced large number of Nepalese and further strained the economy of one of the world's poorest nations. The holding of the April 2008 Constituent Assembly election showed the desire of the Nepalese people for peace and for change. The challenge of consolidating that peace continues. The United Nations has urged renewed focus on outstanding commitments of the peace process, including the effective integration and rehabilitation of former Maoist army personnel and a timely promulgation of a new constitution.[6] However, India has been hesitant to a longer stay of UNIMIN in Nepal as it might become pretext for UN's involvement in other areas of disturbances in the region including Kashmir. Hence, India would like to see the end of UN mission in Nepal as early as possible.

China Factor

China's interests lie in Nepal remaining neutral regarding the Tibet issue. China has developed several infrastructure projects in Nepal and is continuing its support to develop Nepal-Tibet region. China also wants to turn Nepal as 'all weather friend' of China as Pakistan has been for China. China is more keen to have a stable region in its neighbourhood. China sided with former King Gyanendra in February 2005 against the Maoist groups by supplying arms to former Royal Nepal Army so as to enable the former king to deal sternly with the ongoing Maoists war in Nepal. China has been skeptical about the increasing influence of the Maoists group in Nepal's politics. For China, Maoist succeeding in Nepal would have increased the Maoist influence not only in Tibet but also in other parts of China. China's policy towards Nepal is largely guided by its South Asia policy. China sees Nepal as the gateway to its entry in South Asia. The Qinghai-Tibet railway line has brought China closer to Nepal which has significant politico-economic and strategic impact upon South Asian politics including India-Nepal bilateral relations. China has several objectives which shapes its South Asia policy[7] like; China pursuing good neighbourly policy in order to reduce the influence of the US in the region and getting recognition as responsible and great country, China maintaining a balance between Pakistan and India and pursuing policies so as to keep India tied down to the South Asian region only, Maintain cordial relationship with all smaller countries including Nepal to isolate and marginalize India's influence over the region. China has been focusing a lot on the economic development of the Tibetan region which would prove beneficial to many countries of the region including more benefits for the Nepal.

As India's largest neighbour and a key emerging player in the international arena, China remains an important priority of our foreign policy and a key component of our "Look East" policy. The rapidly growing trade and economic exchanges between the two countries are pointers to the fact that India and China are now constantly engaged in mutually rewarding pursuits on the basis of a wide array of complementarities. Frequent high level visits have further contributed to developing mutual trust and understanding. India attaches high importance to its bilateral relations with China. Notwithstanding the complex nature of this relationship, both countries continued their high-level political interaction. Prime Minister Dr. Manmohan Singh met the Chinese President Hu Jintao in Yekaterinburg (June 2009) and Premier Wen Jiabao in Hua Hin (October 2009). The institutionalized dialogue mechanisms between the two countries covering a host of issues have steadily progressed during the period. With a convergence of interests on issues such as Doha Round of WTO negotiations, climate change, global financial crisis etc., both countries have continued to interact constructively on global issues. While India remains fully conscious of its outstanding differences with China, including on the boundary question, the basic paradigm of India's approach is to seek an all-round development of ties, without allowing these differences to define the agenda of the relationship. At the same time, India remained committed to addressing proactively these differences through peaceful dialogue on an equal footing. While some degree of healthy competition between the two countries is inevitable, particularly in the area of trade and commerce, India believes that there is enough space and opportunity in the region, and beyond, for both India and China to grow together.[8] Similar sentiments were expressed by Chinese Premier Wen Jiabao that there is enough space and opportunity in the region and beyond for cooperation between India and China. Keeping in view, the India-China partnership is an important determinant for regional and global peace and development, India must protect its interest in the region by remaining engaged with Nepal and the present policies of the UPA government has started showing improvements between Indo-Nepalese relationships.

'String of pearl' thesis and the fear that China is "encircling" India by building close relations with smaller South Asian neighbours like Nepal and Sri Lanka is not uniformly shared within the government. It is in this context Foreign Secretary Nirupama Rao's view assumes significance to treat India-China as rivals by saying that it is "an over-generalisation and over simplification of a complex relationship which encompasses so many diverse issues."[9] The fears that China is planning to connect Nepal to Tibet by rail has also an economic motive. Till now Nepal imports Chinese goods by sea via Kolkata. The important point is that China's growth is fuelling the increased presence of Chinese companies in South Asia. China has so far provided 1.7 billion Yuan for economic development[10] in Nepal. If India is moving closer to South East Asia and East Asia the same is bound to happen for China in case of South Asia. The sheer volume of trade worth $55 billion approx. in 2010 between India and China speaks in itself the importance of economic issues and likely competition between both in and around the region. For country like Nepal it would continue to look towards both the countries for overcoming its socio-economic problems in near future.

There have been several high profile visits of leaders as well as military officials between China and Nepal. The first ever visit of Prime Minister Pushpa Kumar Dahal was not to India but to China, unlike the past practice of visiting India first by the head of any new government in Nepal. Such a move on part of Maoist leader reflected the keenness of Maoists groups in Nepal to seek closer cooperation with China and at the same time demanding the revision/scrapping of 1950 treaty with India. So far India's approach to this entire issue has been very cautious. China also has been very quick to pronounce its pro-establishment policy towards Nepal.

As discussed in the preceding paragraphs, China and India have been competing for influence along the Nepal-China border. Both are trying to reduce each other's influence in the region. Any announcement of economic aid package by one is responded with bigger aid package by the other, reflecting unfolding of power game in the region. India's development assistance of Rs. 100 million for the remote hill region of Mustang led to China coming out with financial assistance worth Rs. 10 million for construction of a library, science laboratory and school building with computers in Chhoser village (adjoining Jhongwasen district of Tibet) in the same region to counter Indian influence. The ambassadors of both countries have visited the area. China is also opening China Study Centres in Nepal along the Indo-Nepal border. In response to the Chinese attempt to extend the railway link from Tibet till the Nepalese border, India is also planning to extend its rail links to Nepal along the border. India has announced assistance worth Rs. 10.88 billion for the expansion of railway service in five places along the India-Nepal border. The first phase of expansion is scheduled to start from Birjung of Nepal which is about 350 kilometres south of Tatopani, the place to be connected by China through railways.

Implications for India-Nepal Bilateral Relations

Given the experiences of the involvement of external powers like USA, China and the UN in the sub-continental politics has provided important lessons and opportunity to both, that Nepalese as well as Indian government must fine tune their relationship as per the new realties and give preference to improving bilateral relationship in today's interdependent world and should be more willing to accommodate each other's concerns on the basis of equality. Any misgivings and divergence of interests between both of them is likely to increase the role of external powers into the region. The region is already facing serious politico-strategic problems in Afghanistan and Pakistan because of the ongoing power game there which has exposed the vulnerabilities of weak and poor countries in the world.

India has been fully supporting Nepal's historic democratic transition and expressed confidence that Nepal would progress further on the path of peace, democracy and development. India has been extending the highest priority to further developing closed and multi-faceted relationship with Nepal. The statements and official pronouncements made from time to time clearly pointed that India is ready to reconcile itself to the new realities which has swept the Himalayan kingdom for past several years ungrudgingly. India's relationships with Sri Lanka and Bangladesh in past few years reflect significant changes in India's policy towards neighbouring countries. India is all set to experience similar success in its relationship with Nepal also. It can be argued that India has consistently tried to allay the fears of neighbouring countries that India has restructured its relationship with all smaller neighbours as per the new realities and it has deviated from all past doctrines in its dealing with the neighbours. Rather it is the economic issues which assume primacy for the policy makers in India in the 21st century.

Since the formation of the government in Nepal under Mr. Prachanda and his visit to India in Sep 2008, India has been extending full support to the to the peaceful, political, democratic transition in Nepal. The Joint communiqué issued at the end of the visit underlined "the need to inject new dynamism into the relations between the two countries for a forward looking change, in tune with the realities of the time as well as the wishes and aspirations of the people of both the countries."[11] To forge a forward looking relationship the two prime ministers agreed on the need "to review, adjust and update the 1950 Treaty of Peace and Friendship and other agreements, while giving due recognition to the special features of the bilateral relationship." India recommitted itself to continue to extend its assistance towards building economic assets, particularly in the infrastructure sector. As an immediate measure, New Delhi agreed to provide Rs.20 crores as immediate flood relief to the people in Nepal and rebuild the segments of the East-West Highway, damaged in the recent Kosi floods. To tie over the shortage of petroleum products India agreed to provide a credit of Rs. 150 crore and ensure for the next three month uninterrupted POL supplies in Nepal. Thus, India's policy has been to continue to support Nepal in every way possible to achieve the goal of a democratic, stable and prosperous Nepal. India remains steadfast in its commitment to assist Nepal's economic rehabilitation and political stabilization.[12]

For India, changed security perceptions demand continuous negotiations with Nepal on the role of terrorists and religious organizations in making use of Nepalese territory for carrying out anti-India activities including the smuggling of small arms, drugs and other psychotropic substances, breaking of nexus between criminal and extremists groups across the borders and joint management of borders. It is in the light of these concerns, the two day Home Secretary level talks between India and Nepal were held in end of 2008. During the meeting, both sides reviewed the implementation of the decisions taken at the previous meeting and held focused discussion of the issues relating to: (i) Security, (ii) Border Management, and (iii) Training, Provisioning and Capacity Building. The discussions on security related issues centered around effective cooperation in combating terrorist activities including activities of Insurgent Groups, circulation of Fake Currency Notes, and institutionalizing the mechanism for real-time exchange of security related information between the two countries. India also raised the issue of security of Indian aircrafts so as not to repeat the 'Kandahar' type hijacking again. With reference to Border Management, discussions were also held to review of the Nepalganj-Rupaidiha Pilot Project; effective cooperation for combating trans-border crimes including arms smuggling,trafficking of narcotics & psychotropic substances and human trafficking; institutionalizing the mechanism for regular meetings of the Border District Coordination Committees; and coordination and exchange of ground level/operational information between SSB and its counterpart police and security agencies in Nepal. It was also decided that a meeting of the Joint Working Group on various other Border related issues would be convened in early 2009.[13] However the issue of religious institutions of a particular religion being used for nefarious designs against India continues to remain a bone of contention for India.

In keeping with the tradition of regular high-level exchange of visits between India and Nepal, President, Dr. Ram Baran Yadav, First President of Nepal, paid a state visit to India from 15-18 February 2010 at the invitation of our President. Other visits from Nepal to India in the recent years have been by Prime Minister Madhav Kumar Nepal (18-22 August 2009) and Prime Minister Pushpa Kamal Dahal 'Prachanda' (14-18 September, 2008). Foreign Minister Ms. Sujata Koirala visited India from August 10-14, 2009. External Affairs Minister S.M. Krishna visited Nepal from 15-17 January 2010. Government of India will continue to assist the Government and people of Nepal in its peaceful, democratic transition; its economic development and reconstruction. The areas of assistance would include infrastructure, human resource development, health and education.[14] All such visits reflect that India has finally realized the urgency of remaining an active player in the region and not get guided by past hangovers alone. India today has succeeded in establishing important linkages with Nepal to the mutual benefit of both and tried its best to allay the fears of smaller neighbour like Nepal.

In last few years, India-Nepal relationship has grown stronger because of India's ever readiness to allay the fear of smaller country like Nepal. On several occasions the present leadership in Nepal has categorically stated that Nepal has two main tasks to accomplish, first the writing of the Constitution and second, ensuring the economic development of Nepal. It is in light of Nepal's twin policy India's interaction with Nepal has assumed lot of significance which is reflected from the GOI's policy so far. As per the MEA Annual Report of 2009-10, India contributes to the development efforts of Government of Nepal (GoN) by undertaking various development projects in the areas of infrastructure, health, rural and community development, education, etc. The grant assistance extended to Nepal during 2009-10 under 'Aid to Nepal' budget was over Rs 127 crores. In addition, GOI has extended considerable economic assistance to the ongoing peace process in Nepal. The Small Development Projects scheme offered by the Embassy of India delivers development assistance at grass-roots level in sectors identified with the local population. It now covers over 390 projects with an outlay of approx. Rs 3560 crores. As part of India's effort to assist with capacity building and development of Human Resources in Nepal, over 1500 scholarships are offered annually for Nepalese students to pursue various courses in India and Nepal. In 2006, to assist Nepal's democratic transition, India had provided a credit line of $100 million for developmental activities. In February 2010, during the historic visit of Nepal's first President, Dr. Ram Baran Yadav to India, a new line of credit for $ 250 million was announced. To improve cross-border connectivity between India and Nepal, GOI has undertaken to develop an extensive network of roads in Terai region of Nepal at the cost of 776.15 crores. GOI has also agreed to develop cross-border rail links at 5 points across India—Nepal border at a cost of Rs 1327 crores as well as 4 Integrated Check Posts (ICPs) with an estimated cost of Rs. 318.7 crores.[15] All such measures have restored the credibility of India before Nepalese people that India is genuinely concerned about the backwardness of Nepal and it really wants that Nepal and its people should grow economically and do not doubt India's participation in their progress.

Cooperation on issues of mutual security concerns relating to the open border has received due attention on part of both the countries as India through its diplomacy has succeeded in seeking firm assurances from Nepalese side that it would not allow its territory to be used for any activity against India both the countries have used existing bilateral mechanisms to address issues concerning security, including cross-border crime, and establishing effective communication links between and along the bordering districts to further facilitate the exchange of information. Both the countries have shown more sensitivity towards each other on such issues of security concerns. Harnessing of energy from water resources has lot of potential for cooperation between India and Nepal in the field of water resources. Nepal has 42,000 MWs hydropower potential that is known to be technically feasible and economically viable. In recent years, hydropower has emerged as an attractive sector for Indian investments by public and private sector companies. About 25 licenses, having generation capacity of more than 7000 MWs have been issued to Indian companies for their joint ventures. Energy cooperation between India and Nepal has the potential to turn Nepal into the richest country in the region. Harnessing of hydro power and selling of surplus power to India can change the fortunes of the people and country together. India need to make extra efforts for instilling faith in the people and government that it is them who is to benefit more from an open border as they have free access to India's market which might help both to reinforce their economic partnership between both the countries who share a very strong cultural and civilization links with each other. Recently, the controversial audio tape incident came to light where senior Maoist leader was caught asking for $ 50 million for purchasing the support of MPs of the Madhesi parties for supporting Maoist leader Prachanda's candidature as PM once again in the seventh round of voting. This incident eased pressure on the alleged involvement of the Indian Embassy for its intervention in Nepalese politics, the tape controversy has successfully diverted popular attention towards China. Whether the audio tape is genuine or fake, it will affect the contour of Nepalese politics in the days to come. Any Chinese proactive role in Nepal will have to be countered by India as it will definitely have serious implications for India's security. The win-win situation for both India and China lies in respecting the 'buffer-status of Nepal' between them. This will also ensure political stability in Nepal and will serve the security interests of both nations.

As discussed in preceding paragraphs, India's interaction with the new dispensation in Nepal has clearly reflected that Government of India has been willing to accommodate the wishes of Nepalese people to a very large extent which also included the willingness for restructuring of the 1950 Treaty with Nepal as well as splitting the Treaty for Trade and Transit into two carrying out all necessary changes suggested by the Nepalese Government. India need to emulate the Turkey's experience of "zero problem policies" towards the neighbours like Nepal. Time has come when Nepal can emulate the Indian experience of remaining non-aligned between India and China and both the countries should pay heed to the aspirations of people of Nepal in enabling them of maintaining autonomy between two larger neighbour. India should be prepared to treat Nepal as equal and it must not expect from Nepal to behave like vassal state. India must exhibit more soft skills that contribute to political stability in Nepal which in turn is a prerequisite for keeping the wheels of commerce and capital to move effortlessly in the region. Economic aid being given to Nepal for its development remains the main center of focus for any government in India. Apart from this, water resources, food security, renewable energy, hydrocarbons and climate change should also be given attention between India and Nepal.

As per the MEA Annual Report of 2009-10, India continues to be Nepal's largest trade partner, source of foreign investment and tourist arrivals. Bilateral trade between India and Nepal has increased substantially since the signing of the Trade Treaty in 1996. According to figures for the Nepalese fiscal year

2065-66 (ending July 15, 2009), bilateral trade with India accounted for 58.22 per cent of Nepalese total external trade. The bilateral trade in merchandise is expected to witness a growth of over 25 per cent during Nepalese fiscal year 2066-67 and exceed $ 3.5 billion. All such figures strongly support the argument that both the countries and their leaders have realized the futility of strained relations for a longer period of time and taken suitable steps to recover much ground which they had lost after the beginning of pro-democracy movement in Nepal.

As per the report, India and Nepal signed a revised Treaty of trade in October 2009. The new Treaty has provisions that allow Nepal greater access to the Indian market. India and Nepal renewed the treaty of transit for seven years, which confers transit rights through each other's territory through mutually agreed routes and modalities. The two countries have concluded a Rail Services Agreement (RSA) and a revised Air Services Agreement (ASA) to enhance bilateral connectivity. A Motor Vehicles Agreement (MVA) for passenger vehicles is awaiting formal signature. India also remains Nepal's largest source of foreign investment, accounting for 43.14 per cent of the total foreign investments approvals in Nepal. Indian investment approvals in Nepal till March 2010 amount to Rs 1419 crores with 453 FDI projects. A Bilateral Investment Promotion and Protection Agreement (BIPPA) has been finalized and is awaiting cabinet approval on the Nepalese side.

Challenges Ahead for India because of Prolonged Constitutional Crisis in Nepal

India needs to employ techniques of appealing to Nepalese identity as a fellow neighbouring and developing country so as to find an honourable win-win solution for all the groups and help and enable them to end the political impasse. Indian model of parliamentary democracy with the quasi-federal nature of constitution with independent judiciary and very strong presence of fundamental rights ensuring equality, liberty and justice of all kinds can meet the aspirations of all groups and allay the fears of majorities versus minorities or *vice-versa*. Emerging India needs not to pose threat to neighbours like Nepal as it is a democratic, plural and non-irredentist state.

Nepal also needs to adopt a system of governance through its new constitution that meticulously defines the powers and responsibilities of the three branches and regulates relations between center and the states. Second, the Constitution should act a bedrock of Nepal's parliamentary democracy. It must ensure that the governments are made and unmade through universal adult franchise supervised by an independent election commission. Third, the constitution must abolish untouchability in Nepal as seventy percent population living there is Hindu and the new Constitution must serve as a powerful emancipation proclamation ending centuries of caste-based discrimination and social exclusion of 'jan-jatis' or the 'pahari' people. The new constitution must guarantee every citizen important fundamental rights, which may be subject to only certain restrictions. These rights must include the ability to freely speak and express oneself; the freedom of conscience and to profess, practice, and even propagate a religion; basic protection against arbitrary arrest and detention by authorities, and various cultural and educational guarantees. The role of caste Hindu political elite must be diluted and concentration of power among them should be reduced and the inclusion of more than two thirds of Nepal's population constituted by the indigenous nationalities (*Adbasi Janajan*), Dalits and Madhesis in governance and sharing of power must increase through adequate constitutional provisions. It can be concluded on a positive note that the Indian democracy and its socio-economic development processes may hold some significance for Nepal, especially given India's very similar social, cultural and geographic conditions and developmental levels and challenges.

END NOTES

1. Bruce Vaughn, CRS Report for Congress, Accessed through the CRS Web, Order Code RL31599, Nepal: Background and US Relations, February 2, 2006
2. *www.spotlightnepal.com/FacetoFace.aspx?ArticleID=892&IssueID...*, accessed on November 2, 2011
3. *www.nwec.jp/en/data/Darshandari_Nepal.pdf*, accessed on January 1, 2011
4. Government of India, *Annual Report 2009-10,* Ministry of External Affairs, New Delhi
5. *www.observerindia.com/cms/sites/orfonline/.../ReportDetail.html?...*, accessed on February 11, 2011
6. *www.nytimes.com/.../nepal-party-chief-warns-king-to-turn-over-pow...*, accessed on November 5, 2011
7. Abanti Bhattacharya. "Chinese Perception of Developments in Nepal," *World Focus,* no. 331, New Delhi, July 2007, pp.276-78
8. Government of India, *Annual Report 2009-10,* Ministry of External Affairs, New Delhi
9. Nirupma Rao's Interview given to *The Hindu* just few days before Chinese Premier Wen Jiabao's visit to India in December 2010
10. China seeks to play active role in Nepal's peace process: Envoy," June 28, 2007, accessed from *http://68.178.224.54/udayavani/showstory.asp?news=0&contentid=426357&lang=1* cited in Abanti Bhattacharya, "Chinese Perception of Developments in Nepal," *World Focus,* no. 331, New Delhi, July 2007, pg.277
11. Avtar Singh Bhasin, *India's Foreign Relations: 2008 Documents,* Part-I, MEA, Government of India, New Delhi
12. *peace.net/sites/default/files/...docs/Curriculum%20Vitae.doc*, accessed on September 15, 2011
13. *www.spotlightnepal.com/Opinion.aspx?ArticleID=830&IssueID...*,accessed on February 10, 2011
14. *www.spotlightnepal.com/sln/Forum.aspx?ArticleID=628&IssueID...*,accessed on July 28, 2011

26

China's Penetration in Nepal and its Impact

SATISH KUMAR

Introduction

The year 2010 was another disappointing year for the people of Nepal. The peace process was deadlocked, with extreme polarization within and among the political parties on various issues. Despite the extension of the Constituent Assembly (CA) for a year, the parties could not complete even the rudimentary task of drafting a new Constitution. The blame for this unsettled state of affairs was conveniently heaped on the so-called external forces. Throughout the year, the major political parties undertook a number of initiatives to resolve the deadlock. A High Level Political Mechanism (HLPM) was initiated on January 8, 2010 under the leadership of the late G.P. Koirala. His death on March 20 brought the HLPM to a halt. The Maoists announced an indefinite nationwide strike from May 2, after a number of inconclusive dialogues with other parties. After prolonged discussions the Maoists entered into a three-point agreement with the other political parties on May 28 to extend the tenure of the CA for a year. The differences between the political parties widened further with Prime Minister Madhav Kumar Nepal's resignation on June 30.[1] There have been seventeen rounds of elections to form a new government since July 21, but no candidate has been able to attain a simple majority in the CA.

It was difficult to generate consensus among the three main political parties on the issues of PLA integration, restructuring of the country, and formation of a consensus government. The factionalism within the parties and greed for power among the leaders came to the fore and stalemated the process of negotiations. The leaders were seen to be changing their positions in each meeting according to the internal situation within their parties.[2]

Chinese Game Plan

Last year's expose of Chinese funding to buy the MPs in favour of the Maoists had created a new threat not only for Nepal but for India as well. It has been seen as penetrating into the political system of Nepal. Chinese interest in Nepal is to block the penetration of those forces which could pose a serious threat to its interests, especially through Tibet, China's weak belly. Nepal's importance seems to be amplified in terms of regional as well as international power equations. Since the beginning of 'peace process', Nepal's two giant neighbours —China and India and the United States are undertaking activities unmatched in the past. The current political deadlock is a mere reflection of the power rivalry among these three major powers, which are competing for an increased role in the world arena in general, and in this part of Asia, in particular. China has had its interests in the South of the Himalayas from the very beginning. This interest has apparently of late been expanded across the realm of the Indian Ocean in general, and across South Asia in particular. China in the past also had been eyeing its interests in Nepal and beyond. Chinese added presence in Pakistan, Sri Lanka, Myanmar and Bangladesh is clear evidence of Beijing's changed foreign policy, from quiet to an aggressive one. For being linked closely with Nepali territory, China is always sensitive towards Nepal's political affairs. In 1961, the then Chinese Deputy Prime Minister and Defence Minister Marshal Chen Yi had clearly stated that any interference in Nepal's internal affairs from any quarter would be taken as an attack on China itself. This was the first strong stand coming from Beijing that was ever recorded. In the later years, China kept close watch on its interests in Nepal but in a very subtle manner. She never came out openly but adopted quiet diplomacy. China changed its strategies vis-à-vis Nepal after the latter experienced political changes in recent years, especially after the regime change that took place in 2006.[3] During the past four years, more than twenty high-level Chinese delegations have visited Nepal. The Chinese not only come to Kathmandu but more often than not, talk about Nepal at home as well. The policy of quiet diplomacy seems to have turned into an aggressive one.

Chinese interests in Nepal should be analyzed from the regional perspective as well. The political changes that took place in this part of the world of late encouraged China to take an aggressive posture. There have been some noticeable anti-China activities originating from Nepal which have increased exponentially over these years. Nepal has been used by anti-China elements. Anti-China slogans were chanted in the streets of Nepal. Both visible and invisible activities were noticed to have gone against China's national security interests. Such acts have sensitized the Chinese regime that may have concluded that such acts could in the long run pose a grave threat to its national security, particularly through Tibet. The Chinese may have inferred that if Nepal became politically unstable, the society and government being weaker, the chances of foreign forces interfering in Nepalese affairs would be high, which eventually would be counter-productive to its national security. The Chinese have always adopted a pro-establishment policy towards Nepal. Nepal-China relations are based on the Five Principles, or Panchsheel, according to which China will not intervene in Nepal's domestic politics and Nepal will respect China's sovereignty and territorial integrity with respect to Tibet and Taiwan. Thus, China is taking such action in Nepal to confront and counter-balance India and seems to continue to act similarly in other countries in India's neighbourhood as well, especially in Sri Lanka and Pakistan. In the past, China viewed the monarchy as the most stable, credible and dependable partner and the mainstream political parties as pro-India. Chinese security interests, which have been China's prime concern in Nepal, were served by the King in the past.[4]

Nepal: Arena of Global Power Rivalry

The importance of Nepal is geopolitically heightened with the shift of the power equation at the global level. With international relations becoming global, one or other region has become the heartland for rivalry between and among world powers. Nepal is located in a very strategically significant position which is flanked by two emerging world powers—China and India. If China and India continue to develop in the way that they are today, then one fateful day these two powers can challenge the United States, not only economically, but probably militarily also. It is this concern which has been prompting the Americans to avert the looming danger from China, in the short term and India, in long run. Nepal's traditional policy of 'equal distance' between Beijing and New Delhi seems to be fading with the grand entrance of the Super Power in Nepal's domestic power politics. Though present-day power players in Nepal may try to continue with their 'balancing act', they would hardly endure the storm of global powers' rivalry that is in the making. Indians are concerned that Nepal is being used by anti-India elements. This was not the case during the Cold War, though China, India, US and Pakistan were there as they are now. China is seeking more reliable assurance from Nepali rulers, that Nepal would not be used by any anti-China elements. Due to its location sandwiched between global players and probable threats to China and India, Nepal provides a suitable ground for visible as well as invisible strategic activities. Nepal constitutes an important element of China's South Asia policy. One may recall Mao Zedong's five finger policy in which Nepal constituted one of the five fingers along with Ladakh, Bhutan, Sikkim and Arunachal Pradesh. The five fingers were essentially meant to serve as a 'new buffer' zone between India and China after the 'old buffer' (Tibet) came under China's sovereign control in 1951. With growing tensions in Tibet, particularly after the March 2008 uprising, China's conception of Nepal as a new buffer acquired particular significance. Its policy towards Nepal came to be driven by the need to curb the clandestine activities of some 20,000 Tibetan refugees (the second largest Tibetan refugee community in the world) in Nepal. Consequently, China has been increasingly playing a significant role in determining the future shape of Nepali politics. During each of the high-level meetings China has extracted assurances from Nepal that it adheres to the one-China principle, acknowledges Tibet as an inalienable part of China, and ensures that no anti-China activity is allowed on its soil. Underscored in China's South Asia policy is the strategy to marginalize India's influence in Nepal. Marginalizing India would allow China not only to dominate South Asia but also provide easy access to Nepal's roughly 83,000 megawatts of hydro-electric potential.[5]

It is interesting to note that China pronounces its foreign policy towards Nepal in a manner which presents not only a benign image of itself but which also helps assuage Nepal's fears of a domineering India.[6] For instance, Yang Jiechi's assurance in December 2008, to protect Nepal's "sovereignty and independence" not only strengthened Beijing's diplomacy but also sought to obviate India's influence. News reports from Nepal even go further to suggest that "China intended to develop relations with Nepal in a way that would serve as a role model for bilateral ties between big and small countries."[7] China has, in fact, laid down a four-fold policy to strengthen its bilateral relations with Nepal: "First, accommodate each other's political concern. Second, enhance the economic cooperation on the basis of mutual benefit. Third, boost people-to-people and cultural exchanges. Fourth, strengthen the coordination and cooperation in international and regional affairs."[8]

Apart from stating a clear policy towards Nepal, China has been systematically pursuing a multi-dimensional engagement with Nepal. There has been a flurry of visits between China and Nepal in recent times. According to one news report, about 38 Chinese delegations visited Nepal in 2008 alone. China has been cultivating ties with not only the Communist Party of Nepal-Maoist (CPN-M) but also with the Communist Party of Nepal-United Marxist-Leninist (CPN-UML) and the Madhesi People's Rights Forum. Lately, China has begun taking interest in Terai politics. There are reports of a high level Chinese delegation visiting the General Convention of the Madhesi People's Rights Forum in early 2009. In April 2009, a CPN-UML delegation led by Jhala Nath Khanal visited Beijing when China had impressed upon the delegation that it wants "a new kind of relationship" with Nepal.[9]

Besides high level visits, China's inroads into Nepal are being greatly facilitated by the systematic promotion of China Study Centres (CSCs) which are completely funded by China. The number of CSCs in Nepal has increased in recent times. According to the CSC website, there are ten local branches located in Butwal, Banepa, Sankhuwasabha, Pokhara, Biratnagar, Morang, Sunsari, Chitwan, Nepalgunj and Lumbini, besides the central organization of the CSC-Nepal in Kathmandu. According to Bhim Prasad Bhurtel, the executive director of the Nepal South Asia Centre, Kathmandu, "33 China Study Centres have been established in southern Nepal adjoining the Indian border." He also mentions that China Radio International has launched a local FM radio station in Kathmandu with the purpose of bringing China closer to Nepal. Besides CSCs, a Nepal-China Mutual Cooperation Society (NCMCS), funded by the Chinese Embassy in Nepal, was established in March 2005. The primary aim of NCMCS is to strengthen diplomatic relations between the two countries as well as to disseminate an image of a friendly China as opposed to a 'hegemonic' India.[10] Besides, there are other associations like the Nepal-China Executives Council in Kathmandu, the Nepal-China Friendship Association in Lumbini and the Nepal-China Youth Friendship Association in Pokhara. Further, to promote bilateral cooperation and exchanges the Nepal-China bilateral consultation mechanism was constituted in 1996. Such multi-layered engagement enabled China to not only strengthen its diplomacy in the region but also project a benign and cooperative image. It may be noted that India does not have such multi-layered levels of contact and lacks innovative ways (cultural or diplomatic) of reaching out to the Nepali government and people. In fact, similar cultural traditions in Nepal create a kind of extended cultural zone for India and often therefore, many of the natural linkages that exist between India and Nepal are taken for granted.

China's proactive policy in Nepal can also be discerned from the military assistance it has been providing. On December 7, 2008, during a meeting in Kathmandu between Nepal Defence Minister Ram Bahadur Thapa and the deputy commander of China's People's Liberation Army, Lieutenant General Ma Xiaotian, China pledged to provide US $2.6 million as military assistance for Nepal's security sector. Earlier, in September 2008, China had announced military aid worth $ 1.3 million, the first such assistance to the Maoist government in Nepal. It may be recalled that in 2006 China had provided clandestine military assistance to the Maoists in a bid to placate them. In recent times, Beijing has shown keen support for the Maoist government's proposal to integrate some 19,000 Maoist guerrillas with the Nepal Army.[11] China had announced a doubling of aid to Nepal amounting to $21.94 million. To attract Chinese investment in Nepal, on April 7, 2009, the Nepal-China Executives' Council (NCEC) and the Chinese People's Association for Friendship with Foreign Countries (CPAFFC) signed an MoU. The trade volume between the two countries currently stands at $401 million, with China selling goods worth about $386 million, and Nepal exporting goods worth a mere $15 million. To bridge the trade deficit, China has agreed in April 2009 to provide duty free access to 497 Nepali goods in the Chinese market. Also, not to forget, China's initiative in building a road link between Lhasa and Khasa, a border town located some 80 kilometres north of Kathmandu. China has also accepted Nepal's proposal in April 2009 to open up two more custom points in addition to the existing five.[11] China is also building a 65 km second road link, the Syafrubesi-Rasuwagadi road, which is the shortest route from Tibet to Kathmandu.[12] As part of promoting Nepal's hydro-power projects, in 2008, China's Assistant Minister for Foreign Affairs, He Yafei, pledged to provide Nepal a loan of $125 million for Upper Trishuli 3 'A' and $62 million for Upper Trishuli 3 'B'.[13] The plants would start operating from 2012.

In sum, observing the growing trends of Nepal-China ties, it may be argued that Nepal under the Maoist government has been clearly seeking closer ties with China at the cost of India and is far from pursuing a policy of equidistance. Further, Nepal's geo-political location coupled with China's proactive South Asia policy has clearly accentuated the security dilemma in the region. At this juncture, when Nepal is in turmoil, a great deal of dexterity in foreign policy is required on the part of the Indian establishment to preserve its influence in South Asia and at the same time ensure a democratic Nepal that would deter China's inroads into Nepal. Nepal has been without a government since June 30, when former Prime Minister Madhav Kumar Nepal relinquished office under pressure from the Maoists to pave the way for a new power-sharing administration. Since then, political leaders have been unable to agree on the shape of the new government and six earlier attempts to choose a new prime minister have failed, with neither of the two candidates securing an absolute majority. The Maoists, who fought a decade-long civil war against the state before transforming themselves into a political party and winning the 2008 election, hold the largest number of seats in Parliament, but not enough to govern alone. Now, the political crisis in Nepal has further deepened the Parliament. China's construction of a rail link between Lhasa and Xigaze

(Shigatse) in the Tibet Autonomous Region will bring its rail network closer to the Nepal border and to India. The rail link has potential to boost Sino-Nepal trade and tourism; it is also expected to enhance China's already substantial influence in Nepal and bring the Chinese rail system closer also to the contested Sino-Indian boundary. A worried India is looking on as the Chinese railway steams southwards. An added concern for India is the rail's steady approach towards Nepal, a country it regards as lying in its sphere of influence, and its own borders. It is evident that the Chinese rail system will not terminate at Xigaze. In 2008, for instance, Chinese and Nepalese officials announced plans for extension of the rail beyond Xigaze up to Khasa, a small market town on the Sino-Nepal border—and it might not stop even there. Cheng Xia Ling, the Chinese ambassador to Nepal, was quoted in 2008 by *Nepal Weekly* as saying: "We are even planning to link it to Kathmandu in not too distant future." Landlocked Nepal has been eyeing the southward advance of the Chinese rail system with anticipation. It will bring it more tourists from China and Chinese trains loaded with goods will reduce the Himalayan nation's longstanding dependence on Indian imports. To Nepal, the Chinese rail link promises opportunity.

New Delhi also has worries over other proposed rail links that might be constructed up to the Sino-Indian boundary at Sikkim and Arunachal Pradesh. China is contemplating a rail link from Xigaze to Yatung, a trading centre a few kilometres from Nathu La, a mountain pass that connects Tibet with Sikkim.[14] Another rail line will run eastwards from Lhasa to Nyingchi near Arunachal. This southward expansion of China's rail lines is of concern to several Indian security analysts. Much of the Sino-Indian boundary is disputed and the two countries fought a war over it in 1962, which India lost. Incursions by both sides, especially along the eastern sector, are frequent given the fuzziness of the boundary. China had earlier adopted a policy of 'non-intervention' in the internal matters of Nepal and largely stayed out of Nepalese internal politics. However, the demise of the monarchy and the ascendance of political parties has forced China to reshape its Nepal policy. Moreover, frequent protests by Tibetans in recent months alerted the Chinese to the possibility of the China-Tibet border being misused. Consequently, China has sought to engage Nepalese political actors at all levels, primarily to secure the border with Nepal. With the Maoists in power, China also hopes to use its ideological commonalities to suppress the Tibetan movement in Nepal. When the Maoists emerged victorious in the April 2008 elections, China adopted a wait and watch policy because it was unsure of their intentions. After all, the Maoists were backed by India and were catapulted to the political centrestage only after a comprehensive peace agreement in which India had played a substantial behind-the-scenes role. However, media reports reveal that after several interactions with Maoist leaders, China has begun to feel quite comfortable with the Maoist-led government. The Maoists' ideological linkages with China and their keenness to neutralize India's influence in the region have also made them an obvious choice for engagement.

In fact, twelve high-level Chinese delegations, including two military teams, visited Nepal in the course of 2008-09. During these visits, China has repeatedly assured economic, technological and military aid to Nepal. The Maoist-led government was also asked to adopt a 'One-China' policy, not to allow Nepalese land for anti-China activities, take strong action against Tibetan refugees and grant special facilities for Chinese investments in strategic sectors. Beijing has also initiated Track-II diplomacy with Nepal and invited Nepalese scholars to undertake visits to Chinese think tanks. Some of the important visits from China to Nepal were: Nepal's engagements with China have also increased manifold with the visit of delegations both at State and non-state levels. Apart from visits at the official levels, private visits by political leaders, journalists and academicians are also sponsored by China as part of public diplomacy. During these visits Chinese authorities have reportedly assured all kinds of support to the Maoist government in its efforts aimed at laying the foundation for a 'New Nepal'. For the Nepalese Maoists, growing Chinese engagement is a win-win situation in line with their 'policy of equidistance', which has been deliberately adopted to counter-balance India's influence in Nepal.[15]

The nature of Chinese engagements in Nepal goes beyond the political domain. They might also be aimed at influencing the process of drafting of the new Constitution to ensure that China's long-term interests are served, particularly in hydropower and other strategically important projects. China has also assured Nepal help in the modernization and integration of registered Maoist guerrillas into the Nepal Army. Considering the strategic and economic interests Beijing has in Nepal, in terms of energy from hydro projects and as a transit country between China and India, China may expand its state level engagements by entering into long-term agreements at various levels. The proposed new friendship treaty marks the beginning of this process. Moreover, the treaty may enhance the bargaining power of the Maoist government vis-à-vis India to resolve some of the longstanding disputes between the two countries.

Describing Sino-Nepalese ties as being as close as "tooth and lip", the Chinese visitor reiterates that "we have always treated our relations with Nepal from a strategic high and with a long-term view."[16] In plain language, it means that, for China, Nepal is of 'strategic' significance and, furthermore, that the relationship is by no means transient: it is here to stay, permanently. In other words, if, as we are monotonously reminded, India has legitimate security concerns in Nepal, so does China—particularly a China that sees sometimes open and more often clandestine endeavours by extraneous powers to abuse Nepali soil as a convenient base for anti-China maneuovres, mainly in the shape of the 'free-Tibet' movement. A few months back, when Nepal's army chief, Chhatraman Singh Gurung was being feted by the Indian army with the honorary rank of General, his deputy was busy signing military deals with the PLA. The Indian army has always warned the political hierarchy in New Delhi of growing Chinese influence in the region. Economically, China is contributing a lot to improve the poverty-ridden economy of Nepal and in a latest development Beijing is investing around US$ 20 million to build a small 17 km long stretch of mountainous road through the Himalayas that would link Tibet to the Nepalese town of Syabrubesi. This stretch would not only connect Tibet to Nepal but when finished, would also be the first direct Chinese land route to New Delhi. China has been trying to encircle India. It has shown its aggressive postures in Arunachal and Ladakh. Nepal is one of the Chinese strings to encircle India. In fact, weakening political structure and instability in Nepal are providing space to Chinese power. The coming months and year is definitely a test of power between India and China on Nepalese turf.

END NOTES

1. Gopal Sharma, *The Kathmandu Post*, Kathmandu, 25 February 2010
2. Prashant Jha, "India, Nepal, China to collaborate on eco-restoration," *Jairam*, Kathmandu, 11 March 2010
3. S D Muni, "India China and Nepal," *Indian Express*, New Delhi, July 2009
4. Bhartendu Singh "Chinese Influence in Nepal", *www.ipcs.org*, accessed on February 21, 2011
5. Awanti Bhatacharya, China's Rail Route in Nepal, *www.idsa.in*, accessed on September 22, 2011
6. Nihar Nayak, "China in Nepal", *www.idsa.in*, accessed on September 25, 2011
7. *icj.org/dwn/database/NEPAL_ESC_rights_FINAL_30July2009.pdf*, accessed on September 22, 2011
8. C. Raja Mohan, China's Growing Influence in Nepal, *Indian Express*, New Delhi, 17 March, 2010
9. *himalaya.socanth.cam.ac.uk/.../IDEA_Creating_Constitution.pdf*, accessed on February 21, 2011
10. *idsn.org/.../user.../Nepal/Nepal_UPR_session_-IDSN_analysis.pdf*, accessed on September 25, 2011
11. *martinchautari.org.np/research-dis-2009.html?tmpl=component*, accessed on May 15, 2011
12. *monthlyreview.org/.../womens-role-in-the-nepalese-movement*, accessed on February 11, 2011

13. *soas.academia.edu/.../The_Rejection_of_the_Minority_Approach_in...*, accessed on February 8, 2011
14. *southasiamonitor.org/detail.php?type=n&nid=418,* accessed on November 5, 2011
15. *trulynepalivideos.meronepalma.com/people-blame-parties-for-delay-...*, accessed on March 21, 2011
16. *unsr.jamesanaya.org/.../22-nepal-alleged-exclusion-of-indigenous-pe...*, accessed on June 17, 2011

27

Changing Dynamics of China's Nepal Policy

SANJEEV KUMAR

China's Nepal policy was guided by Panchsheel, the famous Five Principles of Peaceful Coexistence when People's Republic of China and Nepal established diplomatic relations on 1 August 1955.[1] The good neighbourhood policy was followed in post-Mao China as a measure to maintain peace and stability for the growth of China. However, China's activism in Nepal especially since 2008 has been primarily driven by political factors including Tibet and geopolitical considerations. This can be termed as a paradigm shift in China's Nepal Policy.[2] The shift has created legitimate concerns in India, the only other neighbour of the Himalyan state, primarily because India and Nepal share a long open border, free movement across the border, and free trade between the two countries. To understand the changing dynamics of China's Nepal policy and the relationship in a holistic perspective, the paper takes an overview of patterns of development in China-Nepal relations since proclamation of the Peoples Republic of China on 1 October 1949.

From "Lean to One Side" to "Panchsheel and Beyond": 1949-78

Mao Zedong announced the policy of 'Lean to One Side' in 1949.[3] This was the time when there was hardly any contact between China and the non-socialist world; China was outside the global community and faced a period of isolation, and containment. The world was ideologically divided into two camps and China was a significant part of the socialist camp which was led by the then Soviet Union. China was leaning to the side of Soviet Union. While Chinese foreign policy emphasized the 'principal contradiction' between United States and the Soviet Union, the world at large especially non-socialist states including neighbouring countries were apprehensive about the intentions of the authoritarian state. Mao Zedong during his conversation with Prime Minister of Nepal B.P. Koirala even acknowledged 'anti-China wave' in neighbouring countries.[4] Nepal had more reasons to get worried. Even during the 1930s Mao had described Nepal, Bhutan, Sikkim, Ladakh and North Eastern Frontier Areas (NEFA) as five fingers of Tibet's palm.

China's incorporation of Tibet into the mainland in 1950-51 created apprehensions about intention of Communist China in Nepal. Nepal continued to maintain its relations with Tibet as independent of China and ignored China's efforts to establish diplomatic relations till 1954.[5] It has also been argued that out of these fears Nepal had signed its historic Treaty of Peace and Friendship with India on 31 July 1950 which established Nepal special relationship with India in the field of trade and commerce, defence and foreign relations. Meanwhile, more than 10000 Tibetans had fled to Nepal during the Tibetan uprising which aggravated China's sense of insecurity in Tibet.[6] Thus, the strategic significance of Nepal was much evident to China. The location of Nepal in South Asia in relation to China has also contributed in shaping China's Nepal policy. Premier Zhou En-lai statesmanship and initiative was largely responsible for establishing ties with Nepal which has been described by many as 'reluctant Nepal' in the early 1950s. It was during the Asian-African Conference at Bandung, that China tried to establish diplomatic relations with non-socialist countries of Asia on the basis of Panchsheel. The Conference was convened upon the invitation of the Prime Ministers of Burma, Ceylon, India, Indonesia, and Pakistan on 18-24 April 1955. In addition to these sponsoring countries, 24 countries including China and Nepal participated in the conference.[7] The first 'Agreement between China and Nepal on Economic Aid' of 20 million Indian Rupees in cash and 40 million rupees for aided projects was signed in October 1956. The economic aid was used as a policy instrument by China.[8] In the early years, Chinese assistance was pledged in terms of projects and no financial involvement therein was mentioned. This policy was changed in post-Mao china. The significant achievements of China's Nepal policy in 1960s was the 'Agreement between His Majesty's Government of Nepal and the People's Republic of China on the Boundary Between the Two Countries' signed on 21 March 1960 and 'China Nepal Treaty of Peace and Friendship' signed on 28 April 1960 under the guidance of Panchsheel principles. The later was even projected as parallel or similar to the historic India Nepal Treaty of Peace and Friendship.

The 1970s was broadly characterized as China slowly expanding its economic cooperation, high level political visits and China's support to Nepal proposal of 'Zone of Peace' in 1973. However, domestic political upheavals during the Cultural Revolution (1966-1976), and the deteriorating Sino-Soviet relations played a role in determining China's Foreign policy. Panchsheel was effectively forgotten during this period largely due to the conflict between India and China and then between China and Soviet Union. During the Cultural Revolution, foreign policy became peripheral and isolation was dominant once again.

Neighbourhood Policy and Economic Diplomacy: 1978-2008

China's foreign policy entered into a new era shortly after the end of the Cultural Revolution. By the end of 1970s (and following the death of Mao), history witnessed the emergence of Deng Xiaoping as the supreme leader of China. Deng initiated bold economic reforms, which required a peaceful domestic as well as external atmosphere. China not only broadened the range of its external exchanges and communications but also tried to create favourable atmosphere in neighbouring countries for peace and development. It signified a change in foreign policy, primarily because of the compulsion of the domestic economy that focused on resource management. From 1978 onwards good relations with other countries, particularly neighbours, became a priority of Chinese foreign policy in official documents. This could be seen as a major change from the Mao's era. Chinese scholars broadly maintain that China's neighbourhood policy (*Zhoubian Zhengce*) is the core of China's foreign policy. China attaches importance to maintain stable relationship with neighbouring countries. It has been argued by Chinese scholars that the neighbourhood policy "even has determined the direction of China's foreign policy."[9]

In post-Mao era, China tried to improve and develop relations with neighbouring countries at the following levels: country-to-country relations, party-to-party relations, external economic relations. Firstly, China dealt with country-to-country relations based on national interests and requirement of economic reforms. China abandoned "the leftist (zuo)" policy, and do not judge other countries by ideology. As early as the beginning of reform and opening up in 1978, Deng Xiaoping emphasized the importance of developing country-to-country relations on the basis of the five principles of peaceful coexistence. Secondly, China tried to construct a new type of party-to-party relations as a part of its diplomacy. Thirdly, China constructed economic cooperation with neighboring countries which also included proposal for free trade agreement and building transportation corridors across the border.

Further, China put forward the approaches of laying aside dispute or peaceful resolution of disputes.[10] Moreover, China gave importance to political stability over other factors in neighbourhood. China's role in South Asia has also been described as 'regime protector' by some experts.[11]

In an attempt to boost bilateral economic relations, China and Nepal established Inter-Governmental Economic and Trade Committee (IGETC) in October 1982. The IGETC meetings have become the main forum for discussions on Nepal-China bilateral economic and technical cooperation. The IGETC meetings focus on economic and technical assistance, bilateral trade and tourism. From mid-1990s, the Chinese Government has been pledging grant assistance to the Nepal Government under the Economic and Technical Cooperation programme in order to implement mutually acceptable development projects. The volume of such assistance is to the tune of around 80 million Yuan every year.[12] Chinese investment in Nepal is growing. Chinese investors are found interested in making investment in hotels and restaurants, electronics, readymade garments, nursing home, hydropower, civil construction, etc. Both countries established the Nepal-China Non-Governmental Cooperation Forum in 1996. The Forum has been meeting regularly. The Forum is being led by Federation of Nepalese Chambers of Commerce and Industry (FNCCI) from the Nepalese side and All China Federation of Industry and Commerce (ACFIC) from the Chinese side. China has completed a large number of projects related to transport and connectivity, industries, water recourses, health, sports and others (see table I)

Table I: China Aided Projects in Nepal (Completed)

A. Road and Transport

Arniko Highway
Arniko Highway (Rehabilitation)
Kathmandu Bhaktapur Road
Prithvi Highway and Surface Pitch Paving
Narayanghat-Mugling Road
Gorkha Narayanghat Road
Kajhuwa-Gorkha-Road
Kathmandu-Bhaktapur Trolly Bus
Kathm Seti River Bridge at Pokhara

B. Industries

I. Bansbari Leather and Shoes Factory
II. Hetauda Cotton Textile Mills
III. Harisidhi Brick Factory
IV. Bhaktapur Brick Factory

V. Industrial Gloves and Apron Manufacturing at Bansbari
VI. Bhrikuti Paper Mills
VII. Lumbini Sugar Mills

C. Water Resources

I. Sunkoshi Hydroelectricity Plant
II. Pokhara Water Conservancy and Irrigation Project (Multipurpose)
III. Sunkoshi Vicinity Electricity Transmission Project
IV. Sunkoshi-Kathmandu Electricity Line Transmission Project

D. Health

I. B.P. Koirala Memorial Cancer Hospital, Bharatpur

E. Sports

I. Sports Complex at Kathmandu and Lalitpur
II. Construction of Sports Facilities for the 8th South Asian Federation Games in 1999
III. Repair of Lighting System in the Sports Complex (April 2005)

F. Other Construction

I. National Trading Complex
II. Warehouse at Kathmandu and Birgunj
III. City Hall in Kathmandu
IV. Birendra International Convention Centre
V. Consolidating Seti River Bridge in Pokhara
VI. A three-month arch bridge training course for 15 Nepalese engineers
VII. Pokhara Sedimentation Pond
VIII. Provision for the Television Truck for NTV

Source: Ministry of Foreign Affairs, Government of Nepal available at *http://www.mofa.gov.np/bilateralRelation/nepal-china.php* accessed on 15 June 2011

There is a large number of ongoing projects related to infrastructure connectivity and industry in Nepal.[13] However, some scholars in Nepal have acknowledged that China has tried to influence political events in Nepal which is against the spirit of Panchsheel principles. Scholars like Kanak Mani Dixit has noted:

> The Chinese planners are alert to Nepal's natural resources and market. The increased attention to Nepal affairs is therefore natural, but *there seems to be a desire in Beijing to influence political events that go beyond market access* (*emphasis added*).[14]

China's Activism in Nepal Since 2008

Various domestic and regional factors explain China's activism in Nepal and changing dynamics of China's Nepal policy in recent past.

Core Interest and Tibet

The rise of China has been one of the most important developments of 21st century. In the past few years especially since China's significant role in global recovery from recession the issue of China's rise has been dominated by a new perspective. It has been argued that China is becoming more assertive on many foreign policy issues. The issue of debate is that whether China's peaceful rise is possible? While many western observers emphasize a potential threat emerging from China's new posture, Chinese scholars depict China's assertiveness in defense of 'core interest' (*hexin liyi*). While spelling out China's core interests in South Asia and the Indian Ocean area, China's Defence Minister General Liang said:

> The core interests include anything that is related to sovereignty, stability, and form of government. China is now pursuing socialism. If there is any attempt to reject this path, it will touch upon China's core interests. Or, if there is any attempt to [encourage] any part of China to secede, that also touches upon China's core interests related to our land, sea, or air. Then, anything that is related to China's national [economic and social] development also touches upon China's core interests.[15]

Thus, the issue of Tibet is certainly a core issue as it has been in the past. In March 2008, protests by Tibetans not just the Tibet Autonomous Region (TAR) but also neighbouring provinces of Qinghai, Gansu and Sichuan presented great challenge to China. Nepal is home of approximately 20000 Tibetan refugee who have protested against China's 'Strike hard' policy in Tibet. Nepal and China's Tibet Autonomous Region have a common border of 1414 km with 34 major passes between the two countries. Nepal adhered to the so called 'Gentleman Agreement' in 1989 which is an informal agreement with the UNHCR. The agreement suggests cooperation among Nepalese police, government officials and the UNHCR to provide safe transit to Dharamshala through Nepal. However, crackdown on protests by Tibetan refugees living in Nepal has been a normal phenomenon since 2008. Secret US diplomatic cables published by Wiki Leaks in December 2010 reveals that Chinese government rewards Nepalese forces by providing financial incentives to officers who hand over Tibetans attempting to exit China.[16] Thousands of Tibetan refugees annually escape into exile by crossing treacherous snow clad passes into Nepal facing threats to their lives. They transit through Nepal in their route to Dharmshala in India where their spiritual leader and Tibeten government in exile is based. However the number of refugees appearing at the Kathmandu reception has decreased from 3000 per year in 2006-08 to 770 in 2010.[17]

The Human Rights Report, 2010 released by United States also highlighted forcible return of Tibetans from Nepal. On February 13, 2011 Nepal police prevented Tibetan community elections for new government in exile by destroying polling stations and seizing ballot papers. It was also reported that the Chinese embassy in Kathmandu compelled Nepal Home Ministry to prevent even the celebration of the Dalai Lama birthday. Thus, it can be said that China's new Nepal policy is primarily based on China's stakes in Tibet and its assertive policy to secure core interest in Nepal.

India Factor

India and Nepal maintain a unique relationship. They share a long open and porous border, free movement across the border, and open and free trade between the two countries. The special relationship is also evident in the fact that around one million people in Nepal receive pensions from the Indian Army and approximately three to four million Nepali citizens work in India.

India factor has always influenced China's Nepal policy. However, it is noteworthy that China's activism in Nepal is directed to counter India's influence in Nepal. Following text by a Chinese scholar narrates the story:

> India has resumed military cooperation with Nepal, suspended in 2005. Under new agreements, India will train and share intelligence with Nepali forces. The Press Trust of India reported on December 7, 2009 that India is to build an air base in Nepal and resume arms sales. *The struggle between pro-India and pro-China forces in Nepal is at the critical stage and China need to pay more attention to its interest there.* (*emphasis added*)[18]

China has opened China Study Centers in Nepal along the Indo-Nepal border. Many Indian Scholars have raised their apprehensions and concerns about the activities of these centres. Most of the China Study Centres are located in close proximity to Nepal's border with India.[19] China also considers Nepal as an extension of its development strategy of Western China promoting sub regional development in South Asia as part of her neighbourhood policy. Nepal accounts for more than 60 percent total foreign trade of TAR. Moreover, China's Geopolitical objectives in South Asia have also created concerns in Nepal. A scholar from Nepal has said:

Geopolitically, Chinese strategists seem to have now decided to make Nepal a part and parcel of their South Asian outreach which includes Bangladesh, Burma, Pakistan and Sri Lanka. While the economic, political and geopolitical imperatives may be important for China, what Beijing is doing about it seems based on an under-appreciation of Nepali political realities and democratic aspirations.[20]

Party to Party Relations

The end of monarchy and the declaration of Nepal as Federal Democratic Republic in 2008 was a momentous occasion in the history of Nepal. China supplied arms during the rule of King Gyanendra to suppress Maoist insurgents for the sake of stability in Nepal. China's support to the Maoist party in Nepal came after its emergence as a single largest party in the Constituent Assembly election of April 2008. A scholar from Nepal has rightly noted:

> While the Chinese were looking for a durable and dependable force in Nepal, the Maoists, looking for support from a strong power in the neighbourhood, approached China for help...China also found it expedient to cultivate the Maoists because of the growing tensions in Tibet, particularly after the March 2008 uprising. ... China was deeply concerned when six Nepalese Parliamentarians visited Dalai Lama in Dharamsala in February 2009. Only after this did China start establishing good relations with other political parties.[21]

There has been unprecedented number of Chinese delegations including Party delegations who visited Nepal in recent past and Nepalese officials have also visited China in their turn.[22] A sixty-member Chinese delegation led by Zhou Yongkang, a senior member of the Standing Committee of the Politburo of the Communist Party of China met caretaker Prime Minister Khanal in Kathmandu on 17 August 2011 and signed economic, technical and other agreements.

Role of the PLA

China's People's Liberation Army has also got involved in the matters of Nepal. The visit by Chinese Army Chief Gen. Chen Bingde to Nepal in March 2011 was significant. The proposal of Chen Bingde was very plain: Deport Tibetan Refugee to China to prevent rise of militant Tibetan émigré force.

Reports in Beijing suggested that Gen. Chen's visit was focused on deepening the military relationship between the two countries and ensuring peace at the Tibet frontier. A memorandum of understanding was signed between the Chief of Army Staff of Nepal, Chhatra Man Singh Gurung and the Chinese Army Chief Gen. Chen Bingde which included bilateral agreement with the Nepal Army pledging assistance worth 1.42 billion rupees China will also provide medical equipment for the Birendra Sainik Hospital and logistics required for rescue operations worth 1.09 billion rupees for the Nepal Army. The visit of the 15-member Chinese Army delegation marks the highest-level of military exchange from China in recent years.

Trade and Economic Assistance

In 2010 Nepal's trade with China was pegged at US$ 500 million with Nepal suffering a trade deficit of US$ 444 million. China and Nepal inked an agreement that will allow duty free access to 350 Nepali goods in Chinese market. This may reduce trade deficit.[23] After his official visit to China in April 2009, Foreign Minister Upendra Yadav informed that that China had agreed to increase its annual assistance to Nepal by 50 percent from 100 million to 150 million Yuan. Recently agreements were even signed with caretaker government for a $50 million economic and technical cooperation, an agreement to provide a $24 million soft loan for a hydropower transmission line project, a $2.5 million security project meant to enhance the capacities of Nepal Police, and a preliminary agreement to provide other concessional loans.

Building Infrastructure

According to a press release dated December 3, 2008 of Ministry of Foreign Affairs Nepal, Nepal and China have agreed to make the best use of the existing geographical advantage to expand relation between Nepal and TAR. Road and transport receives top development priority in Nepal. Government of Nepal and Tibet Hongji Construction Industrial Group had signed an agreement in Kathmandu to implement a Chinese assisted Syafrubesi-Rasuwagadi road project. Yang Jiechi, Foreign Minister of China initiated construction of this road project linking TAR with Nepal during his visit to Nepal in December 2008. Ai Ping, Director General Asia Department of the CPC informed that Chinese government has begun the railway extension project of Tibet railway to Nepal-China border and the railway link would be ready in 2013.[24] Many scholars in Nepal have written about the positive impact of the railway extension on business and trade. However, there is also a view that such infrastructure projects may serve dual purposes. The extension of Qinhai-Tibet railway from Lhasa to Shigatze, and from Shigatze to Nyalam a county in Shigatze prefecture with Khasa (*zhangmu*) as one of its town bordering on Nepal has been listed in the medium and long term railway network planning of China. Apart from road and rail network there is cooperation in the field of telecom network. Nepal telecom has started to link its fiber optic network with China Telecom Network near the Nepal China border in Tatopani in August 2009.[25]

Conclusion

There has been a shift in the dynamics of China's Nepal policy particularly since 2008. Ensuring peace through dictating terms on the issue of Tibetans in Nepal has been the prime characteristic of China's new Nepal policy. Equally important factor is to counterbalance India's special relationship and influence in Nepal by a rising China who has means to do it after 30 years of economic reforms. Many facets of neighbourhood policy of China in Nepal have produced good results. China's cooperation with Nepal in various fields including business, industry and infrastructure has been greatly increased. However, the striking feature of current policy is the role played by the PLA in Nepal and the attempt to influence fate of political issues in Nepal which has implications for India.

END NOTES

1. Five Principles or Panchsheel are: (i) mutual respect for each other's territorial integrity and sovereignty; (ii) mutual non-aggression; (iii) mutual non-interference in each other's internal affairs; (iv) equality and mutual benefit; and (v) peaceful coexistence.
2. Some experts believe that the paradigm shift in China's Policy became evident since Nepal was declared Federal Democratic Republic and which was immediately followed by Anti-China protests in the streets of Kathmandu. Scholars like Kanak Mani Dixit has also termed the proactive role of China following the end of Nepali Monarchy as a paradigm shift. For more details kindly see "Between Sycophancy and Adventurism," *Republica Daily*, 27 July 2011
3. To know more about Mao's 'Lean to one side' policy, kindly see "Is it right to lean to one side", December 8, 1956 in *Mao Zedong on Diplomacy*, Foreign Language Press, Beijing, 1998, pp.215-16
4. See, full conversation between Mao Zedong and PM B P Koirala in *Mao Zedong on Diplomacy*, pp.302-07
5. Rishikesh Saha, *Modern Nepal: A Political History 1885-1955*, vol. II, Manohar, New Delhi, 1990, pg.321
6. Swarn Singh, *China-South Asia: Issues, Equations, Policies*, Lancers Book, New Delhi, 2003, pp.210-11
7. Initially the issue of China's participation was disputed due to opposition from sponsoring countries like Pakistan, Ceylon and Indonesia, but finally Indian and Burmese support championed China's participation.
8. For more details see, Swarn Singh, *op. cit*, no.6, pp.210-31
9. Ma Ying and Zhao Gancheng " Evolution of Guiding Principles and Strategies of China's Periphery Policy", *http://www.siis.org.cn/en/zhuanti_view_en.aspx?id=10012*
10. For more details see, Ma Ying and Zhao Gancheng " Evolution of Guiding Principles and Strategies of China's Periphery Policy", *http://www.siis.org.cn/en/zhuanti_view_en.aspx?id=10012*
11. According to Prof. S D Muni, China has been seen as a regime protector and an economic opportunity in South Asia. He gave this remarks during Conference on "Emerging China: Prospects for Partnership", organized by ICWA at New Delhi, 21-23 November 2009
12. List of assistance available at *http://www.mofa.gov.np/bilateralRelation/nepal-china.php*
13. For details see, Dr Upendra Gautam, "China and Nepal: Closing in for Mutual Interest" *Friendship: Journal of Nepal China Studies*", 2009, Special issue to commemorate 60th

anniversary of founding of PRC, pp.40-42 and *http://www.mofa.gov.np/bilateralRelation/nepal-china.php*

14. Kanak Mani Dixit, "Between Sycophancy and Adventurism", Part I, *Republica Daily*, 27 July 2011
15. "No Naval Build up Says China's Defence Minister," *The Hindu*, New Delhi, 6 June 2011
16. Needless to say, there are questions about credibility of Wiki Leaks.
17. Nidhi Bhardwaj, "Nepal Deporting Tibetans to China" Secretly" available at *http://www.indiandefencereview.com/author/Nidhi-Bhardwaj/1*
18. Dai Bing, "India Building Security Barrier Against China", available at *http://www.china.org.cn/opinion/2010-02/08/content_19387164.htm*
19. Various sources suggest different numbers for China Study Centres in Nepal ranging from 10 to 30
20. Kanak Mani Dixit, "Between Sycophancy and Adventurism", Part I, *Republica Daily*, 27 July 2011
21. Pramod Jaiswal "India-China Power Game in Nepal and the Consequences", *http://www.idsa.in/idsacomments/IndiaChinaPowerGameinNepalandtheConsequences_pjaiswal_160910*
22. Some reports suggest that 38 Chinese delegating visited Nepal in 2008-2009
23. "Nepal China Ink Zero Tariff Deal," *The Hindu*, New Delhi, 15 May 2010
24. Upendra Gautam "China and Nepal: Closing in for Mutual Interest", *Friendship: Journal of Nepal China Studies"*, Special issue to commemorate 60th anniversary of founding of PRC, 2009, pp.40-42
25. *Ibid*

28

Constitutional Progress in Nepal

SAURABH

A constitution is the supreme legal document on which all the laws, acts delegated legislations and regulations of a country are based. Therefore, constitution making is an important part of the process of ensuring justice, peace, security and good-governance. Constitution making is also an exercise of democratic empowerment and can contribute significantly to nation-building. In order to ensure and incorporate the marginal voices, majority articulations and minority aspirations, a large number of key stakeholders at all levels must be involved in the making of a constitution.[1] There should be reconciliation between mainstream and conflicting forces, and consensus among all the political forces on the constitution making process. Without this the constitution thus formed will have little legitimacy.

Rationale for a New Constitution

People need to have a sense of ownership in the constitution. Some people feel that the 1990 constitution failed to represent properly all sections of Nepali society and could not gain support from the general public. Questions were raised about the lack of people's participation in its making. Women, dalits, janajatis, religious minorities and people from remote geographical regions began to assert that the 1990 constitution was not representative and, therefore, a new constitution was needed.[2] The debate gained greater salience as the Communist Party of Nepal (Maoist), which was waging the people's war against the state, started to demand that a new constitution be made through a democratically elected constituent assembly as a way out from the current impasse. The constitution making process, therefore, has increasingly become a means of negotiating apolitical settlement in Nepal. Consequently, the major political forces in Nepal agreed to make a new constitution through the election of a constituent assembly.[3]

Challenges

The making of a democratic constitution is an important but difficult task. It has to incorporate aspirations and demands of the people of different socio-economic status and backgrounds. Sometimes, it must pursue the conflicting goals of representing the people's wills and forging a consensus regarding the future of the state. Besides, it must respect the universal principles such as human rights and the basic norms of democratic governance.[4] Nepal has to overcome numerous challenges while designing and executing an inclusive and participatory constitutional process. First and foremost is the challenge of creating popular pressure to make the constitutional process inclusive and participatory. Different civil society groups have tried to get ordinary citizens involved in the process. But the political parties have shown only a lukewarm response to make the constitutional process more inclusive and participatory. Another challenge is to incorporate and reflect the voices, aspirations, of the diverse groups of people. But, Nepal's tremendous cultural diversity and wide socio-economic variation make the issue of proportional representation more complicated. However, involvement of a large number of people in the making of a constitution is important to promote and strengthen the legitimacy of the constitution. The urgent need is to set out the basic principle governing the constitution making process and ensure that one group doesn't dominate the process.[5]

The third challenge is that of building a consensus among the existing political forces on the content and structure of the constitution. This is a hard task, given that the main actors in the Nepali polity don't feel the need for such a consensus. The king's supporters are demanding space for the monarchy while other political parties are trying to build a consensus on democratic republic.[6] Still there is distrust between the mainstream political parties. The international community, which is very influential in Nepal, appears divided about the constitutional modality. The fourth challenge is of making a democratic constitution in a multicultural state.

Emerging Issues

Nepal has seen political upheavals time and again. The growing political consciousness in the people and the status-quoist character of the state has revealed various socio-economic and political contradictions in Nepali society.

Socio-economic disparities, repression, economic inequalities and the domination of certain socio-cultural groups in the decision making process of the state have prevented the transformation of society into a pluralistic democratic form.[7] A participatory constituent assembly, federal state and proper representation of all caste/ethnic groups, dalits and women in the state are the emerging issues in the current Nepali politics. The question of a ceremonial king and republic has not been answered clearly by the political parties. The interim constitution has not clearly defined what model Nepal should follow while restricting the state. Both political parties and civil society have remained mum over the crucial issue of the redistribution of resources. Without solving these problems people of Nepal cannot hope to be lasting peace and prosperity to the country.[8]

Challenges for a Sustainable Political Solution

The task now is to develop a new model of democracy which considers all socio-cultural groups as equal stakeholders of the state and create a more equitable economic condition by redistributing the resources.[9] A constituent assembly might provide a forum for developing a consensus. But there are some challenges that the political leadership needs to grapple with while making a democratic Nepal. Although the interim constitution has suspended the king, the loyalty of the army and feudal elites of Kathmandu is still with the king. The hue and cry of fundamentalists and the activities of the army show that the ousted ruling clique is yet to fully accept defeat and it will try to recapture power.[10]

Party Politics and its Degeneration

The soul of democracy lies in the smooth functioning of the political parties. Parties not only lead the people but also unite them under the banner of an ideology. But in Nepal, most of the political parties have not created a space for the equal representation of all social groups. It has, more or less, started to degenerate the parties.[11] On the other hand, the political parties like the Nepali Congress and CPN-UML are not clear about how to address the demands of indigenous people, Madhesis, women, dalits.[12] Experiences from around the world have shown that constitution making is not an easy task in countries, which have suffered the trauma of armed conflict. Since it is a blend of political and technical processes, consensus building on a common constitutional framework needs skills and serious commitment on the part of stakeholders engaged in the process.[13] Although Nepal has come a long way since the comprehensive peace accord was signed in November 2006, the political parties have been trying their best to accomplish the task of formulating a new democratic Constitution for Nepal within the stipulated timeframe through an inclusive sovereign Constituent Assembly of 601 members. Like many other post-conflict societies, Nepal is also at war against violence, impunity, lawlessness, discrimination, poverty, underdevelopment and social injustice. The Constitutional Committee of the House is entrusted with the responsibility of preparing the final draft of the constitution by building on the reports of the thematic committees and the recommendations and directions of the full house on the debate of each committee report.[14]

Nepal is following a bottom up approach in its constitution making exercise. It has not engaged experts to draft the constitution with a view to take it to Constituent Assembly for focused discussions.[15] Rather, it started from scratch, and enabled the thematic committees to work on their respective components of the constitution, right from the beginning. All this is being done according to the rules beg laid down by the Interim Constitution of 2007 and the Rules of the Constituent Assembly adopted by it in early 2008. Certain policy prescriptions have been made by the Interim Constitution as well. The final constitutional draft has to be taken to the plenary meeting of the Constituent Assembly for a clause-wise discussion and voting as per Article 70 of the existing constitution.[16] Once an agreement is reached on each provision, the entire draft will be taken for adoption by the House before it is promulgated. The countdown for the promulgation of the new constitution has already started. The concept papers and preliminary constitutional drafts from nine of the eleven thematic committees have been tabled at the Constituent Assembly and discussions have been held in the full House, as well as in the wider civil society. The two remaining thematic committees—i.e. the Committee on the Restructuring of the State and Allocation of State Powers and the Committee on the Determination of the Form of Government—are still working in the issues under their terms of reference.[17]

Over the last three years, the nation has gone through a participative constitutional process emphasizing the importance of public participation in the constitutional drafting process. This has been done as a means to promote legitimacy and encourage the participation of citizens in government. An array of methods has been employed to reach out to members of the public and include their views. The thematic committees have not only tried to discuss major issues of the transition with the public, but have also tried to factor their input into their concept papers and preliminary drafts at the committee level. It will go through the second round of consultative process again after completing the first comprehensive draft of the new constitution. Although Nepal had several constitutions in the past, this method of framing a new constitution through an elected Constituent Assembly is really a new experience for the people.[18]

Nepal is debating on various issues, such as a suitable federal framework or a system of devolution of power, the features of an inclusive state, the nature of secularism to be adopted, the strategic to ensure local control on local resources, and a decent model for the republican form of government. Some parties have favoured giving continuity to the existing parliamentary form of government, while some have strongly emphasized on a presidential system. Another group is keen on a parliamentary system, where the prime minister is directly appointed by the people. Still, another group prefers a model similar to the French system.[19] The challenge here is to find a form of government, which not only gives stability to the nation, but also ensure modern democratic features in terms of its structure and accountability. Electoral issues definitely arise and need due consideration. Most people believe that there must be solid foundations for an inclusive system of representation in the new constitutional set up. The issue of state restructuring, especially the quest for a suitable model for federalization has received serious attention of the Constituent Assembly. There has been considerable debate not just on how many provinces this country should have, but also on how the provinces should be demarcated, and how national power should be shared between federal constituent units. Many people, especially those indigenous communities that have been excluded from the national mainstream, want to be assured of their right to self determination. Similarly, there are issues involving fiscal federalism or sharing of resources between the centre and the provinces, and among provinces in the new set up. The House is as much divided over these issues as the civil society watching it from outside.[20]

The civil society of Nepal is still deliberating on many important features of the reports produced by the nine thematic committees. Important dimensions of fundamental rights and directive principles have been proposed by the Committee on Fundamental Rights and Directive Principles. It is also a time to ensure that the rights guaranteed by the new constitution have adequate sanctions. The system of separation of powers between the main organs of government and checks and balances are important in every constitutional system that is based on foundations of liberty and freedom. There is no doubt Nepal is more or less united in its pledge to resolve all existing problem relating to caste, ethnicity, regional disparity and gender discrimination. But in an era of globalization, in all types of society, regimes of constitutional law and good governance may be regarded as vital as the issues so far touched on. To meet the challenges of globalization, there have been dramatic developments in democratic and legal reforms in different countries since the end of the cold war. Post conflict societies have been faced with the challenges of establishing a system of law and governance that fulfills the new requirement. In addition, societies already firmly based on constitutional changes and experimented with the introduction of modified institutions and new forms of governance. Comparative analysis reveals that constitutional systems worldwide have been subject to varying degrees of cross-fertilization.[21]

The participatory approach of constitution making may have some dangers. Constitution makers should be aware about at least three dangers in this regard. The first is political use of the constitution making process. Politicians may raise issues and take it to the public primarily to get more votes, political ammunition and political support. Often, it takes place in the form of making promises, particularly when the constitution or constitution making process permits referendums. This is usually used and abused for political purpose. Another important area of post-conflict constitution making is power structure and conflicts over different forms of power structures in the constitution. Usually the power structure defined in a constitution, reflects the power structure at the moment of laying out the rules for constitutions making. This is most often the case. The most important issue here is the need for clarity—as much clarity as possible. Too much of checks and balances and high expectations of consensus are dangerous and counterproductive. For example in many countries the president has veto over the legislation and 60 per cent or even a larger majority is needed to overrule the veto.[22] In a parliamentary system, this actually increases the power of small parties will be in an advantageous bargaining position and may ask the winners who need their votes, for a lot of things. It is extremely important, not only to include rights in the constitution but also to have in place protection mechanics fro rights, including individual remedies and civil society institution that will help to protect constitutional rights.

The process of building a constitution is a peace process as well. It must strengthen peace. Therefore, the journey that has started with the signing of 12 point understanding, between the seven party alliance and the Maoists must be reflected in the new constitution for sustainable peace. The need of the hour is to recognize that a new constitution can be made only by giving proper respect to the peace accord. Finally, the most important thing is whether the constitution fulfills the desire of the people of Nepal for forward looking changes. In the economic and social sectors, this change means guaranteeing the basic rights of the people. But it is not possible to instantly change things have been in existence for many centuries. There must be consistent efforts. Nepal can solve the existence problems of society only by addressing the expectations and feelings of all the deprived people who have been left behind for a long time and suffered injustices. They are women, *dalits,* indigenous people, minorities, and marginalized classed and communities. Let's hope that the people of Nepal will be able to solve all problem including those related to class, and those based on ethnic, regional, gender, linguistic discrimination and problems of the *dalit* community through a new constitution. The political movement of 2006 in Nepal led the country towards a fundamental transformation in its system of political governance.[23]

Many path-breaking achievements like the Comprehensive Peace Accord, Interim Constitution, successful conclusion of the Constituent Assembly elections, abolition of the 240-year-old monarchy and declaration of the country as Federal Democratic Republic have been defining moments in its recent political history. These developments have changed the country's decade long status of violence and conflict into a post-conflict era of great political transformation. Restructuring of the state is needed to resolve social and regional inequalities. While it is fundamental to promote democracy, peace prosperity, and progressive economic and social changes, it is imperative to protect territorial integrity, sovereignty and independence of the country as these are vital concerns to us. People of Nepal are determined to ensure that these ideals and goals are materialized through the adoption of a new constitution.[24] The people of Nepal truly expect that promulgation of the new constitution would permanently end conflict and address the widespread grievances afflicting the population. Thus, the drafting process has to address the twin objectives of peace-building and long-term political, social and economic reforms. The broad objectives of its home-driven peace process include, among others, the integration and rehabilitation of the Maoist into mainstream democratic politics and resolution of long-standing ethnic, regional and caste fissures in the society.[25]

The experience of other countries amply indicates that successful constitutional processes require a delicate act of striking a judicious balance and accommodation between competing interest and broad public participation. Nepal can't live in isolation in the modern world, especially in the context of liberalization and globalization of the world economy. As one of the least developed countries with serious resource constraints, country's quest for peace stability and progress would be futile without international cooperation, goodwill and support. India should keep its eyes on the big picture and encourage all parties to build up the momentum on integration and rehabilitation of Maoist combatants, which is at the core of the peace process, and constitution writing. The roots of the present political crisis in Nepal are internal, and can be attributed to the deepening divisions within all parties.

END NOTES

1. Acharya, Bhimarjun, *Making Constitution through Constituent Assembly*, Pairavi Prakashan, Kathmandu, 2006
2. Cottrell, J and Ghai, Yash, *Creating the New Constitution*, IDEA, Institute for Democracy and Electoral Assistance, Stockholm, 2008
3. Dhungel, Surya P S, Bipin Adhikari, B P Bhandari, and Chris Murgatroyed, *Commentary on the Nepalese Constitution*, Kathmandu, LF Publishers, 1998
4. Fluri, Phillip, *From Conflict to Peace in Nepal*, Spect and Embassy of India, Kathmandu, Asia Study Centre for Peace and Conflict Transformation, Kathmandu, 2010
5. *gorkhapatra.org.np/rising.detail.php?article_id=58508&cat_id...*, accessed on January 23, 2011
6. *hdr.undp.org/en/reports/nationalreports/.../nepal/name,3287,en.html*, accessed on January18, 2011
7. Hutt, Michael, "Drafting the Nepal Constitution, 1990," *Asian Survey*, vol. 31:11, Delhi, 1991, pg.1020-39
8. *icj.org/dwn/database/NEPAL_ESC_rights_FINAL_30July2009.pdf*, accessed on September 22, 2011
9. Joshi, Bhuwan Lal amd Leo E Rose, *Democratic Innovation in Nepal: A Case Study of Political Acculturation*, Berkeley, University of California, 1966
10. Kharel, Laxmi Prasad, *Constitutionalism: Under the Interim Constitution of Nepal 2063: an Analysis*, Parichit Chappakhana, Kathmandu, 2010
11. *nepalnews.com.np/contents/2011/englishweekly/.../face2face.php*, accessed on October 17, 2011
12. *nepal.usembassy.gov/ep-12-17-2008.html*, accessed on November 1, 2011
13. *nhrcnepal.org/project1.php?ProjNo=4*, accessed on February 25, 2011
14. np.china-embassy.org, accessed on August 19, 2011
15. *southasiamonitor.org/detail.php?type=n&nid=418*, accessed on November 5, 2011
16. *swiss-nepal.ch/downloads/newsletters/nl_FinalN97-p04.pdf*, accessed on February 16, 2011
17. *The Constitution of the Kingdom of Nepal*, Ministry of Law and Justice, Law Books Management Board, Kathmandu, 2006
18. Tripathi, Hari Bansha, *Fundamental Rights and Judicial Review in Nepal*, Pairavi Prakashan, Kathmandu, 2002
19. *www.ccd.org.np/.../constitution.../Robert_Piper_Address_to_Intl_Co...*, accessed on March 10, 2011
20. *www.cscsarchive.org:8081/.../9002166987F6C15E6525731A00286...*, accessed on January 19, 2011
21. *www.economist.com/blogs/dailychart/.../human_developmentindex*, accessed on January 10, 2011
22. *www.ekantipur.com/the-kathmandu-post/2010/05/03/.../207904*, accessed on November 1, 2011
23. *www.eurasiareview.com/15082011-nepal-deadline-for-constitution-...*, accessed on February 11, 2011
24. *www.gorkhapatra.org.np/gopa.detail.php?article_id=51673&cat...*, accessed on September 19, 2011
25. *www.hindu.com/2010/06/23/stories/2010062353731200.htm*, accessed on April 1, 2011

Index